Applied Linguistics and Language Study

General Editor: C. N. Candlin

To Joan and Kate

Observation in the Language Classroom

Dick Allwright

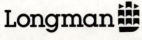

Longman
London and New York

Longman Group UK Limited
Longman House, Burnt Mill, Harlow,
Essex CM20 2JE, England
and Associated Companies throughout the world.

© Longman Group UK Limited 1988

Published in the United States of America by
Longman Inc., New York

First published 1988

BRITISH LIBRARY CATALOGUING IN PUBLICATION DATA
Allwright, Dick
  Observation in the language classroom. –
  (Applied linguistics and language study)
  1. Language and languages – Study and
  teaching – Great Britain – Research
  I. Title   II. Series
  407'.1041   P57.G7

LIBRARY OF CONGRESS CATALOGING IN PUBLICATION DATA
Allwright, Dick
  Observation in the language classroom.
  (Applied linguistics and language study)
  Bibliography: p.
  Includes index.
  1. Language and languages – Study and teaching.
  2. Observation (Educational method)   I. Title.
  II. Series.
  P53.A48   1987   418'.007   87-2698

Set in 10/12pt and 9/11pt Linotron 202 Erhardt

Produced by Longman Singapore Publishers (Pte) Ltd.
Printed in Singapore

ISBN 0-582-55376-8

Contents

Acknowledgements

We are grateful to the following for permission to reproduce copyright material:

American Council On The Teaching of Foreign Languages Inc. for the papers 'The Effects of Training Foreign Language Teachers in Interaction Analysis' by Gertrude Moskowitz from pp. 218–235 *Foreign Language Annals* Vol 1, No 3 (1968) and 'An Observational Method in the Foreign Language Classroom: A Closer Look at Interaction Analysis' by Leona G. Bailey from pp. 335–344 *Foreign Language Annals* Vol 3, No 4 (1975); the author, John F. Fanselow and the editor for his paper 'Beyond *Rashomon*—Conceptualizing and Describing the Teaching Act' from pp. 17–39 *TESOL Quarterly* Vol 11, No 1 (March 1977) Copyright 1977 by John F. Fanselow; the author, Stephen J. Gaies and the editor for his paper 'The Nature of Linguistic Input in Formal Second Language Learning: Linguistic and Communicative Strategies in ESL Teachers' Classroom Language' from pp. 204–212 *On TESOL '77* Copyright 1977 by Stephen J Gaies; the author, Frank M. Grittner for extracts and diagrams from pp. 327–340 *Teaching Foreign Languages*; Julius Groos Verlag for extracts from the paper 'Prescription and Description in the Training of Language Teachers' by Richard L. Allwright from pp. 150–166 *AILA Proceedings Copenhagen 1972 Vol 111: Applied Contrastive Linguistics* (first publ. 1974 by Julius Groos Verlag, Heidelberg) and the paper 'Interaction Analysis and Microteaching for the Training of Modern Language Teachers' by Hans-Jurgen Krumm from pp. 163–170 *IRAL* Vol XI, No 2 (1973) (first publ. 1973 by Julius Groos Verlag, Heidelberg); Harper and Row Publishers Inc. for the paper 'Turns, Topics and Tasks: Patterns of Participation in Language Learning and Teaching' by Richard L. Allwright from pp. 165–187 *Discourse Analysis in Second Language Research* ed. D. Larsen-Freeman (1980); the editor for extracts and diagrams from the paper 'Teacher-Pupil Interaction in the FLES Class' by Sylvia Rothfarb from pp. 256–260 *Hispania* Vol 53 (May 1970); the authors, Michael H. Long, Leslie Adams, Marilyn McLean, Fernando Castaños and the editor for the article 'Doing Things with Words—Verbal Interaction in Lockstep and Small Group Classroom Situations' from pp. 137–153 *On TESOL '76* Copyright 1976 by Michael H. Long, Marilyn McLean, Fernando Castaños and Leslie Adams; the author, Robert L. Politzer and the Executive Director for extracts from his paper 'Some Reflections on "Good" and "Bad" Language Teaching Behaviors' from pp. 31–43 *Language Learning* Vol XX, No 1 (1970); the author, Hubert W. Seliger and the Executive Director for his paper 'Does Practice Make Perfect? A Study of Interaction Patterns and L2 Competence' from pp. 263–278 *Language Learning* Vol XXVII (1977); the editor for the paper 'Problems in the Study of the Language Teacher's Treatment of Learner Error' by Richard L. Allwright from pp. 96–109 *On TESOL '75* Copyright 1975 by Richard L. Allwright; The University of Wisconsin Press for extracts from the articles 'The Pennsylvania Project and the "Audio-Lingual vs Traditional" Question' by John L. D. Clark from pp 388–396 *Modern Language Journal* Vol 53 (December 1969), 'The Teacher in the Pennsylvania Project' by Frank Otto from pp. 411–420 *Modern Language Journal* Vol 53 (Dec 1969) and 'A Behavioral Observation System for Classroom Foreign Language Skill Acquisition Activities' by Gilbert A. Jarvis from pp. 335–341 *Modern Language Journal* Vol 52 (October 1968).

Quoted material

1 Observation 'arrives' in language teaching research
    Clark, J L D (1969)   The Pennsylvania Project and the 'Audio-Lingual vs. Traditional' question
    Grittner, F M (1968)   Letter to the Editor
    Jarvis, G A (1968)   A Behavioral Observation System for Classroom Foreign Language Skill Activities
    Politzer, R L (1969)   Some reflections on 'Good' and 'Bad' Language Teaching Behaviors
    Rothfarb, S H (1970)   Teacher-Pupil Interaction in the FLES Class

2 Observation 'arrives' as a feedback tool in teacher training
    Allwright, R L (1972)   Prescription and Description in the Training of Language Teachers
    Moskowitz, G (1968)   The Effects of Training Foreign Language Teachers in Interaction Analysis
    Grittner, F M (1969)   Teaching Foreign Languages
    Krumm, H-J (1973)   Interaction Analysis and Microteaching in the Training of Modern Language Teachers

3 Second thoughts
    Bailey, L G (1975)   An Observational Method in the Foreign Language Classroom: A Closer Look at Interaction Analysis

Preface

The last decade has seen a rapidly increasing literature in the study of classroom behaviour, written from a variety of perspectives and focused on a range of research topics. Books which offer historical yet critical and evaluative assessments of this research are of inestimable value to teachers and researchers. This need is clear and immediate in the applied linguistic field of language teaching and learning where there are marked divisions between students of the classroom process and experimenters into acquisition, and, more generally, between researchers and language teachers.

A book which seeks harmonization between and convergence of interests and practices, as Dick Allwright's contribution to the *Applied Linguistics and Language Study* series expressly does, is not only desirable but imperative. After all, it is not as if the many studies of classroom processes have been especially coherent in terms of offering either researchers or practitioners a clear and well-charted set of comparable accounts, let alone a consistent commitment to what is being observed or, indeed, to what explanatory purposes the descriptive and interpretive studies were being directed. Even if within language education the divergent tendencies I refer to could be redirected, there is no substantial body of agreed practice and evaluation which could provide a home. This book must, therefore, be judged not only on its imaginatively constructed journey through a decade of research, but on its success as a mediator and as a conciliator. To do this needed task alone, however, would be inadequate since it might sweep important issues under the carpet, and fail thereby to indicate what research and practice in language education must be undertaken to provide a framework in which cooperative activity can thrive. The strength of Dick Allwright's book for many, I suspect, will be its partly-hidden agenda: the issues that this richly-informed account reveals. What are these issues? I shall expand here on *four*: the issue of *Perspective*, the issue of *Paradigm*, the issue of *Responsibility* and the issue of *Goal*.

The first of these, *Perspective*, is inherent in the title of the book.

What is 'observation' and how is it to be done? What perspective should or can the participants take on the goings-on of the classroom? Even to talk about participants in the plural, bringing together teacher, learner and researcher in various configurations, is itself a problematic issue. What framework to choose for description, what significant data, what interpretive procedures, what generalizability of what is 'found'? If in Stenhouse's cautionary phrase, 'there is no telling it as it is', what are the limits on ethnographic and anthropological engagement with and exploration of the data? Such a question, of course, itself encapsulates the problem. The classroom is an attractive research site for a variety of disciplines: sociology, anthropology, social psychology, communicative ethnography, educational research and curriculum management, as well as the legitimate specialist demands of the subject being taught and learnt itself. Perspective, then, is crucial, and contradictory tendencies within language education and research can mask an array of these complex and often concealed vested interests. In posing the key question of what 'understanding' classroom behaviour requires, Dick Allwright skilfully charts a range of responses in order to unmask what is taken for granted in different traditions, showing how over the period covered in his account the observational question has, not unnaturally, been answered according to the particular perspectives of the researcher. The classroom is more than a specific site, however, it is emblematic of many others where the issue of 'description' cannot be easily separated from 'interpretation' and where (though less often pursued) 'interpretation' *always* implies a need for 'explanation', linking texts to ideologies and issues of the social institution and society. After all, no observational schedule is neutral; it embodies a set of norms and purposes not at all transparent to either observer or observed. Nonetheless, despite the wider significance of the classroom for all manner of other-directed discourse analysts and ethnographers of speaking, there is a particular subject focus. What connections can be drawn between patterns of observed interaction and classroom talk with the process of language acquisition in the learner? This is, after all, what interests teachers, what should interest second language acquisition researchers and what should suggest modifications to classroom practice. It is this question that Dick Allwright uses to document how a 'faith in the observable' gave way to a recognition that there was no escaping the need to involve teachers and learners in personal, illuminative introspection of their own classroom behaviour. However difficult it was to undertake and to justify in some circles, it was necessary if we were to explore more fully what was being learnt. This is not to say that the issue of perspective is solved. What this book does is to place it squarely on the agenda.

Issues naturally breed issues as perspectives call up research paradigms that underpin them. Here the historical account is of greatest value to the reader since it enables us to share the author's question: why such and such a 'faith' appealed at the time it was current. The systematic comparison of paradigms of research in language education made possible in this book cannot exist in some epistemological vacuum. Paradigms and methodologies need to be linked more generally to historical moments in research, and in a cross-disciplinary fashion. What Dick Allwright does is address this issue of *Paradigm* not only through his own perceptive commentaries, but by letting the research speak for itself to the reader through his carefully chosen extracts from major studies in the field. Tracing this history we see how a positivistic faith in the measurable found allies not only in the training and management desire to assess 'objectively' teachers' performance, but also in the dominant descriptive linguistic model of the time with its concentration on the identification of discrete items of formal structure. If teaching and learning language were quantifiable, what better mode of measurement than a research paradigm premissed upon the calculation of discrete linguistic and behavioural performances? If one adds to this a view of the teacher's role as the agent of language development, it is not difficult to see how an early and unstructured subjectivism fell prey to positivist forces, however reductionist and causal their conclusions now seem to be. This is not to say, however, that current concerns with ethnographic research with their focus on contextualization, emergent hypotheses and the importance of inferencing informed by an under-standing of participants' sociocultural knowledge, are unproblematic. The issue of explanatory adequacy and generalizability of findings still remains, granted the current harmony of such a paradigm with concerns for learner-centredness and the equalization of participatory significance between teacher and learner. Nor should the accommo-dation between that classroom research paradigm and topical interest in linguistic pragmatics surprise us. The historical point of view taken here would make us expect such cross-curricula harmony. The strength of this book is to demonstrate how we need an integration of research paradigms as part of that general convergence I refer to at the outset of this Preface, rather than some simplistic and unhelpful antagonism.

A reading of these extracts under Dick Allwright's expert guidance reveals another issue, not unrelated to the shift of paradigms high-lighted above. Two perceptive comments provide the clue: 'It no longer made sense to look at classroom interaction as if it was only the teacher's behaviour that mattered . . .' and 'It is odd that class-room teachers seem to see practice as a major concern and to be less concerned about input, whereas researchers typically have their priorities quite the other way round . . .' We might add, just so, to both, but they reveal an issue of *Responsibility* which runs through this historical account. Who is to undertake the observation? Who is to be observed by whom? For whom are the results of the obser-vation formative? What are the objectives of the observation? For whose benefit? These are questions which are not merely academic. Under different conditions they might be asked by any of the possible participants in classroom research: teachers, learners, researchers, administrators and sponsors, although not with the same motives or ends in view. Readers may see it as significant in the light of my remarks about the need for *explanation* above that this issue of re-sponsibility receives least acknowledgement in the extracted studies, despite Dick Allwright's own sensitivity to its importance. It is, of course, not only an issue of perception, but one of power. Undoubt-edly, the divergence of interests and not a little of the disappointment in terms of displaying connections between classroom behaviour and learning stem from a failure to problematize and engage this issue. Accommodations between classroom researchers and second language acquisition specialists might have been matched by productive partici-pation among teachers and learners in the study of language learning processes if these questions had been raised as preliminaries to research rather than as *post hoc* complaints. If the aims are important, whether to chart the process of language learning, or to evaluate teaching, or to appraise methodology or to inform curriculum change, then in terms of Systems Analysis it is worth obtaining a 'rich picture' of what is occurring within and 'behind' classroom behaviour. To do that we need the contribution and cooperation of all, and a range of research instruments. That in turn implies, at very least, an accom-modation of interests and a sharing of power. This may, of course, also be an instance of the historical moment I referred to earlier. After all, if we can have 'community architecture' where the interests and concerns of all are respected and their varying talents harnessed to agreed goals, ought we not also to promote a 'community' approach to classroom observation and action research? It would at least be in harmony with the call in these pages for a study of the 'culture' of the classroom.

Cooperative action needs nonetheless some purposes, some uses to which it must be directed, if it is to be sustained. Addressing this raises the final issue of this Preface, that of *Goal*. Different actors will have different priorities as far as determining the uses to which classroom observation can be put. For some, the focus is on the participants, informing teachers as a necessary part of self-development about the process of their practice, or enabling a greater understanding of the possibilities and limitations of learner interaction. For others, the focus is on more macro decision-making at the level of curriculum planning, evaluating the consequences of educational innovation in the classroom. For others again, such data offer insights into the ways in which cultural knowledge is transmitted or how the 'happening' of teaching is organized and conducted. There will be quite particular objectives, as for example, exploring the relationship between the order of presentation of language items and the order of their acquisition by learners, or more global ones as the links to be made between classroom processes and wider social forces at work outside the institution. Just as the interpretation of the data will be different and the research paradigms various, so will the goals of those responsible for classroom observation diverge. What is advocated here is not a homogenizing of this variation but a making plain of its underlying premisses, relativizing as a means for revealing new ways in which researchers, teachers and learners can cooperate as 'partners in the enterprise' as Dick Allwright puts it.

What then of the reader? I have referred above to the helpful argument provided by the author as a matrix within which the statements from research can be easily presented. This is a novel approach within the *Applied Linguistics and Language Study* series, allowing us to do justice to the historical perspective which characterizes this contribution. More than this, however, Dick Allwright has been able to draw on almost twenty years of experience in the field of study portrayed here to offer readers a set of activities and points for discussion through which they can take further the directions of the documented research. We hope that these initiatives, supported by the ideas contained in the further readings, will encourage researchers, teachers and learners to engage in fruitful cooperative projects in classroom language education.

Christopher N. Candlin   *Lancaster*
General Editor   *January 1987*

Introduction

Difficult as it is now for us to believe, twenty years or so ago it was radically innovative to suggest that people seriously interested in classroom language teaching and learning should actually look systematically at what happened in the classroom itself. At that time it was more 'normal' to introduce a new method as an experiment and then wait for achievement test results to tell the story. It took about a decade to establish systematic classroom observation as a standard procedure in both language teacher training and in language pedagogy research. Then, in the mid-seventies, some even more radical suggestions were made. Instead of just looking at people in the classroom and trying to work out what was going on, we might learn more, it was suggested, if we asked the learners themselves to tell us about what they were doing. Now, after two decades, with no radical new proposals currently on the table, it is time to review the status and role of systematic classroom observation in our field. But such a review would be impoverished – both more difficult to interpret and more difficult to learn from – if it lacked a historical perspective. The purpose of this book is to combine the review and the history in one volume, telling the story chronologically and interweaving a considerable number of key publications, or extracts from them, into the main text.

The story of systematic classroom observation is also largely the story of the changing relationship between teacher training and research over the same years. This is reflected in the structure of this volume. The first five chapters take us from mid-sixties research in Chapter 1 to late sixties teacher training in Chapter 2, and then back into research in the mid-seventies via Chapters 3, 4, and 5. At the start mainstream research and teacher training are working in different worlds, apparently unaware of each other. But we see in Chapter 1 that the introduction of systematic classroom observation into teacher training is accompanied by a new sort of research, based on the detailed study of classroom events. Chapter 3 tells how this new sort of research eventually breaks away from its roots in teacher training, dissatisfied with the limitations of the research procedures in use, and with the lack of a theoretical base. Alternative procedures are devised, as we see in Chapter 4, but new roots are at last found outside pedagogy in studies of second language acquisition. Research, as documented in Chapter 5, then looks forward to a long period of separation from the immediate concerns of teacher trainers. The ultimate goal remains the same for both, however, that of knowing enough about classroom language learning and teaching to be able to help classrooms become more productive places to work in, both for teachers and for learners. Chapter 6 reviews the historical survey of the previous five chapters, brings it up to date, and then looks in more depth at the status and role of observational data in current work.

Each of the chapters ends with some suggestions for follow-up activities and discussions. These have been devised with a group rather than the individual reader in mind, and constitute a basic practical introduction to the conduct of observational studies. They draw attention to papers that are not reproduced in this volume but which it would be valuable to consult.

Finally, it may be as well to say something about the definition of 'observation' adopted throughout this volume. Essentially what is involved in classroom observation is a procedure for keeping a record of classroom events in such a way that it can later be studied, typically either for teacher training or for research purposes. That record does not have to be a visual one, despite the obvious derivation of the term 'observation', since audio-recordings are often entirely adequate as raw data. The record does have to be a 'public' one in some sense, however. The data must either be collected by agreed and explicit coding procedures (such as a set of categories according to which all classroom events are classified – the Flanders model), or collected by electro-mechanical means for later analysis by such explicit procedures. In short, private diary entries about a lesson are not 'observations', for the purposes of this volume, and neither are vague evaluatory statements like: 'You don't give the people at the back of the room enough opportunities to speak'. Such things might well serve as usable data, for some purposes, but they would never constitute 'observational' data. To reinforce this point throughout the volume the term 'observation' will be most often accompanied by the qualifier 'systematic', reflecting these important restrictions on its interpretation.

1 Observation 'arrives' in language teaching research

The role of observation in methodological comparisons

It has not always been considered necessary for research on classroom language learning and teaching to include classroom observation as an integral research tool, and of course in some areas of research, such as aptitude testing, there is no obvious reason why classroom observation should be involved anyway. In the 1960s, however, attention turned away from aptitude, which had indeed been an important focus of attention in the previous decade, thanks to the pioneering work in the USA of Carroll and Sapon (1959). Attention in the 1960s turned towards methods. It became especially important to find out, at least in the USA, what method was the most effective. This concern with effectiveness was not prompted by purely pedagogic motives, however, rather it was part of the general reaction to the first success, in 1957, of the Soviet Union's space programme. Sputnik came as a great and unwelcome surprise to the US government, and had the not entirely predictable but no doubt altogether welcome effect of making greatly increased funding available for education in general and for language education in particular, via the National Defense Education Act of 1958.

With the extra funding came extra responsibility for spending it wisely, for making sure that it meant maximum effectiveness. At the time the best bet for effectiveness was clearly to be found in the work of the psychologists and linguists who had been responsible for the success of the wartime military language programmes. Their work had been grounded in behaviourism, and it was behaviourism that underlay the new effort to produce language teaching materials suitable for state schools and colleges. The simple label 'behaviourist' was not applied to them, however, the term 'audiolingual' being much more descriptive, bearing clearly the intended emphasis on listening and speaking rather than on reading and writing. This was an emphasis that could be derived from behaviourist thinking, and thinking within linguistics, on the primacy of speech, but it was also an emphasis that fitted exactly the perceived capabilities of the newly invented language laboratory, which the extra monies now made a viable proposition for very many educational institutions. With advanced educational technology in support the 'audiolingual revolution' made a great impact, and 'audiolingualism' was adopted very widely in the USA (as might be expected, other parts of the world were not so quick to put their faith in the 'new').

The move from an emphasis on aptitude to one on method can now be seen as altogether understandable, not only for the more or less straightforwardly political and even commercial reasons given above, but also for the 'internal' reason that the natural outcome of aptitude work is selectivity. In an elitist system, as in military education, good aptitude tests make it possible to select for teaching only those who are considered most capable of successful learning. For universal public education in a democracy such elitism is, in principle, and on principle, unacceptable, and therefore some alternative route to success must be found. At a time of increasing optimism about the capabilities of science and technology, as in the late fifties and early sixties, the appeal of a methodological solution combining the science of behaviourist psychology and linguistics with the new technology of the language laboratory was no doubt compelling.

But the scientific and technological spirit of the times, applied to the crisis of confidence engendered by Sputnik, brought with it the additional concern of accountability. It was not enough to be doing what was scientifically and technologically the most sensible and promising thing to do. It was also necessary to establish 'scientifically' that improved results were obtainable. This meant devising empirical studies to prove, hopefully, that the 'new' was indeed to be preferred to the 'old'. Interestingly the first appears to have been Keating's 1963 'Study of the Effectiveness of Language Laboratories', suggesting that the initial focus was on the technology rather than on the method as such. Keating's report was surprisingly negative, however, which only increased the pressure on the proponents of audiolingualism to demonstrate their case empirically. Scherer and Wertheimer took up the challenge at the university level, in Colorado, but their 1964 report was also discouraging. Although it was clear from their results that audiolingualism promoted the audiolingual skills, while the 'traditional' method promoted, naturally enough, the skills of reading and writing, they were unable to demonstrate any overall superiority for the audiolingual method after two years of teaching. Since they had great difficulty in keeping their two learning groups distinct over the two years, these results are not in fact so easy to interpret, however. In addition, since observational records were not kept of the actual teaching involved, it is not possible to determine whether or not the teaching itself was distinctly different for the two groups of learners. At this point observation had clearly not 'arrived'.

Systematic classroom observation was however included as a design feature in the very large-scale experiment that began just as the Colorado team published its report. The Pennsylvania Project team set out quite unashamedly to demonstrate the superiority of the new audiolingual approach in the public school setting. This preliminary bias was admitted in the team's final report, published in 1970, by which time methodological thinking had already moved on and found new reasons in favour of traditional ways of teaching modern languages (brought up to date in the light of a new enthusiasm, initiated by Chomsky's 1959 attack on Skinner's 'Verbal Behaviour', for cognitive psychology). For more of the background to the study, and for a first extract from contemporary documents, we can turn to Clark's 1969 paper in a special issue of the *Modern Language Journal* devoted to the Pennsylvania Project: 'The Pennsylvania Project and the "Audio-Lingual vs. Traditional" Question'.

> The Pennsylvania Project had as its major focus the in-field comparison of three different foreign language teaching methods for beginning and intermediate French and German classes at the high-school level: 1) 'traditional'; 2) 'functional skills' (essentially the 'audio-lingual' approach as broadly defined within the profession); and 3) 'functional skills plus grammar' (similar to the 'functional skills' approach but specifying the use of grammatical explanations by the teacher as a supplement to the regular audio-lingual procedures). Since there has been a considerable history of controversy between proponents of traditional and audio-lingual techniques on the relative merits of these approaches, results of this large-scale study were eagerly awaited by the profession. The reported major conclusion that after two years of 'traditional,' 'functional skills,' and 'functional skills plus grammar' instruction there were no significant differences in student achievement in listening comprehension, speaking, and writing – and slight superiority of the 'traditional' group in reading – was a rather disheartening outcome for the many persons who had placed their faith and developmental effort in the audio-lingual approach. While relatively modest student performance in reading and writing might have been anticipated following one or even two years of audio-lingual instruction, the lack of superiority in speaking and listening

comprehension shown by audio-lingual students in the Pennsylvania study was difficult to accept both in light of teachers' on-going experiences with this method, and in view of the results of two other in-field research studies in the area: one comparing audio-lingual and eclectic methods for beginning college French (Creore and Hanzeli 1960), and another contrasting audio-lingual and traditional methods for first and second-year college German (Scherer and Wertheimer 1964). In both of these investigations, the control groups were found equal or superior to the audio-lingual classes on measures of reading comprehension and writing, but the audio-lingually trained students surpassed the control groups on tests of listening comprehension and speaking ability, usually with quite large mean differences in test score.

It is the intent of the next few pages to arrive at some estimation of the accuracy and import of the Pennsylvania Project findings as they relate to the 'audio-lingual vs. traditional' question. Valette (1969) and Marxheimer (1969) have also commented on various aspects of this study, with particular attention to the classroom texts and language laboratory procedures used in the project.

At the outset of the discussion, it should be emphasized that no experimental study – especially one which uses the real-life school situation as its laboratory – is faultless in the sense that it does not allow at least some adverse commentary on various aspects of its design or execution: furthermore, when findings of a particular study run counter to the sentiment or expectations of a large segment of the profession, that study is often subjected to much more detailed examination and criticism than would be an investigation having more readily accepted results. The researchers on the Pennsylvania Project should be warmly praised for having undertaken a large-scale study attempting to provide empirical data on the relative merits of basic instructional procedures which have been more often accepted on faith than critically and carefully evaluated. If various shortcomings of the Pennsylvania Project can be identified, this should not be considered as a justification to dismiss the entire investigation as fruitless or insignificant or to close the door to continuing investigations in the area.

Description of the study

At the beginning of the study, a panel of prominent foreign language educators was assembled by the project staff to assist in developing close descriptions of and rationales for three language teaching methodologies: 'traditional,' 'functional skills,' and 'functional skills plus grammar' (I, pp. 18–25). From a total of 58 high schools participating in the study, 61 beginning French classes and 43 beginning German classes were assigned to one of the three teaching methods. Since it was not considered desirable to have different methods 'competing' in a single school building, only one method was used in any given school. School equipment and teacher preferences were also usually taken into account in making the assignments.

Before the beginning of the fall, 1965 school term, the project staff held teacher workshops to explain the purpose of the study and to alert the teachers to their responsibilities toward the study. Detailed instructional guides were also developed to help teachers adhere to the pedagogical strategy and laboratory system to which they were assigned.

Classroom instruction under each of the three teaching methods was carried out during the 1965–66 school year and periodic classroom visits were made by project field consultants to monitor teacher adherence to the assigned method.

Student achievement in the four skill areas of listening comprehension, speaking, reading, and writing was evaluated at mid-year and again at the end of the year by use of the *MLA Cooperative Classroom Tests* (Educational Testing Service 1963). Scores on the earlier *Cooperative French and German Tests* were also obtained (Educational Testing Service 1939–1941). Student scores on these measures, when adjusted for certain background variables such as student language aptitude or prior achievement, showed in almost all cases no significant differences among the three teaching methods. The 'traditional' group was found superior to the 'functional skills' and 'functional skills plus grammar' groups on the older Cooperative tests (which are primarily reading-oriented instruments), and the 'traditional' group also scored higher on the reading portion of the MLA Cooperative battery.

A smaller-scale replication of the first-year study was carried out in 1966–67, and showed non-significant differences among the teaching methods for the two skills of listening comprehension and reading ability; speaking and writing ability were unfortunately not evaluated in the replication study.

About half of the French and German students who had participated in the original 1965–66 experiment were also followed through a second year of language instruction (1,090 students participated in the second-year investigation from a first-year total of 2,171). Testing at the end of the second year was based primarily on the MLA Cooperative battery: after two years of instruction, the 'traditional' group surpassed the 'functional skills' groups in reading ability but scored less highly on a test of oral mimicry of short phrases (Valette Sound Production Test). Student achievement in listening comprehension, global speaking, and writing as measured by the MLA Cooperative tests was not significantly different for the three groups.

No fewer than fifty-eight high schools were initially involved in the experiment, then, and more than two thousand students. Aware of the need to differentiate clearly between the different teaching approaches, the team built in systematic classroom observation procedures, using specially developed observational schedules to reflect the expected pedagogic differences in classroom behaviour. It was a very ambitious undertaking, to monitor so many teachers and learners in so many classes across the state of Pennsylvania, but it was crucial to the enterprise, not only for the sake of making sure that the intended methodological prescriptions were indeed being followed, but, as suggested earlier, for making sure, after Colorado, that any results could be confidently interpreted as the results of the application of distinctive teaching methods. Unfortunately, as our second extract from Clark's paper explains, the precautions taken were not entirely adequate. Clark's arguments relate interestingly to the role of classroom observation and the technicalities of observation schedules.

Possible confusion of distinctions among "traditional," "functional skills," and "functional skills plus grammar" groups

Central to an effective comparison of different teaching methodologies is the strict maintenance of the desired distinctions between the methods. If ostensibly different teaching methods tend in the course of the experiment to resemble one another in terms of what actually goes on in the classroom, the likelihood of finding significant differences in student performance is accordingly reduced.

The Pennsylvania Project staff appears to have been sensitive to the need for exercising strict control of classroom procedures within each of the three method groups. The project reports indicate that the following steps were taken, among others: detailed inventories of suggested teaching procedures and expected student outcomes were prepared for each of the instructional methods and distributed to participating teachers; for each textbook system, detailed teacher guidelines were prepared by the project staff; participating teachers received information about appropriate teaching methods and the general aims and procedures of the project in a four-day pre-experimental workshop and at other general meetings throughout the year; project field consultants made periodic class visits to evaluate teachers' adherence to the instructional procedure specified in each case.

Although the procedures followed by the project staff in defining, developing materials for, and training teachers in the three teaching methods seem to have been well conceived, the classroom observation procedure – which would have offered the most direct way of determining teacher adherence to a particular teaching method – was somewhat less precise and thus less useful than would have been desired. The observation technique used by the project was to have a project coordinator visit classes randomly, each teacher being observed about once every two weeks. For each class visited, the observer noted the extent of conformance to the assigned strategy by rating – on a 5-point scale ranging from 'excellent' to 'very poor' – each of a number of possible classroom activities such as 'vocabulary drill,' 'writing – free composition,' 'reading as direct communication,' 'average use of tapes – ten minutes per day.' Unfortunately, quite different rating scales were used for the 'traditional' and 'functional skills' classes.[1] The 'traditional' rating scale listed such activities as 'vocabulary drill,' 'translation of reading lesson' and other procedures typical of the 'traditional' approach; the 'functional skills' scale, by contrast, contained entries for 'students speak foreign language,' 'vocabulary taught in context only,' and so forth. As a consequence of this lack of overlap between the 'traditional' and 'functional skills' rating scales, there was little or no provision for the observer to note the occurrence of 'functional skills' activities in nominally 'traditional' classes, or *vice versa*. For example, the 'traditional' rating scale contained no entry for 'teacher speaks foreign language': it is not difficult to imagine that in some 'traditional' classes occasional or even extensive discourse in the foreign language would have gone unreported. By the same token, use in the 'functional skills' classes of 'traditional' procedures such as vocabulary drill would have not been noted on the observer's report sheet.

There are peripheral indications in the two project reports that 'traditional' project teachers used, at least to some extent, instructional procedures appropriate to the 'functional skills' method and *vice versa*. In the October 1968 report it is noted that 'field consultants observed students in TLM ("traditional") classes pronouncing the foreign language more than had been anticipated' (II, p. 41). During the replication study the teachers and students in the 'traditional' classes 'spoke the second language more than was expected. In the "functional skills" strategies the students did not speak as much as might have been expected but were rated as "good" to "fair" in the amount of time spent in speech production' (II, p. 53). The transcript of a combined teacher-project staff evaluation meeting in May 1968 shows somewhat mixed teacher opinion

1. 'Functional skills' and 'functional skills plus grammar' rating lists were identical except for one entry involving classroom approach to grammatical explanations.

on the extent to which they had been able to adhere to the assigned strategy: while some teachers reported that they were able to follow closely the instructional procedures specified for their group, others had reservations such as 'the teacher will use what he thinks is most important regardless of the textbook,' or 'the TLM strategy was not really defined. Was the TLM teaching that went on not a combination of Direct Method as well as everything else?' (II, Appendix H).

In order to afford an objective comparison of the instructional procedures actually used in the 'traditional' and 'functional skills' classrooms, it would have been much more appropriate to use a single rating form which would have allowed the observer to rate not only those activities considered characteristic of the teaching method nominally in use but also activities more appropriate to another type of teaching strategy. Using a combined rating form, close adherence to a particular method would be shown by a high score on 'positive' aspects for that method *together with* a low score on 'negative' aspects. It may of course be the case that 'traditional' and 'functional skills' distinctions were fairly well maintained throughout the study; nonetheless, the use of a more sensitive rating scale capable of noting both 'pro' and 'con' activities would have allowed for much more objective support of the claimed distinctiveness of the teaching methods as they were actually implemented in the classroom.

Following Clark's arguments it seems hardly reasonable to claim that classroom observation had 'arrived'. It had certainly appeared on the scene at last, but only in such a way as to further indicate its potential importance, and the importance of doing it some other way in future. At least, though, it was now quite clear that research on methodological comparisons in the natural classroom setting had to include a systematic observational component, if its results were to be interpretable. Clark addresses this issue more directly in his final comments.

Discussion

A number of factors have been identified which suggest the need for a rather cautious interpretation of the Pennsylvania Project findings as they relate to the comparison of 'audio-lingual' and 'traditional' teaching methods. Many of the points raised – as, for example, the possible differences in teacher experience among the experimental groups – could be investigated using data which are probably already available in project files. Statistical re-analysis incorporating (as necessary) controls for teacher background and other variables discussed would appear quite feasible, as would the removal of present covariate adjustments for mid-year achievement.

The presentation of convincing evidence for the operational distinctiveness of the three teaching methods would probably be a more difficult undertaking, but even in the absence of the 'hard' data that would have been provided by detailed classroom records, a more thoroughgoing description of classroom activities as perceived by the project coordinators would be of considerable value. Perhaps the Pennsylvania Project staff would be willing to address some of these procedural and analysis questions in a future document; the arduous activities already carried out and the great quantity of data assembled would appear to justify further analyses incorporating these and other comments by interested persons in the field.

Before we leave the Pennsylvania Project entirely, mention should be made of the important fact that Clark's comments, along with those of several other critics, were published in the *Modern Language Journal* before the Project's own report (Smith 1970) was generally available. The reader is referred to Smith's report not only for a more comprehensive picture of the whole study, but for a fascinating appendix in which Smith addresses the issues raised by the Project's critics. Mention should also be made of a form of criticism that went well beyond the technicalities of observation schedules to attack the whole idea of methodological comparisons as a viable way of investigating classroom language learning. Grittner had already made the point, in 1968, in a letter to the editor of the *Newsletter of the National Association of Language Laboratory Directors*.

'The validity of the research design used by Smith and Berger is being increasingly questioned by educational psychologists and curriculum specialists. For example, Stephens in *The Process of Schooling* (1967) documents 780 such studies involving control and experimental groups. Of these 580 showed 'no significant difference' or 'NSD.' The remaining 200 students were rather evenly divided between positive and negative results. *In short, a half century of such 'research' has told us almost nothing about the relative superiority of one educational strategy or system over another!* (Examples of the areas which Stephens reported on are the following: large vs. small schools; large vs. small class size; accredited vs. non-credited teachers; progressive vs. traditional education; live teachers vs. TV; lecture method vs. discussion method; team teaching vs. traditional teaching; and homogeneous vs. heterogeneous grouping of students.) Tables showing standard deviations, covariance, F-ratios and the like are very impressive; however, if the ultimate result of such studies is that they cancel one another out, perhaps we should ask for a cease fire while we search for a more productive means of investigation.'

Perhaps the most significant conclusion that can be drawn from studying the Pennsylvania Project is that we must have better research regarding the processes of learning a foreign language and the subsequent patterns of teacher-student interaction.

Grittner's letter was quoted by Otto in his contribution to the *Modern Language Journal*'s special issue of criticism directed at the Pennsylvania Project, an indication of further support for his worries about the essential validity of methodological comparisons as a research procedure, but these worries, it should be noted, were not accompanied by constructive suggestions for new or at least radically different procedures that would meet the criticisms levelled at Smith and his team. What was needed was an alternative approach to the whole problem of conducting practically worthwhile research on classroom language learning, but first there had to be a change in the sorts of questions asked. The research so far had been conducted on the assumption that it made sense to ask 'Which is the best method for modern language teaching?', and that presumably on the additional assumption that once the answer was determined it would then make sense to simply prescribe the 'winning' method for general adoption. Both these assumptions were now themselves being questioned. The first was being questioned by those who tended to believe, curiously enough, in the validity of the methodological comparison studies so far conducted, and who therefore felt drawn to the conclusion that perhaps the inconclusiveness of the results of these studies should be taken as evidence that method itself was not nearly as important a variable as had been so confidently assumed. It no longer made so much sense to ask which method is 'best'. The second assumption, that methods could be simply prescribed, was also now called into question, if only because the criticisms of the Pennsylvania Project had revealed the immense practical difficulties of introducing a new method and of ensuring its systematic and faithful adoption.

The time was ripe, then, for an alternative approach to classroom language learning research, an approach that would no longer see the language teaching world in terms of major rival 'methods', and one that would be more respectful of the complexities of the language teacher's task. It is to such an approach that we now turn.

Observation as the basic research procedure

The obvious radical alternative to methodological comparisons was to be found in general educational work, where observation was already the key procedure for a number of researchers, notably Flanders (see Flanders 1960), who were interested not so much in comparing 'methods' as in investigating 'teaching styles' in the hope of being able to find which one was the most effective. Ultimately this was no less prescriptive in intent, of course, but now the immediate focus was not on telling teachers which method to use for an experimental period but on producing detailed studies of actual classroom behaviour, and on relating aspects of teacher behaviour directly to learning outcomes, regardless of the 'method' employed. Language teaching was in any case peculiar, it seems, in having a number of labelled methods to concern itself with, and to wish to be able to choose between.

One of the most interesting of the people who brought systematic classroom observation to language teaching research was Jarvis, who made a number of very distinctive contributions to the field. His 1968 paper (his work was therefore contemporary with the Pennsylvania Project, and published before it) begins by taking the observational perspective for granted as 'the most obvious approach to research on language teaching' and continues with an acknowledgement of the practical problems standing in its way. He then draws attention to the necessity of devising an observational system that will properly reflect the special characteristics of the language classroom, chief of which is the fact that language is used there both for 'real' and for 'drill' purposes. Our first extract from 'A Behavioral Observation System for Classroom Foreign Language Skill Acquisition Activities', presents Jarvis's observational schedule, his 'instrument'.

> Although the inauspicious history of research on teaching effec-
> tiveness can appear intimidating to the prospective researcher, the
> recent widespread recognition of the need for systematic obser-
> vation of what actually does happen within the classroom does seem
> to provide an alternative to the futilitarian approach. While it is the
> most obvious approach to research on teaching, it is very expensive
> in terms of time, money, and the skill required of the observers. In
> the literature one finds many pleas for more systematic observation
> but fewer reports of research utilizing the technique.[1] Recently
> Moskowitz (1968a) has attempted to adapt the Flanders system of
> Interaction Analysis to the foreign language classroom. The

1. A concise treatment of the entire subject can be found in Medley and
   Mitzel 1963.

ingenious Flanders system, now being extensively used in research
in other academic areas, categorizes classroom verbal behavior into
various types of teacher talk and student talk. Teacher talk categories reflect the directness or indirectness of the teacher's influence. Matrices of behaviors observed and recorded at three second
intervals provide a graphic abstraction of the classroom behavior
in terms of the categories used. Foreign languages were among
those subject areas excluded from the early extensive work of
Flanders because the interaction analysis data 'were too variable
for efficient analysis' (Flanders 1961). Moskowitz suggests (p. 219)
that this lacuna in interaction research may be due to the need for
the researcher to understand both the system of interaction analysis
and the peculiarities of the foreign language classroom. While this
need is certainly critical, a fundamental factor may be traceable to
the objective of any behavioral description system, which is to
abstract behavior into kinds which in the classroom are significantly
different from one another in terms of learning consequences. A
valid system of behavior analysis must in the foreign language classroom differentiate between types of behaviors which are monolithic
in other classrooms. For example, when a student verbalizes, 'it's
cold outside,' he may do it in English or in the target language.
When it is in the target language, he may be making the utterance
because the temperature is in fact below zero that day, and the
teacher has asked him how the weather is, or he may be making the
utterance because it is simply an item in a pattern drill on idiomatic
expressions about the weather. Moreover, the utterance may be an
answer to the teacher's question about the weather despite its being
a warm September afternoon, because it is the only way the student
has learned to respond to that question. He may not yet have
learned to say that it is hot outside. These semantically identical
utterances are not identical behaviors in terms of the language
learning outcomes.

Thus, one is led to the need for a system for classifying behaviors
in terms of language skill acquisition consequences of the behaviors.
The instrument proposed below is derived from the psychology of
second language learning as it is generally understood at present
and from experiential knowledge of how these theoretical
considerations do actualize in today's classrooms.

The instrument

Inherent in any system of behavior classification is the *a priori*
postulating of a teaching model. The defined categories peremp-
torily represent judgments about which aspects of behavior to
observe and which to ignore. In order to avoid a restrictive model
the instrument here proposed presumes merely that language skill

acquisition means optimal student skill development in each of the four language skills: listening, speaking, reading, and writing. (The instrument is intended for use only in language skill acquisition activities; it is not applicable, for example, to testing or a lecture about culture.) The implied model assumes that in language skill acquisition the student must proceed through the stages of 'encountering' (hearing or seeing) elements of the language, imitating them, manipulating them, and finally using them in innovative real communication language. Above all, the model assumes that teaching effectiveness is in part attributable to the teacher's choice of behaviors and their frequency of use.

Use of the instrument requires that an observer record a time sample of classroom behaviors in terms of the categories defined below. At regular intervals of a predetermined number of seconds the observer records an entry in terms of what is occurring at that particular instant. Using a ten second interval the first five minutes of a class might appear as: A A 2 2 D 2 A H C 2 A 8 E E P A 2 4 1 B A D 2 2 G 4 3 3 A A. At the end of the class period one has a sequential graphic sample of what occurred. The frequencies of each category are then totalled and easily converted to proportions or percentages of the class period. A table of the behavioral categories appears in Figure 1 [p. 15].

The format of Figure 1 can also be adapted to that of a table for recording totals and proportions of time for each behavior. Proportions of the larger divisions of the instrument, such as teacher talk and student talk, target language, English, real communication language, or drill language can be summarized from the individual categories.

The major dichotomies are required by the nature of meaningful verbal behavior. Further divisions are related to learning activities. Target language activity can involve either written language or spoken language which can be further dichotomized into 'real' or 'drill' language. 'Real' language categories are those where language is used to communicate. Control of the language is in the speaker's intent or meaning rather than in the structure of the language. The utterance is not invariably predictable by a potential auditor. It has furthermore, a meaningful and immediate context. The student's response about the weather depends upon what he really believes the weather to be.[2] This 'real' language occurs in the following categories.

2. The need for this type of behavior in the classroom has been a recurring theme in the professional literature especially since the publication of Rivers 1964, *The Psychologist and The Foreign-Language Teacher.*

Real language categories

A *Teacher evokes student response.* The teacher utterance results in a verbal response by the student (or is intended to elicit such a response). The utterance is intended to result in an interaction. Most entries would be questions either personalized to individual students or relating to material studied. Typical examples would be: 'How are you?' 'What time is it?' 'What color is your shirt?' (English examples are used merely for convenience.)

B *Evoked by student.* The teacher responds to a student utterance (which is evoking), thus making an interaction; e.g. 'Yes, Mary, Marseilles is in the south.'

C *Management.* The teacher uses the target language in the mechanics of running the classroom; e.g. 'Open your books to unit ten.' 'Would you go to the board, John?' 'You must study much more.' 'Change the verb to the past tense in this drill.'

D *Reinforcing or facilitating student performance.* The teacher uses real communication language in a way that has a positive affective influence on students; e.g. 'You did very well, Paul.' 'Good.' 'I know how difficult this is.' 'Would it help you to remember what John said?' This category is differentiatied from categories J and P by its communicative nature. The focus is on the meaning of the teacher's utterance.

E *Explanatory information presentation.* The teacher gives an explanatory presentation which provides information to the students. The focus is the meaning of what is said and not the language forms used to express it. The time involved can range from that of a short utterance to a lengthy lecture. Typically the teacher may be conveying information about material studied (e.g. a story read), explaining a grammar pattern, or explaining the meaning of an item.

The 'real language' student utterances are all individual as opposed to choral. The very nature of choral work excludes its communicative use.

1 *Student evokes response.* The student initiates an utterance to which the teacher (or another student) responds. Direct dialog which is communicative is included.

2 *Student responds.* The response is to an evoking utterance, thus completing an interaction; e.g. 'Yes, I do have a sister.' 'I'm sixteen years old.'

'Drill language' is language for the purpose of facilitating the use of that language. It has meaning but is not uttered for the purpose of communication in this instance. It is 'practice language.'

	Teacher	Student
	Target language	
Real	A Evoking student response	1 Evoking response
	B Evoked by student	2 Responding
	C Classroom management	
	D Facilitating performance or reinforcing behavior	
	E Information explanation	
Drill	G Evoking stimulus	3 Individual response
	H Repetition reinforcement	4 Choral response
	J Prompting	
	P Modeling or correcting	
Reading and writing	W Presenting written language	5 Writing
		6 Reading silently
		7 Reading aloud
	English	
	K About target structure or sound system	8 Question about target
		9 Answer about target
	M About meaning	
	N Management	

+ Silence or English not in the above categories but which seems to facilitate learning
− Silence or English not in the above categories but which seems to impede learning

FIGURE 1

Drill language categories

G *Stimulus evoking response.* The teacher gives a drill stimulus for any type of pattern drill including repetition (e.g. dialog repetition). It does always elicit student response.

H *Repetition reinforcement.* The teacher approvingly repeats (echoes) student utterance. Both informational feedback (about the accuracy of the student utterance) and effective reinforcement are inherent in the repetition. It may be slightly correctional; however, it does not evoke an additional student repetition.

J *Prompting.* The teacher provides the student with language forms he has momentarily been unable to produce. The prompting is associated with encouragement and should not be a correction of forms already uttered by the student.

P *Modeling or correcting.* The teacher presents examples of language forms so that students can hear them, however, they do not evoke a student response; or, secondly, the teacher provides a corrective representation of a student utterance.

3 *Individual response.* The student utters practice language forms individually.

4 *Choral response.* The students utter practice language forms chorally (two or more students).

The reading and writing categories are essentially self-explanatory. These behaviors can in certain circumstances occur simultaneously with spoken language. A decision must then be made as to whether the learning is primarily centered in an oral skill or in a written skill. A transformation drill which requires major changes in the stimulus is not being read when the student is looking at the printed stimulus. Reading a sentence where the central task is simply the placement of a correct verb form into a blank is, however, essentially a reading task.

Categories W and 6 can also occur simultaneously. Here again judgment must be made about which is dominant. 'Teacher presenting written language' involves a small segment of classroom behavior when the teacher simply turns on an overhead projector; but when a sentence is written on the chalkboard, the shift to student reading logically occurs only when the teacher completes the writing. In category 5 the source initiating the student behavior can be written language (as in a writing drill), spoken language (as in dictation), or it may be innovative writing (student writes a description of an object).

The categories in English refer to all English talk. Included are all the uses of target language words, phrases, or sentences within English frames. For example, 'You should say, "Il en a besoin." '

K *About target.* All teacher talk about 'grammar' and the sound system. Most commonly this category represents generalizations about structure.

M *About meaning.* The teacher clarifies meaning by the use of English. The teacher either gives or asks for an English equivalent. The English portion of 'translation drills' is included in this category.

N *Management.* The same as C but in English.

8 *Student question about target.* The student begins an interaction by inquiring about any aspect of the target (including meaning).

9 *Student response about target.* The student completes an interaction by talking about any aspect of target language.

Any behavior not appropriately classified into the above categories is considered in the following dichotomy. These behaviors all involve either a use of English not subsumed by the above categories or a state of silence or confusion.

+ – *Lack of verbal behavior or English which seems to have a positive effect upon learning* (in its broadest sense); e.g. appropriate amount of time spent on administrative activites; joking, laughing, comments, all of which seem to contribute to the situation; other necessary English.

– – *Lack of verbal behavior or English seeming to impede learning;* e.g. excessive pauses for any purpose, irrelevant digressions, excessive teacher hesitancy.

These latter two categories require observer inference. The observer must make a judgment in categorizing the behavior occurring. All other categories require a relatively low degree of observer inference. The only other use of inference involves the duration of pause following a verbalization. When, for example, the teacher asks a question, there is frequently a pause of varying length before another behavior (such as a student answer) occurs. In recording the behavior the pause is, of course, considered a part of the question, the prior behavior. However, inference is involved if the pause is judged to be excessive. After this point the behavior occurring belongs to the final negative category.

In order to make a determination about the validity of the instrument's categories as indicating differences in teaching effectiveness a correlational study was made.

Jarvis seems to have been one of the first to see the importance of attempting to capture the special characteristics of the language classroom, and of distinguishing between what we might now call 'communicative' as opposed to other uses of language. His work is also interesting for its concern with the justification of the observational categories in the light of current thinking, but without reference by name to any particular method, another indication of the apparent gulf between such researchers and those whose work was described in the previous section. Jarvis's paper continues with another distinctive contribution. He sets out a procedure for using his 'instrument' to describe the teaching behaviour of teaching assistants in relation to a hypothesized ideal model, which he validates with reference to the 'attainment of course objectives' by the learners involved in the study.

Procedures and findings

Fourteen graduate teaching assistants in French at Purdue University were ranked according to their effectiveness as judged by their two most immediate supervisors. A third ranking was obtained from the teaching assistants themselves by using a 'pair comparison' technique.[3] Effectiveness was defined in terms of attainment of course objectives. High reliability existed between the rankings of the three judges. Using an analysis of variance for ranked data (Winer 1962) a Kendall Coefficient of Concordance of .9365 was computed. From this the average intercorrelation between the judges was calculated. It was .9047.

On a theoretical and experiential basis a model of an ideal average frequency for the various behaviors was then postulated for the teaching situation involved. The model took into account the nature of the course: objectives, text materials, contact time, methodology used, type of student, teacher qualification, and time of the semester. The model then served as a standard to which the behavior of the teaching assistants could be compared.

Following this, the teachers were observed and their teaching behaviors recorded. It was not feasible to obtain a large random sample of their teaching patterns. Therefore, the classes to be observed were chosen in a very restricted manner. Each teacher was to be observed for at least two hours. To provide standardization the total time for the two classes had to be approximately equally divided between teaching structure and teaching vocabulary. If dialogue work (primarily vocabulary) required eighty percent of a class hour with the remaining twenty percent grammar pattern instruction, the second observation was selected so that the class was made up of approximately eighty percent grammar instruction. This careful selection of classes was made possible by the existence of a very detailed course outline which specifies the content for each class hour of the course. Furthermore, if a teacher felt that a class was atypical, the class was eliminated from the data, and further observation was made. If the observer suspected that the class did not represent the typical pattern of the teacher, it was retained in the data; however, an additional observation was made and included in the mean profile of that teacher.

Following the observations, a classroom behavior profile was made up for each teacher. It consisted of the mean proportions of the classes devoted to each behavior. It was then relatively simple to determine each teacher's congruence to the model which had been postulated. A deviation-from-the-model score which consisted of the sum of the absolute deviations within each category was computed. Each percent deviation (.01) was counted as 1.00 in obtaining a deviation score. Figure 2 represents the model profile and that of one of the teachers (broken line). The deviation score of 61.10 is then the sum of the absolute differences between profiles at each category. A deviation score of zero would indicate exact congruity to the model. The maximum possible score is two

3. An adaptation of the technique found in Guilford 1954.

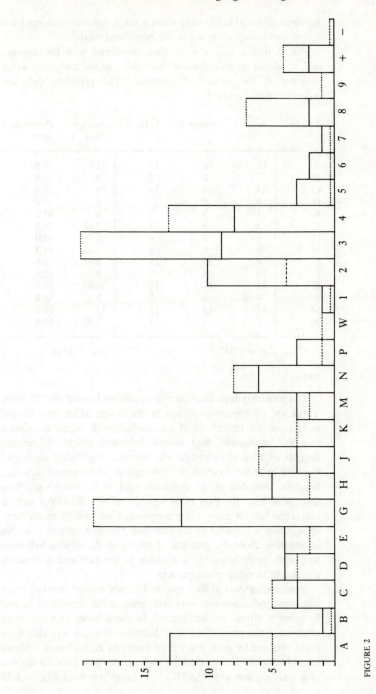

FIGURE 2

hundred. It could occur only when a single behavior observed was a zero percentage category in the postulated model.

The deviation scores were then correlated with the average rank to obtain an indication of the validity of the categories as an indicator of the judged effectiveness. The complete data are represented in Figure 3.

Teachers	Judge 1	Judge 2	Judge 3	Average Rank	Deviation Score
A	12	12	12	12	92.5
B	7	3	2	4	42.8
C	14	14	14	14	87.4
D	1	1	1	1	33.8
E	4	5	9	6	61.6
F	3	2	3	2.67	40.9
G	5	7	6	6	48.0
H	6	6	5	5.67	64.3
I	8	10	11	9.67	60.6
J	10	9	8	9	52.8
K	11	11	10	10.67	55.1
L	9	8	7	8	68.8
M	13	13	13	13	91.1
N	2	4	4	3.33	60.8

$$r_3 = .9047 \qquad\qquad r_{RD} = .8275$$

FIGURE 3

The strikingly high Pearson r is significant beyond the .01 level. There are no apparent artifacts in the design which have tended to increase the magnitude of this coefficient. It seems to indicate that the instrument does record behaviors which differentiate degrees of what is judged as effectiveness. Significant aspects of teaching behavior do seem to be recorded. The instrument is not, however, intended as an evaluative tool. It is, rather, strictly a descriptive tool, the data from which, can be utilized not only in evaluation but for many other purposes. Undoubtedly much more information is included in the data than has been utilized here. No information about the patterns or timing of the various behaviors was used; nevertheless, it is available in the data and is certainly a factor in learning consequences.

In recording data at five, ten, and fifteen second intervals there was some indication that very little information seemed to be lost by using a fifteen second interval. In three hours of five second observation the proportions of all behaviors differed very little from those obtained by using every third entry, the equivalent of a fifteen second interval. The mean difference per category between the two time intervals was .0048 (.48%). The range was from 0.00 to 2.33

percent. A classroom observer who wishes to record additional information (e.g. a supervisor) can make brief notes identifying structures, activities used, language errors, or other comments while using a fifteen second interval.

Recording data was greatly facilitated by the use of a small electronic device which indicated by a high frequency 'beep' the intervals at which entries were to be made.[4] Its use freed the observer from watching a timepiece and permitted concentration upon what was occurring in the classroom. Moreover, the observer did not have to transfer his attention from a visual cue to an instantaneous decision about verbal behavior which is primarily auditory. The interval indicator 'beep' was directly superimposed upon the verbal behavior.

Reliability in terms of observer agreement presented no particular difficulties. The degree of observer agreement seems to be strictly a function of observer training. After approximately three and one-half hours of familiarization and practice in using the instrument two graduate students and I viewed three one-half hour segments of videotaped high school classes. Making simultaneous entries the coefficient of the number of agreeing entries to total entries (a most conservative approach) was .84. Using an analysis of variance of the category summaries for the three classes over the three observers the reliability was .98.

Jarvis concludes his paper with some comments that are particularly interesting in the light of subsequent developments in the field.

The use of the instrument to reflect congruence to a model is but a single, if not novel, application. The instrument can, of course, be used to determine and construct such a model for a particular teaching situation. It seems to have particular relevance to any research involving teaching behavior change. The data obtained is immediately quantifiable and amenable to statistical analysis. The very use of such instruments may, in fact, be a causal factor in behavior change.

Jarvis's interest in congruence to an overall model brought him very close to the needs identified in the previous section in respect of research on methodological comparisons. As we saw, this was precisely what they needed, a way of characterizing the teaching entailed by particular teaching methods, and a way of establishing the degree of fit between the actual teaching and the ideal model. But this potential connection between the two approaches to research

---

4. The instrument, basically an audio oscillator, was designed and built by Harry Smith, technician for the Department of Modern Languages, Purdue University.

does not appear to have been realized at the time, and the moment soon passed, as large-scale methodological comparisons were abandoned in favour of smaller-scale comparisons of individual teaching techniques that did not pose the same descriptive problems.

There are two other particularly interesting points in Jarvis's concluding paragraph. First there is the suggestion that his work could be of relevance to 'any research involving teaching behaviour change'. This hint of a connection with teacher training was well taken up at the time, as we shall see in the next chapter. Second there is the intriguing reference in his final sentence to the 'very use' of such instruments being perhaps 'a causal factor in behaviour change'. What exactly Jarvis had in mind cannot be entirely clear from such a cryptic statement, but perhaps it can be interpreted as a suggestion that the precise characteristics of observation schedules might be less important than we would otherwise suppose, that it might not in practice matter very much whether a given schedule was particularly aptly designed for any particular purpose, because the mere fact of using any systematic observational tool would serve to raise consciousness and this might itself be the major factor in the promotion of behaviour change.

Jarvis's perspective was comprehensive in scope, even though his own study was limited in scale. Meanwhile an even more ambitious project was in progress at the University of Stanford, California, and more precisely at the Stanford Center for Research and Development in Teaching, where a team was already engaged in attempting to identify the 'characteristics and behaviors' of successful teachers. Their work was primarily conceptual originally, since they started by identifying these 'characteristics and behaviors' with reference to professional opinion rather than to actual teaching behaviour, but Politzer published in 1970, two years after the publication of Jarvis's paper, an empirical study designed to distinguish between 'good' and 'bad' teaching behaviours. The behaviours he focused on were drawn directly for the most part from the audiolingual materials in use by the teachers being observed, but again no explicit connection was made by the author between his work and the contemporary work in methodological comparisons. It is as if the two research approaches existed in two quite separate worlds. Our first extract from Politzer's *Language Learning* paper, 'Some Reflections on "Good" and "Bad" Language Teaching Behaviors', gives a very brief statement of his research procedures and a much lengthier one of the instrument used for analysing the videotapes made of the seventeen teachers involved. He refers to 'ratings' and to 'general impressions' but it is clear that his procedures were much more systematic than the use of such terms would normally imply.

The study of the 'Characteristics and Behaviors of the Successful Foreign Language Teacher' (Politzer and Weiss 1969a) utilized the classes of 17 French teachers all teaching elementary French (first semester) on the high school level and using the so-called 'A-LM' Audio-Lingual Materials (Thompson 1961). The classroom performances of the teachers were videotaped (4 tapings of 15 minute sequences) during the semester. At the end of the semester the students of the teachers were given achievement tests in French, which were specifically designed to measure language skills that could be expected to have been developed as a result of the exposure to the A-LM materials. One of the main goals of the study was to investigate the correlations between student achievement in French and selected teaching behaviors observed by the analysis of the videotapes of the teachers' performances.

The instrument used in the rating of teacher classroom behaviors was designed to record objectively on three dimensions: (a) Categories of drills, (b) Time, and (c) Frequency. The raw data thus obtained could be expressed in terms of proportions or ratios.

a   *Categories of drills*: Six types of drills were specified for observation and rating: (1) Repetition drills, (2) Substitution drills, (3) Dialogue drills (in other words, cuing of one line of a dialogue by another), (4) Translation drill (English cuing for a French response), (5) Conversion drill (cue and response are structurally different), and (6) Free Response (response not predictable from the cue).

b   *Time*: The rating sheet contained 15 columns, one for each minute of observed time. During the rating sessions, an audio tape recorder was set up in each video room and synchronized with the videotape recorder. At the end of each 60-second interval, a voice on the tape spoke the number of the following minute. This served as a signal for the rater to move on to the next column and also removed any question as to which one of the 15 minutes was being rated.

c   *Frequency*: The rater recorded a tally for each drill event, that is, for each pair of stimulus/response involving teacher and students. An exchange was considered an 'event' whether it was between teacher and individual or teacher and class.

In addition to their objective rating of drill activities, raters were asked to put down, at the end of each 15-minute observation, their general impression of other classroom behaviors. There were three columns labeled: Never, Occasionally, and Frequently. The cut-off point between Occasionally and Frequently was established for each behavior during the raters' training sessions.

During the training sessions, the raters agreed completely on these variables. The four categories of classroom behavior were:

1 *Direct reference to book.* How often did the teacher refer to the textbook or to cue cards during the drill activities? Five times or less was considered 'Occasionally,' more than five times was considered 'Frequently.'

2 *Use of visual aids.* How often did the teacher use visual aids such as pictures, realia, overhead projector, chalkboard, and so on during the drill activities? Ten was considered the cut-off point between 'Frequently' and 'Occasionally.'

3 *Student/student interaction.* How often during the drill period did the teacher arrange for communication in French between students rather than between teacher and students? This category subsumed the use of the A-LM dialogues as well as free exchanges between students. Four or more occasions given to students to interact was considered as 'Frequent.'

4 *Variation of structures.* How often during the drill period did the teacher change the structures that were being drilled? Although a variety of structures is provided by the textbook, it is quite possible for a teacher to drill extensively on only one structure to the point of fatigue and boredom. It was therefore considered important to take note of the number of grammatical problems the teacher treated during the observed time. The cut-off point for this measure was four.

Politzer's next step was to relate the observations (although it must be noted that he does not use this term) to fourteen variables derived from his observational categories.

The raw data collected from the rating sheets were converted to proportions or averages to form the basis for the following fourteen variables of observed classroom behaviors. (For the table of scores for the 17 teachers, see Table 1.)

Variable 1: *Proportion of time spent in drill activity.* A count was made of the number of columns in which there were any tallies (regardless of category) in the four observation sheets for each teacher. The total was divided by sixty to arrive at the proportionate amount of time each teacher spent drilling during the four observations. This in itself tells us little except the teacher's propensity for conducting drills. It does not tell us about the speed or type of drill conducted.

TABLE 1 Ratings of teacher behaviors

Teacher	Variable													
	1	2	3	4	5	6	7	8	9	10	11	12	13	14
1	0.42	4.60	3.0	0.52	0	0.12	0.98	0	0.26	0.19	0	4	2	4
2	0.80	10.02	4.71	1.50	0	0	2.89	0.91	0.61	0.96	2	6	2.7	6
3	0.73	9.16	6.47	1.59	0.09	0.32	0.68	0	0.08	0.24	5.3	2.7	2	3.3
4	0.58	4.57	2.85	0	0.37	0.08	1.26	0	0.38	0.24	5.5	4	2	3.5
5	0.85	6.32	1.37	1.76	0	1.81	1.16	0.21	0.28	0.73	2	4.7	3.3	4.7
6	0.93	5.13	2.39	2.48	0	0	0.25	0	0.05	0.10	4.7	3.5	3	4
7	0.77	4.20	3.45	0.43	0.17	0	2.30	0	0.56	0.24	4.5	3.5	3	4
8	0.97	7.23	4.04	0.66	0	0.20	2.05	0.27	0.47	1.59	4	4.5	2	6
9	0.62	6.21	1.29	1.12	1.86	0	1.43	0	0.30	0.16	4	4	4.7	4
10	0.93	5.26	3.07	0.37	0	0.34	1.48	0	0.39	0.56	2.5	4.7	3	4
11	0.68	8.17	3.02	3.19	0	0.61	1.34	0	0.19	0.17	5	4	2	4.5
12	0.68	6.22	2.56	0.85	0.34	1.63	0.80	0	0.15	0.11	4	4.5	2.5	3.5
13	0.75	6.35	4.62	0.53	0	0.15	1.04	0	0.20	0.13	4	3.5	3	3.5
14	0.85	8.09	2.37	2.37	0	0.02	3.86	0.02	0.92	0.89	2.5	4.5	3	4.5
15	0.55	7.78	6.47	0.61	0	0.24	1.57	0	0.25	1.54	2	3.5	2	3
16	0.90	7.22	0.81	2.09	1.62	1.42	1.24	0.02	0.21	0.02	4.5	4.5	2.5	4
17	0.93	9.66	4.19	2.14	0.38	0.34	2.37	0.23	0.37	0.37	2.5	5.5	3.5	5.5

Variable 2: *Average number of drills per drill minute (pdm)*. This variable tells us something about the speed with which the teacher conducts his drills but nothing about the type of drills he conducts. This figure was arrived at by adding all the tallies in all the cells and dividing the sum by the number of minutes during which the teacher drilled throughout the four observations.

Variable 3: *Average Repetition drills pdm*. This figure was arrived at by dividing the total number of Repetition drills for each teacher by the number of minutes the teacher drilled during the 60 minutes observed. The same process was used for variables 4, 5, 6, 7, and 8 that follow.

Variable 4: *Average Substitution drills pdm*.
Variable 5: *Average Dialogue drills pdm*.
Variable 6: *Average Translation drills pdm*.
Variable 7: *Average Conversion drills pdm*.

Variable 8: *Average Free Responses pdm*. The data gathered for this variable were disappointingly meager. Only seven of the teachers allowed for any free response at all and only one of these was of slightly more than negligible frequency. Teacher 2 allowed 18 free responses out of 48 minutes of drill; teacher 5 allowed 4 responses out of 38 minutes of drill; teacher 8 allowed 8 free responses out of 44 minutes of drill; teacher 2 allowed 2 responses out of 56 minutes of drill and the rest allowed one response each. Nevertheless, this variable was included in the numerator of the following variable.

Variable 9: *Ratio of 'Free' to 'Controlled' drills*. In Repetition, Substitution, Dialogue and Translation drills the student response is very highly controlled. Free Response drill and to some extent also Conversion drill represent a loosening of control in which the response is less highly controlled by the stimulus. Conversion and Free Response drills were grouped under the heading 'Free' drills as opposed to the other more 'Controlled' drills. Variable 9 was thus arrived at by dividing the tallies for variables 3 (Repetition drills), 4 (Substitution drills), 5 (Dialogue drills), and 6 (Translation drills) into the total number of tallies for variables 7 (Conversion drills) and 8 (Free Response).

Variable 10: *Proportion of Switched drill to Exclusive drill*. This variable is an indication of the frequency with which the teacher switched from Controlled drill to Free drill and *vice versa*. The figure was obtained by dividing the number of minutes during which the teacher worked exclusively in either Controlled or Free drill activities into the number of minutes during which the teacher switched from one type of drill to another.

Variable 11: *Reference to book.* For this variable as well as for variables 12, 13, and 14 that follow, a numerical score was given to the general impressions of frequency of occurrence. A score of 2 was assigned to 'Never,' a score of 4 was assigned to 'Occasionally,' and a score of 6 was assigned to 'Frequently.' The scores for the four observations were totalled and divided by four to arrive at the average score. In one case (Teacher 1) it was often impossible to see the teacher and the score of zero in this case represents 'Not observed.'

Variable 12: *Use of visual aids.* This variable measures the frequency with which the teacher used pictures, realia, overhead projector, and chalkboard during the drill activities.

Variable 13: *Student to student interaction.* This variable measures the amount of student to student interaction in French as part of the drill activities and includes the recitation of dialogues as well as the rather rare instances of free interchange between students.

Variable 14: *Variation of structures.* This variable measures the variety of structures (grammatical problems) the teacher introduced within a 15-minute segment.

Politzer then describes all the criterion measures used to establish the levels of performance of the learners involved, making clear the close relationship of these measures to the audiolingual materials on which the teaching had been based. Then he goes straight into a presentation and discussion of his results.

Great care was taken to construct criterion measures specifically designed to measure the student's performance in French after one semester of A-LM level 1. Vocabulary and structures used in the tests as criterion measures were restricted to those appearing in the first six units of A-LM – the material covered during the first semester by all teachers participating in the experiment. A very brief description of the tests follows:

1 *Listening.* The test consisted of ten questions, each followed by three response choices. Of the two distractors for each item, one was based on a slight difference in meaning and the other on a slight difference in sound. The questions and responses were recorded on audio tape and the students were required to mark their choice on a specially prepared answer sheet. (Maximum score: 10)

2 *Reading.* The purpose of this test was to measure the student's comprehension of a written paragraph, based on his ability to identify correct grammatical forms rather than rote mastery of certain

sentences contained in the dialogues and drills. The student was presented with a short paragraph of 57 words, seven of which had been deleted. These seven words, along with seven distractor-words, were listed in random order in a column to the right of the paragraph. The student was to choose the correct word and write it in the proper space. (Maximum score: 7)

3   *Grammar*. In this test, the student was required to rewrite five sentences from plural to singular form. The task involved several grammatical principles: (a) the singular/plural relationship of nouns and verbs, (b) the singular/plural relationship of nouns and modifiers, (c) the agreement in gender of nouns and their modifiers. (Maximum score: 16)

4   *Base* and 5   *Free writing*. A test was designed to measure the student's writing ability on two levels: Base and Supplemental. The student was presented with five questions, four of which were closely related to sentences found in the A-LM dialogues. A fifth question: 'Pourquoi n'écoutes-tu pas tes disques?' was intended to provide an opportunity for the more proficient students to respond. Students were instructed to answer each question with a complete sentence. A maximum value of five points was given to this initial response with a deduction of one point for each error, not to exceed five. That is to say, a student could receive a zero for a completely incorrect response but never a minus score. In order to arrive at the supplemental score each additional clause or phrase that could be considered as a thought group relevant to the question was given a value of 5 (again with a deduction of 1 point for each error).

6   *Base* and 7   *Free speaking*. This test was designed to measure the student's speaking ability on two levels: Base and Supplemental. The grading on this test was exactly the same as that of the writing test with errors in speech replacing errors in writing. Questions and answers were recorded on tape.

For criterion measures 1, 2 and 3 the reliability was computed according to the Kuder-Richardson formula (1: .84, 2: .85, 3: .92) and correlations of scores given by two independent graders was used as a measure of reliability for the speaking and writing tests. (4: .96, 5: .98, 6: .98, 7: .99).

The validity of the instruments used derives from the fact that they were based directly on the materials taught. Obviously, equally rated tests of different nature and different emphasis could have been devised. Scores on such tests would quite possibly have related to teaching behaviors quite differently from the test scores used in this study. But the criterion measure problem – another important difficulty in assessing the value of any teaching behavior – is not the main concern of this article.

TABLE 2 Adjusted class means on criterion tests in rank order (Figures at left of each column signify class number)

1 Listening	2 Reading	3 Grammar	4 Writing, Base	5 Writing, Free	6 Speaking, Base	7 Speaking, Free
11 (7.96)	11 (4.91)	8 (11.74)	2 (18.69)	2 (47.88)	2 (46.50)	2 (5.40)
15 (7.47)	1 (4.45)	1 (11.11)	11 (16.33)	11 (27.81)	15 (42.77)	15 (4.76)
2 (7.24)	12 (4.37)	11 (10.89)	14 (13.98)	15 (22.94)	8 (41.06)	5 (4.56)
10 (6.92)	8 (4.32)	15 (10.76)	1 (13.38)	14 (19.13)	11 (40.43)	8 (3.15)
9 (6.81)	15 (4.02)	14 (10.68)	12 (13.07)	8 (17.92)	14 (37.55)	10 (2.92)
1 (6.78)	2 (3.92)	2 (10.44)	15 (13.05)	5 (17.39)	1 (36.47)	1 (2.57)
14 (6.62)	14 (3.80)	4 (10.27)	8 (12.73)	10 (14.67)	4 (35.53)	9 (2.19)
7 (6.31)	10 (3.69)	12 (9.54)	5 (12.07)	1 (13.86)	9 (35.43)	11 (1.83)
12 (6.30)	13 (3.62)	13 (9.20)	17 (11.07)	12 (11.00)	13 (33.13)	16 (1.64)
5 (5.87)	3 (3.40)	10 (9.14)	4 (10.97)	6 (9.40)	10 (31.03)	12 (1.61)
6 (5.68)	4 (3.28)	6 (8.37)	7 (10.72)	9 (8.81)	17 (30.11)	6 (1.53)
4 (5.31)	9 (3.23)	9 (8.22)	10 (10.70)	3 (8.58)	6 (28.10)	14 (1.31)
13 (5.24)	6 (3.22)	7 (8.05)	6 (10.33)	13 (8.53)	5 (27.98)	17 (1.09)
8 (5.17)	17 (3.06)	17 (8.03)	13 (9.39)	7 (7.26)	7 (25.63)	13 (1.03)
7 (5.05)	7 (2.96)	3 (7.62)	3 (9.07)	4 (7.13)	12 (25.04)	7 (.80)
16 (4.34)	16 (2.71)	5 (7.60)	9 (8.17)	16 (3.58)	16 (23.87)	4 (.60)
3 (4.00)	5 (2.38)	16 (7.59)	16 (7.02)	17 (3.44)	3 (25.58)	3 (.14)

The students in all classes used in the experiment were given Modern Language Aptitude tests (MLAT – Carroll-Sapon). The criterion measures were correlated with the aptitude tests.

1	Listening	.48	5	Writing, Free	.49
2	Reading	.51	6	Speaking, Base	.54
3	Grammar	.56	7	Speaking, Free	.26
4	Writing, Base	.57			

On the basis of these correlations the average scores observed in each class were adjusted for aptitude in order to make the scores of classes of different aptitudes comparable. The adjusted scores obtained by the classes of the 17 participating teachers are summarized in Table 2.

Table 3 is the one that is central to the argument of this article. It shows the correlation between the observed teaching behaviors and the criterion measures.

As will be seen from the inspection of Table 3 there are some teaching behaviors which show no significant correlations with any of the criterion measures and which we might classify as belonging to category A (neutral). Behaviors (1), (2), (3), (4) and (9) belong to that category.

Others, classified as belonging to category B, show significant negative correlations with one or several of the criterion measures. Category B includes behaviors (5), (6), (11) and (13). Category C is made up by the behaviors which show significant positive correlations with criterion measures. Behaviors measured by (8), (10), (12) and possibly (7) and (14) might be included there.

But what can be concluded from this categorization? That behaviors in category A (e.g. Repetition drill or Substitution drill) are irrelevant to pupil achievement? That all behaviors in category B (e.g. the use of Dialogue or Translation drills) are 'bad'? That behaviors in category C (e.g. Free Response drills and the use of visual aids) are 'good'?

There may, indeed, be some behaviors observed in this study to which labels like 'good' or 'bad' can – perhaps – be applied. The reference to the open textbook may (but I say *may*) indicate some insecurity or rigidity on the part of the teacher. At any rate, it is difficult to see that the teacher's consulting the open textbook in class will benefit the student. It is possible that the behavior measured by variable (10) – Ratio of Switched to Exclusive drill – indicates a sort of flexibility – an ability to adjust the type of drill used to the situation – which is an 'absolute good.' But even this seems doubtful. Ultimately, a very high score on variable 10 would indicate that the teacher is in the habit of sticking to any one type of drill for less than one minute. It is hard to visualize that this would be a good quality under any or all circumstances.

TABLE 3 Correlations of teacher behaviors and criterion measures of student achievement

	Listening 1	Reading 2	Grammar 3	Base Writing 4	Free Writing 5	Base Speaking 6	Free Speaking 7
A (1) Prop. dr. Time	−.34	−.37	−.33	−.15	−.07	−.26	−.01
A (2) Ave. dr./min.	−.01	.14	.04	.35	.45^a	.33	.20
A (3) Rep. dr. pdm	−.08	.31	.21	.24	.22	.28	.01
A (4) Sub. dr. pdm.	.08	−.04	−.22	.13	.17	−.04	−.06
B (5) Dial. dr. pdm	−.21	−.39	−.43^a	−.58*	−.35	−.26	−.18
B (6) Trans. dr. pdm	−.18	−.22	−.31	−.10	−.14	−.49*	.14
C (7) Conv. dr. pdm	.28	.05	.30	.42^a	.40^a	.45^a	.19
C (8) Free Resp. pdm	.15	.06	.20	.61**	.73**	.50*	.62**
A (9) Ratio Cont/Free	.26	.02	.33	.37	.35	.40^a	.16
C (10) Ratio Sw./Excl.	.28	.25	.53*	.46^a	.55*	.65**	.68**
B (11) Ref. to book	−.46^a	−.20	−.29	−.42^a	−.34	−.30	−.61**
C (12) Use vis. aids	.26	−.08	.15	.36	.48^a	.57*	.59*
B (13) St/St interac.	.14	−.50*	−.47^a	−.28	−.09	−.09	.07
C (14) Var'n of struc.	.03	.00	.17	.42^a	.42^a	.35	.39

^{a} approaching significance
* significant at .05 level
** significant at .01 level

A: no significant relation with criterion measure
B: negative correlation with criterion measure
C: positive relation with criterion measure

With most teaching behaviors measured it is quite obvious that the correlations cannot possible indicate 'the more the better,' 'the more the worse.' Driven to the logical conclusion, such an assumption of straight linear correlation between achievement and observed teaching behaviors would lead us to conclude, among others, that in a dialogue based course like A-LM, the best teacher should not use Dialogue drills and that in a beginning course achievement could be maximized by allowing the student to respond 'freely' all the time.

Obviously, the correlations obtained in the experiment must be interpreted with reference to a specific teaching situation and the teaching method which was utilized by the teachers. It was this specific teaching method which moved various teaching behaviors observed into the A, B or C category.

Average drills per minute (12), Repetition drills (3), and Substitution drills (4) are 'neutral' in the sense that the very method and textbook utilized by all teachers taking part in the experiment requires them so often that variation in the frequency of their use made no significant differences in achievement.

The appearance of Dialogue drills (5) in category B seems to indicate that the dialogue based method moved the teaching behaviors of the 17 teachers into a range where the use of dialogue memorization was overemphasized. The correlation of dialogue drill and achievement measure thus turned out to be negative.

The fact that behaviors like Free Response drills (8) or the use of visual aids (12) appear in category C can also be explained by the method. Both the use of free response and of visual aids are not emphasized in the A-LM materials (at least in their first edition, utilized in this experiment). As a result visual aids and free response were evidently not used enough and the 17 teachers operated within a range in which the correlations between achievement and the utilization of visual aids or Free Response drills was positive.

I should, therefore, like to suggest that there are probably very few teaching behaviors or devices which can be classified as intrinsically 'bad' or 'good.' Ultimately, most teaching activities undertaken by a language teacher in a language class have probably some value; but each activity is subject to what might be called a principle of economics. Each activity consumes a limited resource – namely time. Thus the value of each activity depends on the value of other activities which might be substituted for it at a given moment. If, in the experiment discussed in this article, the correlation between Dialogue drills and achievement were negative, this does not mean that Dialogue drills are 'bad.' It does mean that the majority of teachers taking part in the experiment used Dialogue drills with more than optimal frequency – given the alternatives, and the time limitation of the course. In the same way Free Response drill was a 'good' teaching behavior, in the sense that within the same time limits and given the same alternatives it was evidently not used frequently enough.

Politzer's emphasis on interpreting his results with close regard to the teaching situation studied, and to the particular nature of the teaching materials employed, is important and interesting, especially when one considers again the lack of reference to the contemporary attempts to validate audiolingualism. Politzer's conclusions are especially interesting, however.

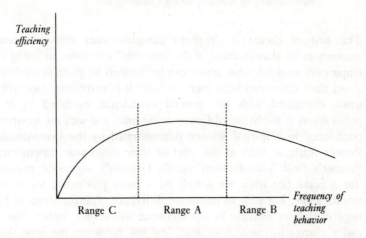

DIAGRAM 1: Relation of teaching efficiency to frequency of teaching behaviors

I should like to conclude, therefore, with the observation that most likely the relation between student achievement and most teaching behaviors or devices is not a simple linear correlation but a curvilinear or curve type of relationship as illustrated in Diagram 1. There is frequency range within which the relation is positive (C) – there may be a range within which there is no significant relation (A) and – at the higher frequencies – a range of negative correlation or diminishing return (B). Within the latter range the teaching device is used at the expense of other more profitable alternatives. The exact nature of the curve and the frequencies falling within each of the above ranges depend on other variables – notably the overall method and – among others – probably also individual characteristics of the student. In other words, the very high complexity of the teaching process make it very difficult to talk in absolute terms about 'bad' and 'good' teaching devices.

The conclusion of this article may thus lead us to two different but perhaps complementary considerations: (a) If there are few 'absolutely good or bad' teaching devices, the choice of devices and the optimal frequency of a device are the matter of individual judg-ment by the teacher. The 'good' teacher is the one who can make the right judgment as to what teaching device is the most valuable at any given moment. Good language teaching is an 'art.' (b) Only models for the investigation of the process of language teaching which are more sophisticated than those used at present will enable us to pass any absolute judgment as to what constitutes 'good' and 'bad' devices of teaching foreign languages.

The first of these two 'perhaps complementary considerations' amounts to an abandonment of the 'scientific' enterprise of trying to empirically establish what advice can legitimately be given to teachers about their classroom behaviour. As such it is surprising, especially when contrasted with the general confidence exhibited by the publications of the Stanford Center at the time, and with the apparent confidence in empirical science demonstrated by the Pennsylvania Project team, at least at the start of their multi-year experiment. Politzer's final 'consideration' recalls Grittner's suggested request 'for a cease fire while we search for a more productive means of investigation', but with an important difference. Politzer seems to be hopeful that an increase in sophistication will suffice, rather than a major change in research strategy, and still holds out the hope that his original research question will one day be answered in absolute terms. It is difficult to go along with such optimism, and much easier to accept Grittner's more pessimistic interpretation of the 'state of the art' of classroom language learning research in the late 1960s, and of its future development.

If we now compare Politzer's work to Jarvis's we can see how both contributed to the development of observation as a basic research tool. Jarvis was much more concerned with the development of valid observational categories, while Politzer, hardly using the term observation at all, was much more concerned with validating particular teaching techniques which happened to be quite narrowly associated with a particular teaching method, but both depended on observation as the fundamental procedure for data collection. Neither seemed to see their work as related in any way to contemporary work on methodological comparisons.

When we turn to Rothfarb's work we find a third approach being adopted. Rothfarb was trying to investigate how well modern language teaching was being conducted in her area, starting with the assumption that 'maximum time given to oral interaction in the target language leads to near-native proficiency'. Unlike either Jarvis or Politzer, however, Rothfarb felt no need to attempt to validate this assumption by relating teacher behaviour to learning outcomes. Her intention was simply to provide a picture of local teaching practices. In her paper, 'Teacher-Pupil Interaction in the FLES Class', we seem to have the first simply descriptive study, although the emphasis on her initial assumption concerning the benefits of oral interaction suggests an implicitly prescriptive stance underneath it all.

Rothfarb's work is also interesting for its close relationship with the tradition set by Flanders. Although she was not perhaps the first to see the potential usefulness of Flanders' system of interaction analysis in language classroom work (Moskowitz had already published on the subject in 1968, but in the context of teacher training), Rothfarb does seem to have been the first to use Flanders' system as the basis for something specially adapted for the language classroom research. Our first extract sets out Rothfarb's own system and details her observation techniques.

Instrumentation

The instrument to be used in eliciting data on interaction in the elementary foreign language class is based on thirteen categories of a taxonomy, representing certain prescribed activities generally found in a FLES class. These activities can be listed as units of behavior involving teacher stimulus and pupil response plus teacher reaction and/or reinforcement, and form the basis of the interaction instrument. The instrument, according to Medley and Mitzel, 'should determine a convenient unit of behavior, and construct a finite set of categories into one and only one of which every unit observed can be classified. The record obtained purports to show, for each period of observation, the total number of units of behavior which occurred and the number classifiable in each category' (Medley and Mitzel 1963). It includes eight categories of teacher talk, four of student talk, and one of silence or confusion. The Flanders scale was used in establishing Categories 6, 7, 9, 11 and 13.

Briefly, the Flanders system provides a classification of ten categories of teacher-pupil verbal interaction. These are teacher talk, indirect influence: (1) accepts feelings, (2) praises or encourages, (3) accepts or uses ideas of students, (4) asks questions; direct influence: (5) lectures, (6) gives directions, and (7) criticizes or justifies authority. The next two categories represent student talk: (8) student talk-response and (9) student talk-initiation. The final category is (10) silence or confusion (Amidon and Flanders 1962). A matrix is provided for recording these categories of classroom behavior, thus enabling the teacher or observer to note frequency of patterns and whether the teaching style is direct (limits pupil response) or indirect (more flexible). No attempt is made to establish direct or indirect teaching behavior patterns in the present study, although it is possible that these will emerge by closely examining the data with respect to interaction occurring in English in, for example, Categories 7 and 11.

The taxonomy further provides for two sub-categories for describing the type and nature of pupil and teacher talk. These are (1) whether a response occurring in Categories 9–12 (student talk) was given by an individual or by a group and (2) whether teacher talk (Categories 1–8) or student talk (Categories 9–12) occurred in the target language or in English. No attempt is made to evaluate pupil responses in the foreign language at this stage, although this could feasibly be done at a later stage by replaying taped sessions. The effort here is solely to describe, in adequate terms, the type and amount of interaction in a *beginning* foreign language course.

Categories for interaction in an elementary school foreign language class

Teacher talk
Target language   *English*
1. *Modeling.* Include here any utterance teacher is modeling in the FL.
2. *Giving directions.* Include also eliciting repeats, commands, direct dialog.
3. *Asking direct questions.*
4. *Guiding structure drills.*
5. *Rephrasing pupil response.* Note all corrections and reinforcements, in structure, vocabulary or pronunciation.
6. *Reacting to pupil performance.* Praise or criticism should be noted here. (As the instrument is tested further, this category may be altered to 6_1 Praise, 6_2 Criticism.)
7. *Lecturing.* Any presentation of new material, review, explanations in grammar, culture, etc., should be included.
8. *Reading-writing-spelling.* Include any activity related to these skills, i.e., oral sound-letter identification, reading a narrative, completion exercises, etc.

Student talk
Target language   *English*
I.   G.
9. *Responding.* All student responses to teacher-initiated directions, structure drills, repeats, commands, directed dialog.
10. *Answering direct questions.* Responses to teacher contact.
11. *Student initiating talk.* Include here all unexpected answers or statements or questions, not prompted by teacher, on material being learned, language in general, structure, vocabulary, culture, etc.
12. *Reading-writing-spelling.* Any activity relating to these skills.
13. *Silence or confusion.*

Observation techniques

The inter- and intra scorer reliability is being ascertained for the instrument, as well as reliability and validity for the categories used. Regarding observation techniques, Flanders recommends training observers to the point where (a) they have memorized all the categories on the instrument and (b) they can tabulate a unit of behavior approximately every three seconds (Amidon and Flanders 1962, p. 12). An observer would thus orient himself for about 5–10 minutes and then begin to note categories, pausing only when there is a shift in classroom activity, which is then indicated by a double line between categories.

The trained observer would, in addition, have to be knowledgeable in foreign language teaching methods and fluent in the language in use. He could be a student teacher, a foreign language teacher at the elementary, secondary or college level, or an FL supervisor. There is no doubt that previous experience in some of these positions would prove beneficial in observation, particularly those directly involved with teacher preparation. However, observation is not limited to 'trained observers.' The teacher himself can tape a segment or an entire FL class in an effort toward finding out more about the way he teaches. In effect, one of the aims of interaction analysis is to discern 'What are the *fewest* concepts and understandings that a person needs in his beginning year (of teaching) that would normally take two or three years of experience to find out?' (Flanders 1967).

Coding

As the preliminary hypothesis of the 'research design' was to assess (a) the extent and nature of teacher talk, (b) the extent and nature of individual and group pupil responses and (c) the extent and nature of the use of the target language and English, each unit of interaction was scored with a number, a letter and a pair of letters. The number represents the category used (1–13); the letter T indicates whether the teacher is talking (although all categories 1–8 are teacher talk, the letter is noted to facilitate reading of tabulations); and the letter I or G indicates whether the student talk was *individual* or *group*. If the interaction occurred in the target language the abbreviation Fr. (French) or Sp. (Spanish) is used, otherwise one letter E (English) was marked. A typical entry might look like this: 1 T Fr. = Category 1, Teacher talk: Modeling the utterance in French; 4 T Fr. = Category 4, Teacher talk: Guiding structure drills in French; 9 I Fr. = Category 9: Student response to teacher initiated talk, individual response and in French.

Of particular interest is Rothfarb's statement of her research aims, at the beginning of the last paragraph of the above extract, in terms of a 'preliminary hypothesis'. This use of the term 'hypothesis' is not, clearly, to be interpreted in a narrowly 'scientific' sense. There is no intention here test a hypothesis derived from a particular theory. Instead there is an intention to improve the database for intelligent pedagogic decision making by providing an objective and relevantly detailed 'picture' of the state of things in the modern language classroom. If we may call the 'classical' type of hypothesis 'explanatory' then what we have here is not 'explanatory' but 'descriptive'. As we shall no doubt see throughout this volume, classroom observation research has frequently opted for descriptive hypotheses, and very rarely for explanatory ones.

The final part of Rothfarb's paper documents the results of the application of the new observation system to three junior high school classes in California, two studying French and one Spanish.

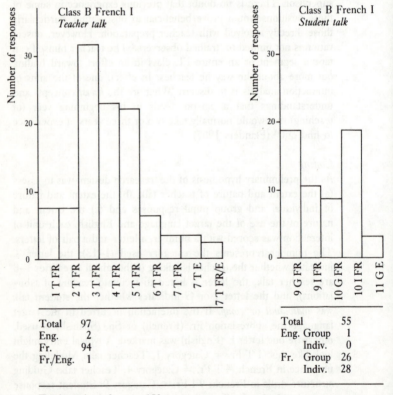

Total	97
Eng.	2
Fr.	94
Fr./Eng.	1

Total		55
Eng.	Group	1
	Indiv.	0
Fr.	Group	26
	Indiv.	28

Total number of entries 153
Unclassified   1

FIGURE 1

Samples and discussion of preliminary data.

The instrument was pre-tested in three junior high school classes in California, where the material was the same as that taught in the sixth grade. The population consisted of 120 students in the middle and upper middle socio-economic groups. The degree of training in modern audiolingual methods of the three teachers visited is not known; however, it was noted that two of the teachers were native speakers.

Class A – French I: Observation time – thirty minutes.
As this was the first class visited, the writer spent the time absorbing FL class atmosphere and observing interaction patterns without writing them down. Keeping in mind the major concerns which prompted this study, it was noted that the teacher, although a native speaker, used English throughout the period of observation, with the exception of a question answer drill. Individual participation and classroom spirit seemed high, but here an important question arises: Should the instrument include a category for noting whether the interaction continually involves the *same* students? Perhaps this type of observation could be noted marginally.

Class B – French I: Observation time – fifteen minutes.
The teacher in this class was not a native speaker, but continually used the target language, as seen by following data. Three or four minutes were spent by the observer's 'getting the feel of the class,' during which time the teacher was guiding the class through dialog drill (1 T Fr. – 9 G Fr.) The remaining activities were then recorded. Categories most used by the teacher were Category 3 (asking direct questions), Category 4 (guiding structure drills), and Category 5 (rephrasing pupil response). Student interaction shows an almost equal amount of group and individual responses, in French.

Class C – Spanish I: Observation time – forty minutes.
It would appear that the more time spent in a beginning foreign language class, the more categories of interaction emerge. The teacher here was a native speaker, and tended to use English mostly as a vehicle for grammatical explanations. The categories she used most were Category 1 (modeling utterances in the FL), Category 3 (asking direct questions), Category 5 (rephrasing pupil response), and Category 6 (praise). The largest amount of entries for Teacher talk was in Category 4 (guiding structure drills) – there were 48 units recorded.

Fifty-seven units were recorded for group responses in Spanish; eighteen for individuals responding to direct questions. There was an extended period of interaction during which several 11's appeared, (student initiating talk), which the observer notes in the margin: The teacher was explaining a grammatical point (*esa, esta, aquella*) and the pupil prompting the discussion (11 I E.) did not understand her explanations in Spanish (given with gestures to clarify meaning). The teacher then switched to English and, when asking if the class understood it then, several (5) pupils offered examples in Spanish! These responses were classified as 11 I Sp. as they were not a direct response to her direct question, but rather attempts to put the language to use creatively.

The only time Category 13 appeared (silence or confusion) was when the bell rang. The ratio of student talk to teacher talk in this class was 88 to 183 responses.

Conclusion

The thirteen categories of the taxonomy would appear to yield useful information as to the extent and nature of interaction in a beginning foreign language class. Consider, for example, a basic tenet of the audiolingual method, which calls for near 'total immersion' in the target language. In trying to achieve this, few teachers are able to assess accurately the amount of time they use English or the language being taught. Native-speaking teachers, for instance, usually assume, and are usually assumed to converse more extensively in their native tongue while teaching it. Yet an interesting aspect emerging from the initial data was that the two native-speaking teachers used far more English than the non-native-speaking teacher.

While further research is needed to determine the reliability and validity of the instrument, there is evidence that teachers working with this process of self-assessment have become more cognizant of their teaching styles.[1] This awareness, coupled with the teacher's desire for self-understanding and improvement, is essential to the process of professional growth. Toward this end, interaction analysis – theory and practice – has been presented in teacher workshops and FLES in-service classes in Dade County schools, in conjunction with microteaching, principles of applied linguistics and children's learning styles.

Of particular interest here is Rothfarb's conclusion, not explicitly derived from her own research findings, that there is practical promise in the use of such observation instruments for teacher development. This clearly echoes Jarvis's conclusion, already drawn attention to earlier, and Rothfarb's final sentence explicitly makes the connections with in-service teacher training, and leaves the reader suspecting that Rothfarb's own interest was more in developing procedures for in-service teacher training than in pursuing descriptive research itself.

1. See, for example, Dodl 1965, Clements 1964 and Moskowitz 1968a.

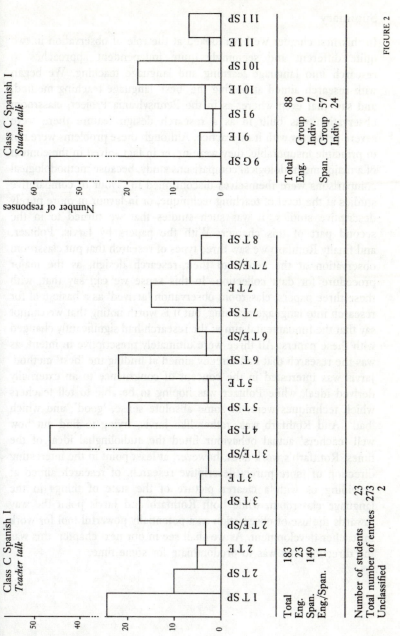

Class C Spanish I
Student talk

Number of responses

	Total	Group	Indiv.	Group	Indiv.
	88	0	7	57	24
Eng.					
Span.					

Class C Spanish I
Teacher talk

Number of responses

	Total	
	183	
Eng.	23	
Span.	149	
Eng./Span.	11	

Number of students   23
Total number of entries   273
Unclassified   2

FIGURE 2

Summary

In this first chapter we have looked at the role of observation in two quite different and seemingly quite independent approaches to research into language learning and language teaching. We began with research aimed at finding the 'best' language teaching method, and saw that even where, as in the Pennsylvania Project, classroom observation was built in as a research design feature there were severe problems with it in practice. Although these problems were not in principle insuperable, they were never in fact solved in the context of a major methodological comparisons study, because methodological comparisons were themselves discontinued in favour of comparative studies at the level of teaching technique, or in favour of more purely descriptive studies. It was such studies that we turned to in the second part of this chapter. With the papers by Jarvis, Politzer, and finally Rothfarb we saw three types of research that put classroom observation at the centre of their research design, as the major procedure for data collection. In this sense we can say that, with these three papers, classroom observation 'arrived' as a basic tool for research into language teaching, but it is worth noting that we cannot say that the fundamental aim of the research had significantly changed with these papers. All three were ultimately prescriptive in intent, as was the research that had directly aimed at finding the 'best' method. Jarvis was interested in the concept of congruence to an externally derived ideal, while Politzer was hoping to be able to tell teachers which techniques were, in some absolute sense, 'good', and which 'bad'. And Rothfarb was, rather like Jarvis, trying to find out how well teachers' actual behaviour fitted the audiolingual ideal of the times. Rothfarb's work does, however, at least point in the interesting direction of more purely descriptive research, of research aimed at providing us with a clearer picture of the state of things in the language classroom, while both Rothfarb and Jarvis point the way towards the use of observation as a potentially powerful tool for work in teacher development. As we shall see in our next chapter, this was the direction that was to predominate for some time.

Follow-up activities and points for discussion

1. Form two groups (A and B). When each group has prepared its response to its own group task (see below), bring the two groups together and try to outargue each other. Finally, look for common ground between you.

> **Task for Group A**: make the strongest possible case *for* a prescriptive approach to language classroom research.
> **Task for Group B**: make the strongest possible case *against* a prescriptive approach to language classroom research.

2. Form three groups, one to look at Jarvis's observation categories, one at Politzer's and one at Rothfarb's. In each group, plan how you would need to modify the categories to reflect current ideas about what should happen in language classes. Finally, bring the three groups together to compare the changes you have proposed, and to see if there is consensus among you. If there is consensus, is this a reason for satisfaction or for suspicion? If there is no such consensus, consider why not, and if such a consensus would in principle be desirable?

3. Make a preliminary proposal for a descriptive project using observation as the basic research tool. Your proposal should address the following questions:

1. What aspect of language classroom behaviour is to be focused upon?
2. Who needs to know descriptive facts about this aspect of language classroom behaviour?
3. For what sorts of reasons?
4. What purpose, if any, is the resultant description to serve?
5. Of what use, if any, could either Jarvis's, Politzer's, or Rothfarb's descriptive systems be to your project?

4. Form three groups, one for Jarvis, one for Politzer, and one for Rothfarb. In each group, make out the strongest possible case in favour of your researcher's general research aims. Finally, compare notes and attempt to convince each other, before discussing your real views on these three research projects.

2 Observation 'arrives' as a feedback tool in teacher training

Observation as problem

In Chapter 1 observation was seen either as a much needed component of experimental research or as the basic research tool for entire projects. It may well seem odd, in the circumstances, to start this second chapter with observation as a 'problem', but it does make sense to do so in the context of teacher training, because, long before Sputnik 1 took to the air, observation was recognized as a problem in teacher training work, where for decades it had been taken for granted that teachers on teaching practice should be visited by supervisors who would later evaluate their supervisees' teaching ability in the light of their observed classroom performance. The problem was, of course, how to observe trainees in such a way that the necessary final evaluations of their teaching ability would be valid.

The problem of validity, in this area as in any other, was necessarily highly complex. Firstly, any classroom observations had themselves to be valid in the sense that they would accurately capture the events of the classroom. 'Accurately' meant here 'objectively', the need for observations to get away from 'mere' impressions and produce something that was incontrovertibly a factual record of the classroom lesson observed. It was well recognized that supervisors' impressions could be unreliable, and that they could only with difficulty form the basis for discussions between supervisor and supervisee, let alone the basis for final evaluations of professional ability. This need for 'objectivity' was a major driving force behind many of the developments we shall be recording in this chapter. The second aspect of the problem of validity was even more recalcitrant. Classroom observations needed to be valid not only as *accurate* records of classroom events but also, and in a sense more importantly, as records that properly focused on aspects of classroom behaviour that were known to be causally related to learner achievement. There was not much point in objectivity for its own sake. Objectivity needed to be directed only to the things that actually mattered, that actually made a difference to learning, whatever they were. But what were they? We have already seen, in Chapter 1, that it was proving impossible to provide a 'scientific' basis for believing any one method to be the 'best', and that even where the focus was on individual teaching techniques, as in Politzer's work, it was proving impossible to 'pass any absolute judgment about what constitutes 'good' and 'bad' devices of teaching foreign languages'.

It is against this background that we move to a consideration of the role of observation in teacher training. My own 1972 paper, 'Prescription and Description in the Training of Language Teachers', concentrated on the second aspect of the problem of validity outlined above, the problem for the teacher trainer of apparently *needing* to know, but not actually knowing, what really matters in classroom language instruction. It put the problem in terms of a contrast between 'prescription' and 'description', the distinction drawn in Chapter 1 to characterize different approaches to research.

> There is a story that Anton Chekhov was once asked, during rehearsals for the first production of one of his plays, how a certain role should be acted. His brief but somewhat devastating answer was simply: 'Well!' One might feel some sympathy for Chekhov, whose answer was perfectly sincere, if not very helpful; but one is more likely to feel sympathy for the actor concerned, who probably felt that he had a right to expect not only an *authoritative* response but also an *informative* one.
>
> Chekhov had, in the circumstances no reason to be at all ashamed of the cryptic vagueness of his answer, however. He simply did not wish to impose his own interpretation of the play. He was dealing with a professional actor whose own professional opinion could be expected to be worth respecting. The situation is not so simple for the teacher trainer. He must be both authoritative *and* informative, since he is dealing with student-teachers who, by definition, do not have '*professional* opinions' that are developed and informed, and are thereby worthy of his respect. Indeed it is no doubt from the teacher trainer that the student-teachers expect to get what will eventually become their 'professional opinion'.
>
> The situation is different therefore but teacher-trainers may well feel that at present there are some very good reasons why they might wish they could just follow Chekhov and give the answer 'Well' to the question: 'How should something be taught?'
>
> As I have outlined it the teacher training situation essentially involves 'prescription' – the notion that the trainer 'knows best' and can prescribe what it is best for the student-teacher to do in any given teaching context. But 'prescription' has acquired unfortunate

associations in recent years. To some extent this is no doubt due to a not altogether necessary 'spin-off' from developments in theoretical linguistics, where much has been made, and quite legitimately, of the undesirable effects of prescriptivism. In language teaching in general 'anti-prescriptivism' has probably been largely beneficial, but it is of somewhat restricted relevance, being limited, basically, to 'anti-prescriptivism' in the area of linguistic content and usage. Anti-prescriptivism, as a slogan, however, is clearly related to anti-dogmatism in general, and it is never surprising if a measure of successful anti-dogmatism brings along with it a further measure of loss of confidence in general among large sections of the affected population.

But there is more than this to sap the teacher-trainer's self-confidence. There is, and this must surely be of much greater importance than the 'spin-off' from a change of orientation in theoretical linguistics, an ever-increasing accumulation of experimental evidence failing to show that it even matters what the teacher does in the classroom. Stephens (1967) surveyed the history of experimentation on teaching methods in general and found that out of 780 experiments 580 had inconclusive outcomes, and that the other 200 had mutually contradictory ones. Dubin and Taveggia (1968), reviewing forty years of research on college teaching methods, were forced to a similar conclusion, even after they had gone to the trouble of going right back to the raw data in each of the experiments reviewed in order to provide comparable statistical treatments.

Such comprehensive and yet discouraging research reviews must surely cause great concern to teacher trainers, whose self-respect and in the last resort, credibility as trainers would appear, at least, to rest rather crucially on the notion that *someone*, at least, 'knows best', that *someone* can tell the teacher what to do.

It could be argued, of course, that what is true of teaching in general might not be true of the teaching of any particular subject. The inconclusiveness of research in general might be an artefact of dealing with all teaching situations together. Unfortunately the results of recent method research in the field of language teaching only serve to confirm the general pattern of inconclusiveness. The reports of the best known of the major experiments in foreign language teaching methodology, those at Colorado between 1960 and 1962, and in Pennsylvania between 1965 and 1969, make equally depressing reading for the teacher-trainer who feels it is his job to know what method a teacher should adopt for maximum efficiency. One might be excused for adopting the attitude that the only reasonable inference to be drawn from such research is that, generally speaking, students learn the things they *are* taught better than the things they are *not* taught. J. B. Carroll, in answer to a question at the first meeting of the German Applied Linguistics Association[1], seemed reduced to an equally pessimistic but related view – that language learning varies in direct proportion to the amount of time devoted to it, and that this is the only reliable relationship that can be inferred from more than twenty years of research experience.

In the circumstances we might wish to say, not that the teacher-trainer might be excused some small loss of confidence in his prescriptive role, but rather that the really conscientious teacher-trainer will have no confidence left at all, and that perhaps he should find a way of avoiding prescription altogether since he will be unable to find research support for anything he says about teaching methods, about what a teacher should or should not do in the classroom.

Are we really prepared to believe, however, that it does not matter at all what a teacher does in the classroom? Surely not. Surely we cannot believe that no teacher is any more effective than any other teacher? Surely the good teacher's success depends somehow on what happens in his or her classroom? Surely research that appears to deny the validity of such points must have its own validity questioned? We could of course fall back on the notion that teaching is an art, and as such not open to objective analysis, and that therefore anything that might reasonably be called scientific research into teaching is just not possible. But this would seem, to me at least, to be as unhelpful as accepting that what happens in classrooms is of no importance, that it just does not matter what the teacher does.

We need, I suggest, to look again at the whole question of research on methodological comparisons in language teaching. We cannot afford simply to ignore existing research. First, of course, we must learn what we can from it, but we must also question the essential validity of the general inference drawn from it, that the inconclusive results of such research so far can be held to indicate that method just does not matter.

When we do look again at the recent research projects, we might first need to consider, I suggest, the concept of 'method' involved. So far I have been using 'method' to refer simultaneously to many different aspects of language teaching, from the most particular items of teacher behaviour to the most global conception of method in terms like the 'Audio-Lingual Method', the 'Cognitive Code Learning Method', the 'Direct Method', or the 'Modified Traditional Method'. It is clear that the major research projects such as those undertaken in Colorado and Pennsylvania were based on a global conception of method. They were designed to compare the

1. Held in Stuttgart, November 1969.

overall effectiveness of overall teaching strategies derived more or less rigorously from competing *theories* of language learning and teaching.

It could be supposed, and it presumably was supposed, that making comparisons at this most global level would give the experimenters the best chance of obtaining significant results, since comparing a method based on one theory with a method based on a competing theory should maximize the differences between the elements in the comparison, and it is by doing so that significant differences are most likely to be obtained. So, at first sight, global methodological comparisons would appear to offer the most promising area for fundamental research on language teaching. And yet the results of such global methodological comparisons have, as we have seen all too often, been inconclusive. It is easy to say, with hindsight, that this inconclusiveness could have been foreseen. Variables in educational experiments are notoriously resistant to proper experimental controls, and global comparisons offer the largest possible number of variables to control. It could have been predicted then, simply on the grounds of the overwhelming difficulty of the enterprise, that significant results would not be forthcoming. More interestingly, perhaps, this inconclusiveness could not have been predicted on other grounds as well. It could have been noted that the methods to be compared were not really derived at all rigorously from the competing theories claimed to underlie them, that these methods were in fact relatively ill-defined to the extent that a considerable amount of overlap could be expected in the actual behaviour of the teachers involved, and that it was perhaps unrealistic, in any case, to expect a number of teachers to all stick closely for at least two years to any particular teaching method, however well-defined, given that the conscientious teacher will wish to adapt his teaching to suit the developing characteristics of his students and is thus unlikely to persevere for very long with any aspect of any method that seems to be unproductive.

In such complex circumstances it seems quite plausible to maintain that 'method', as conceived globally by the experimenters, is unlikely to prove the crucial factor one might otherwise have expected. This does not mean that 'method does not matter', but it does mean that we should not expect to be able to *prove*, by large-scale global methodological comparisons, that 'method matters'.

In place of large-scale global methodological comparisons, smaller-scale experiments have been proposed and many attempted. It must be emphasized that 'smaller-scale' does not necessarily imply that fewer subjects need to be used for example. It refers mainly to the concept of method involved. Instead of all aspects of language teaching, only a restricted number are investigated. The linguistic content may be severely restricted, the total duration of the experiment may be relatively brief, and exclusive attention may be paid only to one or two of the language skills, for example.

The results of such small-scale investigations have certainly been less discouraging overall, than those of the major global projects. Stefan Fink has already described, at this Congress, such an investigation, where the results have certainly lent strong support for a methodological preference with regard to three different presentation strategies for dialogue memorization (Fink 1972). Nevertheless very many small-scale investigations have been as inconclusive as the major global projects. Some of the earlier work on the GUME project in Sweden[2], for example, brought the not altogether expected finding that, in teaching by drill sessions, it just did not matter whether or not explanations were provided. But this sort of inconclusiveness is more serious, in a way, than that resulting from the major global projects, precisely because it is far less easy to dismiss this sort of inconclusiveness as being the product of a mass of poorly controlled variables. We can, and perhaps we should, ignore the results of the Colorado and Pennsylvania Projects entirely, given the poor control of crucial variables, but we cannot afford to ignore the results of the Swedish work so easily.

And yet we may feel we want to, because, in this as in many other small-scale investigations, the teacher variable has been controlled to the point of where the teaching has been done purely by prerecorded tapes. This neatly eliminates one of the trickiest variables, the teacher, but it introduces crucial problems of interpretation. This is necessarily true of any investigation where, in order to get meaningful results, the teaching situation has been considerably idealized.

Such experiments may be useful in that they stand a chance of pointing up those factors that seem most likely to be worth further investigation, but in fact the relationship between such artificial teaching situations and 'real-life' is not really very clear, and there is an obvious need for such investigations to be integrated into a very substantial research programme designed to reintroduce, step-by-step, all the variables that have been eliminated at the earlier stages, until finally meaningful statements can be made about the real-life situation.

Such comprehensive research programmes may be conceivable, and perhaps even possible in such contexts as the GUME investigations, but generally speaking small-scale research has not received the sort of support it would need if it were to get at all far beyond the very early, and very artificially limited, stages. It is probably true that a really comprehensive programme of small-scale

2. See especially Lindblad 1969.

research would be far more expensive of research resources in the long run, than global projects such as that in Pennsylvania, and it would certainly take far longer to produce its findings.

Small-scale research, in the sense used here, then, is the obvious alternative to work based on a global conception of method, but results so far have been far from universally encouraging with respect to the notion that method matters, and, in addition, such research necessarily involves integrated research programmes on a scale for which the necessary financial and administrative support seems unlikely to be often available.

Politzer [1970; this volume Chapter 1] has taken the conception of method a stage further in his investigations of the relative effectiveness of particular teaching 'behaviours' as he calls them. Most of these 'behaviours' investigated are standard drilling techniques, but Politzer was also interested, for example, in such teaching behaviours as direct reference to the book, the use of visual aids, and the arranging of communication between student and student.

Instead of using these behaviours as independent variables to be manipulated, Politzer made the interesting decision to simply observe their frequency in the normal work of experienced teachers, and then to attempt to correlate the observed frequencies with a number of performance measures, in the hope that it might be possible thereafter to designate some teaching behaviours as 'good' and some as 'bad'.

The results did not support so simple a view of course, but they did produce some intriguing preliminary findings; that in an overall method characterized by dialogue memorization, frequency of dialogue drills correlated negatively with achievement, for example. Or that, of the fourteen behavioural measures involved, no less than five showed no significant correlation, either negative or positive, with achievement, four showed negative correlations (so that, as I have just mentioned, it would appear to be a 'bad' thing to use dialogue drills, or to use translation drills, to refer to the book while teaching, or to attempt to foster interstudent communication), and five showed a more or less positive correlation (so that it would appear to be a 'good' thing to use free response drills, and to use visual aids, for example).

Politzer wisely avoided taking these preliminary conclusions seriously and indeed made two interesting observations. One, that no doubt it is the relative rather than the absolute frequency of any teaching behaviour that really matters, if frequency matters at all, and that, two, much less crude ways of investigating teaching behaviours will need to be used before meaningful conclusions can be obtained.

To return to our teacher-trainer, we can see that, certainly at the global level, and even at the level of particular teacher behaviour, there is little research support for any prescription he may wish to make, and Chekhov's 'Well' would seem to be about as good an answer as any other to the question of how to teach 'X'. He could come, from all the available research evidence, to the strong conclusion that method, defined either globally or in terms of isolated teaching techniques, just does not really matter, or he could come to the alternative conclusion simply that it is extremely difficult to *show* that method matters. A third possibility is available, however; he could conclude that method probably doesn't really matter very much, if it is thought of in the terms used here, but that what happens in the classroom still must matter. All the research so far described has involved the implicit assumption that what is really happening in the classroom is simply that some particular method or technique is being used, and that more or less efficient learning might be taking place accordingly.

It is however clear that much more than this is happening. People are interacting in a multiplicity of complex ways, as people, getting bored or even excited, getting encouraged or discouraged, more confident or less confident, and so on. It is commonplace to assume that such events are important to learning, probably crucial, but this seems to have been largely left out of research on methodological comparisons.

Research, then, has been based on an all too simple notion of what the teacher does and of what really happens in the foreign language classroom. We need studies of what actually happens, not just of what recognizable teaching methods, strategies or techniques are employed by the teacher, but of what really happens between teacher and class.

'What really happens' is a loaded term, and might appear to suggest we already know what we mean by it. All we can mean at this stage is 'what happens that is important to learning' as opposed to the method and technique variables already studied that appear not to be particularly important to learning. Moving away altogether from a prescriptive approach, therefore, we need descriptions of classroom events, descriptions that are sufficiently comprehensive so that we stand a chance of discovering, by correlating observed events with performance criteria, the variables that really matter in the classroom.

To be fair to previous research on methodological comparison we ought to look at what has been done in such investigations at this descriptive level. In such research description is crucial in two distinct areas. One, in the specification of the teaching method or technique to be used, and, two, in the reporting of the teaching actually done. The second area is of the greater general interest perhaps but it is worth noting that even in the specification of the teaching to be done the major global research projects appear to have left much to be desired. The fact is important enough to the reader of the reports but of much greater consequence, no doubt, to the teachers actually involved in the projects, who cannot have obtained a sufficiently precise indication of the sort of teaching required of them. It is of course probable that the global conception of method makes sufficiently precise specification of teaching behaviour impossible. It is certainly difficult to conceive of a specification that would in practice give a teacher a principled and precise way of coping with all the possible situations that normal teaching over a couple of years is likely to throw up. In any case it could be further objected that not even a fully comprehensive and precise specification would be of any real use to a teacher not also fully trained to use the teaching behaviours specified. In the Colorado report, I should perhaps make clear, there is little direct information relevant to the above points, and we are left with the distinctly optimistic sounding and perhaps deliberately vague weak assertation that 'by the time classes began . . . . we felt that everyone was reasonably well prepared for what was ahead' (Scherer and Wertheimer 1964, p. 23).

The reporters of the experiment in Pennsylvania are much more informative and thus more open to detailed criticism. Frank Otto supplied this in 1969, finding contradictions and overlap in the operational definitions of the various teaching strategies, and also commenting unfavourably on the way these descriptions were communicated to the teachers involved in the experiment, emphasizing the need for training rather than just information and non-participatory demonstration.

Here was a situation where prescription was essential as a consequence of the experimental design employed, and where adequate prescription was not obtained, due, fundamentally, to a perhaps unavoidable failure at the level of description. If, even when such massive resources are employed, failure at the descriptive level makes prescription in some way impossible, then the ordinary teacher-trainer is likely to feel even less confident in his prescriptive role. How is he to prescribe successfully, when teams of experts especially employed for the purpose have failed?

But we should return to the more fundamentally interesting second area where description is crucial in such experimentation, to the area concerned with the description of the everyday teaching behaviour of the teachers involved. Here again the Colorado report is insufficiently precise and disturbingly optimistic. It is clear that a major effort was made to ensure that teachers conformed to the intended teaching strategies but a statement such as the following, about group leaders' visits to observe teachers in action: 'these visits convinced the leaders that a reasonable uniform mode of instruction was being pursued within each of the two groups' (Scherer and

Wertheimer 1964, p. 25) is clearly not very helpful. Again the Pennsylvania report is more precise and thus more open to specific criticism. John D. Clark (1969) made the most interesting observation when he pointed out [this volume Chapter 1] that, since two different observation schedules were used for recording the events in the classes intended to be using the two basic method types (the Functional Skills Method and the Traditional Method), any use by a teacher of a technique appropriate only to the opposing strategy could have gone unreported. He further noted that in fact the report contained separate evidence of such overlap.

Again, then, we have evidence of an important failure at the descriptive level. In the case just described it would seem to have been a somewhat easily avoidable failure, but we shall return to the practical problems of classroom observation later. For the moment it is perhaps more important to make the point that the two descriptive failures I have just described would serve to vitiate the experiments concerned, even if they had been perfectly conducted in all other respects. Whatever the numerical results, we would have had no way of translating them into practical recommendations, or prescriptions, for language teaching, since we would not have known precisely what sorts of teaching had *produced* the results.

I would like to claim, therefore, that the problem of description is a fundamental problem in research on language teaching. It has been easiest to criticize the global research, but it should be clear that all research on methodological comparisons must remain strictly speaking uninterpretable if it is accompanied by a failure at the descriptive level, whether this be a failure in teacher preparation or in subsequent classroom observation, or both.

Clearly, prescription is inappropriate if descriptive techniques are inadequate, and, equally clearly, all methodological comparisons using the standard type of experimental design so far most commonly employed, rely crucially on the twin notions that prescription is possible within the experiment (for the teachers involved) and that prescription will be possible, for all other teachers, as a natural consequence of the publication of the results.

It seems to me, since our work at the descriptive level is so crude at present, and since methodological comparisons rely crucially on success at this level, that it is precisely at this level of description that a major research effort should be aimed. Frank Grittner, in 1968, with the Pennsylvania Project in mind, wrote 'perhaps we should ask for a cease-fire while we search for a more productive means of investigation' [this volume Chapter 1]. I would suggest that we modify the object of our research on language teaching to concentrate on coping with the problem of description, and I would suggest that it is in this area that we should search for a productive means of investigation.

How, then, can the problem of description be tackled? What means of investigation can we suggest that might prove to be productive? Can we in fact sufficiently delimit the problem of description itself? I have already suggested two aspects of this problem of description, one concerning the specification of instructional procedures for the direct purpose of prescription, and the other concerning the recording of the events occurring in the foreign language classroom. This second aspect is of greater fundamental importance to language teaching research, it seems reasonable to suggest, and is thus the obvious candidate for the research effort. But we still have not considered how we are going to decide which events it will be worth attempting to describe, which aspects of what happens in the foreign language classroom will be the important ones. Some preliminary remarks can certainly be made here. Firstly, it will clearly not be sufficient to attempt to describe merely the instructional procedures (as commonly understood) employed by the teacher. We will need to take seriously the possibility that it does not much matter what instructional procedures are employed, that perhaps other, no doubt more subtle, aspects of the teachers' behaviour will be more important.

This may be a good point to refer back to my discussion of the descriptive failure in methodological research so far. It may well have been noted that I did not deal with the problem of description in small-scale research, where, at first sight at least, the problem of description might appear to be minimized. It is possible, for example, if all instruction is by pre-recorded tapes, to describe precisely, in commonly understood terms, the instructional content of those tapes, to know that given techniques are employed for a given proportion of the time, and so on. But this is dealing with the problem of description as if it were exclusively concerned with the specification of instructional procedures, in traditional pedagogical terms. We have already seen that this is hardly likely to take us far enough. In addition, and this brings in the second of my preliminary remarks concerning the nature of the definition problem, it seems reasonable to suppose that it is not only the teacher and his contribution to the situation that need to be adequately described, but also the learners and their contribution. Small-scale methodological research of the kind outlined above has not begun to cope with this aspect of the problem, any more than large-scale global research. My third preliminary remark concerns the important point that it will clearly not be sufficient to describe separately the behaviour of teachers and learners.

The fundamental problem of description, then, centres on the problem of characterizing accurately and adequately the nature of the interaction between people in a teaching/learning situation. If I am right then, before we can hope to reach any meaningful decisions about methodological preferences, we must first deal with language teaching at the level of group interpersonal psychology, and then, much later perhaps, we may be able one day to relate choices of instructional procedure, at some more or less particular level, to such more fundamental, more important factors.

To put it more simply perhaps we may look forward to going beyond our present concern with instructional procedures, and teaching methods or techniques, towards a study of teaching *style*.

Until a means of investigation is found for this aspect of language teaching, I would suggest a moratorium on methodological comparisons.

To return to the situation of the teacher-trainer, it seems clear that prescription on the basis of research evidence is just not currently available to him. Prescription on the basis of experience and 'knowledge of the literature' is of course still possible. It must be up to the individual conscience, of course, and the teacher-trainer owes it to his students to make clear the lack of research support for such prescriptions, but prescription on the basis of experience must still be a very important notion for many teacher-trainers. Following my arguments, however, the teacher-trainer will not merely admit that he does not 'know best' (in any rigorous sense), he will positively assert that *no one* 'knows best', and that in the circumstances he will be best able to train his students, not by asserting any methodological dogma, but by eschewing dogma in general and then trying to help his students study just what goes on in the classroom.

If I am right then, the techniques needed by the teacher-trainer in his attempts to help students study what goes on in the classroom (and in his attempts to analyse – and even perhaps grade – the teaching performance of his students) are precisely those needed in fundamental research on language teaching.

Some teacher-trainers, but not many yet, are already exploring the possibilities of Flanders' system of interaction analysis for the training of language teachers. There is already evidence that even the use of such a relatively crude device can be very instructive (Moskowitz 1968a [this volume, pp. 58–74] and Wragg 1970). We should expect to need to develop systematic observation techniques that are much better tailored to the specific characteristics of the language teaching situation.

The teacher-trainer clearly has a professional and immediate practical interest in developing such techniques, and is also, by virtue of his contact with student teachers, teachers and classes, in a particularly favourable position for contributing directly to the research work himself and thus making a very significant contribution to language teaching research in general.

What I find interesting now about my own conclusions in 1972 is firstly the absence of any clear sense of what the descriptive alternative to prescription might really amount to. There is a strong sense that prescription is out of the question, but no equally strong sense that description provides a viable alternative. There is even a suggestion perhaps, as in Politzer's paper in the last chapter, that the problem with prescription might be a temporary one, and that we will one day be able to discover 'the variables that really matter', by 'correlating observed events with performance criteria'. My own stance in 1972 could be characterized as ultimately prescriptive therefore, being based on the hope that one day it would indeed be possible to tell teachers, authoritatively, what to do in their classrooms. More positively (with the benefit of hindsight), the general anti-dogma stance does lead to the still useful suggestion that student teachers should themselves study 'just what goes on in the classroom'. Most positive, I find now, is the suggestion of common ground between teacher training and 'fundamental research'. It seems to have been already apparent that there was a need to bring the two together, that there was a danger of their drifting apart, something that does appear to have happened in subsequent years, as later chapters will document.

My own paper was originally delivered in Copenhagen, to a largely European audience. In the United States, however, much had already been done to bring systematic observation techniques into teacher training as a major solution for its problems.

Observation as solution

In the same year that Jarvis published his paper setting out a system for systematic classroom observation as a research tool, Moskowitz published what was to be a far more influential paper, 'The Effects of Training Foreign Language Teachers in Interaction Analysis', setting out the immediate benefits of systematic classroom observation for teacher training purposes. She saw beyond the supervisors' problem outlined above, and went straight for the potential value of training both pre-service and in-service trainees to systematically observe their own classroom behaviour. In short she was looking at systematic observation not as a solution to a supervisor's *evaluation* problem but to a trainee's *feedback* problem. Hers was, in this sense, a trainee-centred approach to teacher training. (She had already published, in 1967, a programmed manual for teachers to teach themselves how to use Flanders' system of Interaction Analysis, and would publish, in 1971, a paper putting forward 'interaction analysis' as a solution to supervisors' problems.) What Moskowitz was offering was a solution to the fundamental problem of securing *behaviour change*, to which the key was seen to be the provision of accurate and relevant feedback.

Her paper is in two parts, the first reporting a study involving pre-service language teacher trainees, the second devoted to in-service teachers. Of particular interest is the point that with the pre-service trainees she used Flanders' Interaction Analysis system without modification, while with the in-service teachers she used three systems: the unmodified Flanders again, her own extensive modification of Flanders' system, and Galloway's system for analysing non-verbal behaviour. It may also be worth drawing attention at this point to the fact that although Moskowitz used a great variety of measures to determine the effects of training in feedback systems, she did not employ any achievement measures. This was a major break with the experimental tradition exemplified so far in this volume, both in the work on methodological comparisons, and in Politzer's and Jarvis's more descriptive work. It does unite her with Rothfarb, however, who, it will be recalled, relied on the pedagogic assumption that language learning achievement could be expected to relate directly to the quantity of oral interaction in the classroom. Moskowitz's underlying assumption was based on Flanders' earlier research on other school subjects, where a correlation had been found between learner achievement and certain so-called 'indirect' patterns of teacher behaviour.

It is not easy to know now whether this break with tradition was consciously and deliberately made (it was not put forward as anything requiring explicit justification in the paper), but it was certainly a productive move for the whole field of language classroom research. It was also a risky move, of course, since it left classroom researchers wide open to the charge of neglecting what was generally accepted, for obvious reasons, as the major dependent variable, but it had the very beneficial effect of freeing classroom researchers to concentrate on trying to understand language classrooms, instead of trying to prove that they already understood them. In fact it facilitated the move away from prescriptivism and towards a more purely descriptive approach to language classroom research (although 'exploratory and explanatory', cumbersome as they are, would not doubt be better terms than 'descriptive').

Our first extract is the entire first part of Moskowitz's paper.

Part 1. A study of preservice teachers

The problem

'It is essential to relate knowledge of human behaviour to the area of foreign language teaching.' (Bailey 1965, p. 116)

'The overall quality of the nation's language program has taken a large step forward. What is now needed is emphasis on the personal aspect.' (ibid., p. 118)

'We can only agree with . . . . a plea for the specific application of such research approaches as those taken by Ned A. Flanders, Donald M. Medley, Harold E. Mitzel, *et al.*, to the foreign language teaching situation.' (Politzer 1966, p. 253)

So go the appeals of those who realize that recent findings in research from the field of educational psychology are being bypassed in the field of foreign language.

As a means of improving teaching, increasing attention is being devoted to the study of the actual classroom behavior of teachers. Category systems have been developed, *not* to evaluate teaching but to *describe* it, the assumption being that before you can evaluate the teaching act, you ought to know what the act consists of. Studies have been conducted to determine typical teaching patterns teachers use as they interact with pupils. Such studies have been done in elementary schools (Furst and Amidon 1963), in junior high mathematics and social studies classes (Flanders 1960b), in classes of teachers rated as 'above average' or 'below average' (Amidon and Giammateo 1965), and in the classes of secondary school student teachers (Amidon 1966) and cooperating teachers of English, science, social studies, and mathematics (Moskowitz 1967b).

Foreign language has been almost totally forgotten in these studies, perhaps because of the need not only for researchers to understand systems for analyzing classroom interaction, but to understand the peculiarities of the foreign language class as well. Those in the foreign language field are primarily steeped in developing newer methods for its communication and are not necessarily formally involved in the behavioral sciences. No wonder the twain have not met.

An observational system which has been used in a considerable number of research studies since its inception in the early 1950s is the Flanders system of interaction analysis. This system has been referred to as 'the most sophisticated technique for observing classroom climate' (Medley and Mitzel 1963, p. 271). The Flanders categories were used first to determine normative patterns of classroom interaction between teachers and pupils and later in the inservice and preservice training of teachers as a tool for self-analysis and self-improvement.

The Flanders system consists of ten categories: seven designate teacher behavior, two are for student behavior, and one is for silence or confusion. The teacher behaviors are divided into two types of influence, indirect and direct. The indirect categories are those which expand the freedom or opportunity of the students to participate. The categories of indirect teacher influence are: (1) accepts feelings of pupils, (2) praises or encourages, (3) accepts ideas of pupils, (4) asks questions. The categories of direct teacher influence are: (5) gives information, (6) gives directions, (7) criticizes or justifies authority. The two categories of student talk are: (8) student response-predictable, and (9) student response-unpredictable. The tenth category is for silence or confusion. These categories are summarized in Figure 1 [p. 60].

To obtain a complete descriptive picture of what behaviors are used during a lesson, a trained observer tallies every time a different category is used and when the same category is repeated for a consecutive period of time, he records this category every three seconds. The tallies are entered into a ten by ten matrix, resulting in a graphic picture of the lesson. The matrix preserves the general time sequence of the interaction by illustrating which behaviors immediately preceded or followed others. By studying the matrix, teaching patterns can be discovered and analyzed.

The following is an example of how an observation is tallied and entered into a matrix:

The teacher begins by saying, 'Open your books to page 160 and answer the first question, Bill' (category 6). Three seconds pass while the students get out their books and open them (category 10). Bill responds to the teacher's direction: 'Spain and Portugal form the Iberian Peninsula' (category 8). The teacher reacts with, 'Very good, Bill' (category 2). 'Who has the answer to the next question?' (category 4). A pupil raises his hand and says, 'I don't know where we are' (category 9). The teacher remarks, 'We are on page 160, the second question under Exercise 1 (category 5), and if you had been paying attention, you would have known where we are' (category 7). 'Martha, continue by reading your answer to the second question and be very careful to watch your pronunciation as you read' (The observer records two 6's in a row because the length of the statement is longer than 3 seconds). But Martha asks the teacher a question instead. 'They don't pronounce the "h" in Spanish or in French, do they?' (category 9), and the teacher responds, 'That's right, Martha (category 2) "h" is a silent letter in both of those languages' (category 3).

Observations automatically begin and end with category 10. An observer, therefore, would have tallied the above interaction in a column in the following way: 10-6-10-8-2-4-9-5-7-6-6-9-2-3-10.

Every number except the first and last 10 is then entered into

Teacher talk	Indirect influence	1.*Accepts feelings*: accepts and clarifies the feeling tone of the students in a non-threatening manner. Feelings may be positive or negative. Predicting or recalling feelings are included.
		2.*Praises or encourages*: praises or encourages student action or behavior. Jokes that release tension, not at the expense of another individual, nodding head or saying, 'um hm?' or 'go on' are included.
		3.*Accepts or uses ideas of student*: clarifying, building, or developing ideas suggested by a student. As a teacher brings more of his own ideas into play, shift to category five.
		4.*Asks questions*: asking a question about content or procedure with the intent that a student answer.
	Direct influence	5.*Lecturing*: giving facts or opinions about content or procedure; expressing his own ideas, asking rhetorical questions.
		6.*Giving directions*: directions, commands, or orders to which a student is expected to comply.
		7.*Criticizing or justifying authority*: statements intended to change student behavior from non-acceptable to acceptable pattern; bawling someone out; stating why the teacher is doing what he is doing; extreme self-reference.
		8.*Student talk – response*: a student makes a predictable response to teacher. Teacher initiates the contact or solicits student statement and sets limits to what the student says.
		9.*Student talk – initiation*: talk by students which they initiate. Unpredictable statements in response to teacher. Shift from 8 to 9 as student introduces own ideas.
		10.*Silence or confusion*: pauses, short periods of silence, and periods of confusion in which communication cannot be understood by the observer.

* There is *no* scale implied by these numbers. Each number is classificatory; it designates a particular kind of communication event. To write these numbers down during observation is to enumerate, not to judge a position on a scale.

FIGURE 1   Categories for interaction analysis, Minnesota 1959

the matrix twice, which is how the sequence of events is preserved. Each of the 100 cells in the matrix contains an event and what happened directly afterwards. If the behaviors just described are entered into a matrix, they would be paired in this way first:

1st pair (10
           6) 2nd pair

3rd pair (10
           8) 4th pair

5th pair (2
           4) 6th pair

7th pair (9
           5) etc.
           7

The rows in the matrix designate the first events; the columns are the second event. A tally is placed for each pair of numbers in the corresponding cell at the intersection of the appropriate column and row. The first pair above to be entered will go in the 10-6 (read 'ten-six') cell. The second will be placed in the 6-10 cell; the third, in the 10-8 cell; the fourth in the 8-2 cell; and so on. When all the tallies for an observation are entered into the matrix, the columns and the rows are each totaled. The totals for the columns

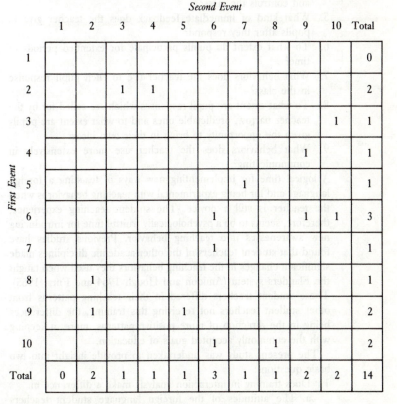

| | | Second Event | | | | | | | | | |
	1	2	3	4	5	6	7	8	9	10	Total
1											0
2			1	1							2
3									1		1
4									1		1
5						1					1
6						1			1	1	3
7						1					1
8		1									1
9		1									2
10						1		1			2
Total	0	2	1	1	1	3	1	1	2	2	14

First Event (row label)

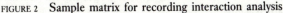

FIGURE 2   Sample matrix for recording interaction analysis

and the rows are identical, i.e., the total for column 1 will be the same as the total for row 1. Figure 2 illustrates where the above tallies will be placed on a matrix; the totals for the columns and the rows are also indicated.

When the matrix is complete, percentages for each category are calculated as well as the percentages of teacher talk, student talk, and silence or confusion. Ratios of the amount of indirect or direct behaviors the teacher used are also determined. There are nine of these ratios, which are referred to as I/D ratios, each focusing on a different relationship.

From the matrix a teacher may find out many specific things about his teaching. A few of these are:

1. What percentage of the class time does the teacher talk?
2. What percentage of the class time do the pupils talk?
3. Does the teacher use more indirect or direct influence during a lesson?
4. Is the teacher more indirect or direct in the way he motivates and controls the class?
5. What kind of immediate feedback does the teacher give to pupils after they respond?
6. To what extent do pupils participate for extended periods of time?
7. What behaviors does the teacher use to elicit pupil response in the class?
8. To what extent are pupil responses which are called for by the teacher narrow, predictable ones and to what extent are pupils given the opportunity to bring in their own ideas?
9. What behaviors does the teacher use more extensively in communicating?

A logical time for implementing new ways of teaching a foreign language and for being experimental with teaching behavior is when the teacher is still a novice. The student teaching experience, therefore, seems to be a psychologically fruitful time for introducing new awarenesses into teaching behavior. Previous studies have found that student teachers of the other academic disciplines made significant changes in the teaching behaviors they used when taught the Flanders system (Amidon and Hough 1964 and Furst 1965). These student teachers differed in their teaching patterns from other student teachers not receiving this training, the differences being in the direction of more positive patterns, more in keeping with the commonly accepted goals of education.

The present study was undertaken to provide insight into two basic questions:

1. Does training in interaction analysis make a difference in:
   a. The attitudes of the foreign language student teachers toward teaching?

    b. The teaching patterns of the foreign language student teachers?

    c. The attitudes toward foreign language of the pupils in the student teachers' classes?

    d. The attitudes of the foreign language student teachers toward their cooperating teachers?

    e. The attitudes of the cooperating teachers toward the foreign language student teachers?

2. Are the results obtained from training foreign language student teachers in the Flanders system similar to those obtained from training teachers of the other academic disciplines?

Procedures

Spring term of 1966 was the first semester that there was a sizable number of foreign language majors at Temple University taking their second and final student teaching experience. In their professional education courses, student teachers in secondary education are required to take one of two possible courses concurrently with their student teaching. It was decided that the fourteen foreign language student teachers should all be placed in the course in which they would learn the Flanders system. Two hours a week for fifteen weeks they attended the lecture for this course together with student teachers from the other academic disciplines. In addition, two hours a week, while the other student teachers had a seminar, the foreign language student teachers met in a seminar of their own in which the concepts of interaction analysis were then related to the teaching of foreign language. The author of the present study was the seminar instructor, having had experience in both the teaching of foreign language and the teaching of the Flanders system.

    In order to investigate the problem, a number of instruments were administered before and after training the foreign language student teachers in interaction analysis. All of the instruments were administered two weeks after the student teachers began to teach (which was the fourth week of student teaching) and again eight weeks later. Following are the measures which were used in the study.

Teaching Situation Reaction Test. Commonly referred to as the TSRT, this instrument was developed at Temple University by James K. Duncan and later refined by John B. Hough and has been found to have some potential for predicting teacher performance and to be resistant to faking. The TSRT assesses the teacher's reactions to classroom situations along the direct-indirect dichotomy and was administered to determine whether any changes in attitude occurred after the training. Other research has found that with the passage of time, student teachers tend to develop less favorable attitudes towards teaching when they do not receive training in interaction analysis (Hough and Amidon 1964; Furst 1965; Kirk 1964; Hough and Duncan 1965; Amidon *et al.* 1967).

The Foreign Language Attitude Questionnaire (FLAQ) is a questionnaire devised by the author of the present study to assess the attitudes of pupils toward learning a foreign language. There are three dimensions to the questionnaire:
1. How the student feels about the foreign language he is studying.
2. How the student feels about the foreign language teacher.
3. How the student feels while in the foreign language class.

There are fourteen items in the questionnaire. The pupils are directed to check along a seven-point scale their responses to each item. The highest possible total score is 98, with an upper score indicating a more positive attitude. The Hoyt technique for estimating reliability by analysis of variance was used to determine the reliability of the attitude questionnaire. The reliability of each individual questionnaire was found to be .76, so for a given class or group, the corrected reliability using the Spearman-Brown formula is .93. Comparisons were made on the total questionnaire, on all three subscales, and on the individual items to determine whether any changes had occurred in the attitudes of the pupils of these student teachers during the eight week period.

Since one often hears it said that females react more favorably to foreign language than males, the attitudes of the male pupils were compared with those of the female pupils to note whether there were differences in how the two sexes reacted to foreign language learning.

The Student Teachers' Attitude Questionnaire (STAQ) and the *Co-operating Teachers' Attitude Questionnaire* (CTAQ) were devised by the author of the present study to assess the attitudes and the degree of satisfaction of student teachers and their cooperating teachers toward one another. These questionnaires consist of items which were analyzed from favorable and unfavorable comments made by student teachers and cooperating teachers about one another. The attitude questionnaires are made up of parallel items, so that the same questions the cooperating teachers answer on the CTAQ are rephrased to apply to the student teachers on the STAQ. Each questionnaire contains eleven items. Subjects are to check along a nine-point scale their reactions to each item. The highest possible score is 99; the higher the score, the more positive the attitude. The following were the reliabilities for these questionnaires as estimated with the Hoyt technique: STAQ .87; CTAQ .92. These questionnaires were administered to determine whether training in interaction analysis affected the attitudes of the student teachers and the cooperating teachers toward one another.

The Flanders System of Interaction Analysis. The student teachers tape-recorded four class periods, a grammar lesson and a conversation lesson which they taught at the beginning of each semester and then again after their training in the Flanders system. The tapes were tallied by reliable observers who knew French and Spanish and who were trained in the Flanders system. Inter- and intra-reliability were always .85 and above. The individual observations of the student teachers were then summed to form four group matrices: a pre-grammar and a pre-conversation matrix and a post-grammar and a post-conversation matrix. Comparisons were then made to determine whether any changes occurred in the teaching patterns of the foreign language student teachers in grammar and conversation lessons after training in the Flanders system.

Findings

A t-test for correlated means using the direct difference method was used to test the significance between the post-test differences on the TSRT, the STAQ, the CTAQ and the teaching behaviors examined on the grammar and the conversation matrices. A conventional t-test was used to test the significance of the differences on the FLAQ.

TSRT. The mean score on the pre-test was 108, while on the post-test it was 99 (the lower the score, the better the performance on the test). The t-test run on pre- and post-TSRT scores was statistically significant beyond the .01 level, the value of t being 3.24. This group of foreign language student teachers, therefore, became significantly more positive in their attitudes toward teaching after the training in the Flanders system.

FLAQ. An examination of the scores concerning the attitudes toward foreign language held by the pupils in these classes indicates that over the eight-week period no statistically significant changes took place in the total score or in any of the three subscale scores. There was, however, a slight increase in the total score from a mean of 68.72 to 69.77 (the highest possible score being 98 and considered the most positive, while the lowest possible score is 14). Each of the subscale scores also became somewhat more favorable, with the greatest increase being in the attitudes toward the foreign language student teachers.

Statistically significant differences did occur in two of the individual items, however. In the second administration of the FLAQ, the pupils perceived that the student teachers (1) praised them significantly more and (2) minded less when they, the pupils, made mistakes. And, although this item did not achieve a statistically significant difference, the pupils indicated that they now liked reciting alone in the foreign language somewhat more. It appears that the student teachers were using behaviors which communicated less dissatisfaction with and more approval of the pupils; these behaviors, in turn, increased in a positive direction the attitudes toward the foreign language and toward the student teachers.

In examining the attitudes of the male and the female pupils both at the beginning and at the end of the study, the females had significantly more favorable attitudes toward learning a foreign language as well as on all of the dimensions of the three subscales. On eight of the fourteen individual items the females had significantly more positive attitudes. In the post-test the attitudes of the females were more positive on nine of the individual items. In the eighteen comparisons made, the degree of difference between the males and the females was greater in the post-test, becoming even more favorable for the females in twelve of the comparisons.

Since the pupils in the study were either first-, second-, third-, or fourth-year students, it appears that whatever the level of the foreign language the *females still had more favorable predispositions than the males toward foreign language learning*. This finding is consistent with those of a study conducted by the author at the college level in which a related questionnaire was used to assess student attitudes (Moskowitz 1966a). Further research should be done to determine reasons for this phenomenon.

Although the attitudes of the pupils as a whole did not increase significantly, on the other hand *they did not become less favorable*. More research is needed to find out what happens to the attitudes of pupils in classes of foreign language student teachers who do not receive training in interaction analysis. It may be that the attitudes of these pupils become more negative.

A possible source of contamination operating here is that because of having studied foreign language from their regular classroom teacher for the first half of the academic year, the pupils no doubt had already formed a number of their reactions toward learning a foreign language. Although the items called for reactions to the foreign language as taught by the student teachers, it is still possible that the student teachers were not the sole determiners of the attitudes present among their pupils.

STAQ. After four weeks of working together, the mean attitude score of the student teachers toward their cooperating teachers was 71.83, while eight weeks later the mean score decreased to 68.23. It may be that the training in interaction analysis caused certain changes in the student teachers which, in turn, caused their attitudes to become less favorable toward their cooperating teachers. The difference was not statistically significant.

A comparison here is possible with data collected in a study conducted in the spring of 1965 (Moskowitz 1966b). Four groups of student teachers from other academic areas responded to these questionnaires. One half of the student teachers and one half of the cooperating teachers were trained in the Flanders system. The student teachers and cooperating teachers were paired in the four possible combinations of training and no training in interaction analysis. *The group with the most negative attitudes toward their cooperating teachers was that with student teachers trained in interaction analysis whose cooperating teachers did not have this training.*

By inspection, the mean score on the STAQ in the present study ranks in consistent order with those in the above-mentioned study in that the post-mean attitude score of the foreign language student teachers, whose cooperating teachers were not trained in interaction analysis, was also much more negative than those of the other three combinations of cooperating teachers and student teachers. It appears as though training only the student teachers in interaction analysis causes some measure of frustration in the student teachers since they do not have a common frame of reference with which to communicate with their cooperating teachers.

CTAQ. Between the pre- and post-administration of the CTAQ there was no significant change in the attitudes of the cooperating teachers toward their student teachers. The first administration was given four weeks after the student teachers had been working with the cooperating teachers. The mean attitude score of the first administration was 79.15 and of the second, 79.62. The attitudes of the cooperating teachers tended to remain stable.

The attitudes of the cooperating teachers in this study were much more positive toward their student teachers than were the attitudes of the student teachers toward these cooperating teachers. (The mean score on the post-CTAQ was 79.62, compared to 68.23 on the post-STAQ). This finding is also consistent with that of the study just discussed. In the present study, when only the student teachers were trained in interaction analysis, the attitudes of the cooperating teachers did not change substantially, whereas the attitudes of the student teachers became less favorable toward the cooperating teachers.

The Flanders System. A major concern of this study was whether or not the teaching behaviors of the foreign language student teachers would change in the actual classroom situation after training in interaction analysis. It may be that certain behaviors are more difficult to incorporate in the teaching of foreign language because of a number of special factors which are present. When the class is conducted in a foreign language, limitations may be placed on the behaviors the teacher can use aside from the actual content of the lessons by (1) the level of pupil comprehension of the foreign language, (2) the ability of the teacher to speak the foreign language, and (3) the ability the pupils have attained in conversing in the language. For example, it is more difficult for a teacher in beginning foreign language classes to produce a 3-3, which means extended use (six seconds worth) of the students' ideas, for the students are not as a rule expressing their ideas in the foreign language. Also the teacher may have difficulty using a student's idea extensively because the students' understanding of the foreign language is so limited that they might not necessarily understand six seconds of such conversation by the teacher. Yet research with other academic disciplines has related high usage of the 3-3 cell with positive pupil attitudes and high achievement, so this is still a critical area to note as it does or does not appear in the foreign language class.

Some people have wondered whether the foreign language teacher is, by necessity, inclined to be direct. They pose the question, 'Is it possible for the foreign language teacher to be indirect?' Certain types of lessons, when conducted primarily in a foreign language, may be more restricted as to the possible behaviors produced. It is for this reason that a grammar lesson was chosen as one of the two kinds of lessons to be tape recorded: to determine whether in certain types of teaching, which may be more restrictive, the foreign language student teachers would make any changes after receiving training in interaction analysis. The other type of lesson selected was a conversation lesson because the possibility of using a greater variety of behaviors might be more feasible.

Yet when the pre- and post-group matrices for the grammar lessons were compared with the pre- and post-group matrices for the conversation lessons, *a similar pattern of changes occurred in the teaching of both types of lessons.* These differences are summarized below; in each case a difference indicated as significant represents the .05 level or beyond. Whether or not the differences were significant, all of the changes in behavior listed below did occur in *both* types of lessons. Note that the term 'extended' means six continuous seconds of the behavior referred to.

1. Student teachers in both grammar and conversation lessons used significantly:

   a. More indirect behaviors in motivating and controlling their classes. (Revised I/D)[1]

---

1. The items in parentheses which follow each description of behavior represent the terminology used in the Flanders system to refer to these measures.

    b. More extended indirect influence. (Extended Indirect Area)

    c. More extended indirect behaviors in proportion to extended direct behaviors. (Extended I/D)

    d. More extended acceptance of pupils' ideas.

2. Student teachers in grammar lessons used significantly:

    a. Fewer directions. (Column 6)

    b. Fewer extended directions (6-6 cell)

    c. More broad questions, which elicited original pupil responses, in proportion to narrow questions, which elicited predictable pupil responses. (4-9 cell/4-8 cell)

3. Student teachers in conversation lessons used significantly:

    a. More indirect behaviors in their overall interaction patterns. (I.D.)

    b. More extended praise. (2-2 cell)

4. Although the differences were not statistically significant, in both conversation and grammar lessons student teachers used:

    a. More indirect behaviors immediately after their pupils participated. (8–9 I/D)

    b. Less extended direct influence. (Extended Direct Area)

    c. More acceptance of pupils' feelings. (Column 1)

    d. More acceptance of pupils' ideas. (Column 3)

    e. Less criticism. (Column 7)

5. The pupils in the classes taught by the student teachers also revealed certain changes. All those reported below were significant at the .05 level or beyond. After the student teachers were trained in interaction analysis, the pupils in both types of lessons:

    a. Initiated their own ideas more, immediately after the student teachers presented information or lectured. (5-9 cell)

6. Pupils in conversation lessons:

    a. Gave fewer narrow, predictable responses. (Column 8)

    b. Presented more of their own ideas and initiated the conversation more. (Column 9)

    c. Talked for greater lengths of time when they expressed their own ideas. (9-9 cell)

The items which were statistically significant in the grammar and conversation lessons are summarized in Tables 1 and 2 [p. 70].

In spite of whatever difficulties might be inherent in producing changes of behavior in a foreign language grammar lesson, *these student teachers did change their interaction patterns*, and *they did become more indirect*. It is important to note that the changes which did occur in these two types of lessons appear to be in keeping with the goals of such lessons. For example, in a conversation lesson, an objective of the foreign language teacher is to get pupils to talk extensively, to express their own ideas, and to feel free enough to initiate these ideas even when the teacher does not specifically call

TABLE 1 Comparisons of teaching behaviors of foreign language student teachers before and after training in interaction analysis: grammar lessons (N = 14)

Variable	Mean Difference	t	p
Revised I/D-ratio	0.10	2.35	0.025
Extended I/D-ratio	0.16	2.48	0.025
Extended Indirect Area	1.37	2.68	0.01
4-9 Cell/4-8 Cell	0.09	1.78	0.05
Column 6	-2.82	-2.32	0.025
6-6 Cell	-1.28	-1.78	0.05
3-3 Cell	0.39	2.53	0.025
5-9 Cell	0.75	2.44	0.025

TABLE 2 Comparison of teaching behaviors of foreign language student teachers before and after training in interaction analysis: conversation lessons (N = 12)

Variable	Mean Difference	t	p
I/D-ratio	0.13	1.92	0.05
Revised I/D-ratio	0.16	2.73	0.01
Extended I/D-ratio	0.31	2.73	0.01
Extended Indirect Area	1.96	1.89	0.05
Column 8	-10.46	-3.20	0.01
Column 9	12.86	3.73	0.01
2-2 Cell	0.44	2.09	0.05
3-3 Cell	0.44	2.09	0.05
9-9 Cell	6.19	2.43	0.025
5-9 Cell	1.15	2.05	0.05

for them. These objectives were achieved more fully in the *post* conversation lessons, as evidenced by the assessment of the classroom interaction.

Discussion

Some may ask of what value is the knowledge of interaction analysis to the foreign language teacher? After all, the newer methods are quite structured often dictating precise behaviors and their exact sequences to the foreign language teacher. What right, if any, does the individual foreign language teacher have to deviate from the prescribed recommendations of those who have carefully thought through and developed pattern practices, drills, and conversations? Yet one serious problem encountered with the teaching of newer curricula is the retraining of teachers accustomed to teaching more traditionally. Although many teachers have received training in these newer approaches, a study by E. Muriel J. Wright (1967) indicated that *teachers are not making the behavioral transitions* necessary to teach these newer programs. Her study found teachers to be using the *same behaviors they used in teaching more traditionally*. Why does this problem exist? Behavior is difficult to change, but without a structure for understanding how to translate new practices into behavior, the task becomes an even greater one.

Using the Flanders categories, model lessons which have different goals can be exemplified on a matrix. As he sees which verbal behaviors are involved in specific types of lessons, the goals become concrete, visual and clearer to the teacher. Goals become more readily attainable as the teacher *sees* which verbal behaviors are involved in each kind of lesson. It is as though the teacher has been given an added sense with which to tune in, enabling him to have better control and understanding of his participation. By analyzing the behaviors he uses, comparing these with behaviors considered desirable for specific types of lessons, and then making changes in his behaviors to approximate the model, the foreign language teacher can come closer to making his behaviors match his intentions, and, in turn, the goals of language learning. Through this type of analysis, desired goals can be translated into reality in the classroom.

The foreign language teacher can therefore benefit from the Flanders system by attaining an additional way of viewing his interaction with pupils. He can be much more aware of the exact nature of the teaching patterns recommended in various types of lessons by using the Flanders categories as a descriptive frame of reference to make the behaviors operational.

On the other hand, if foreign language teachers find that they tend to restrict themselves to fewer behavior patterns than teachers in other disciplines, they might wish to experiment by using additional behaviors which would not interfere with specified drills, but would increase the range of the behaviors they use instead. There are certain additional behaviors, which are somewhat lacking in the foreign language class, that researchers have found relate, in other fields, to pupil achievement. It seems important, therefore, to expand the repertoire of behaviors used by foreign language teachers in an attempt to incorporate such behaviors also.

For example, instead of using solely the classic words of brief praise such as *bueno* or *très bien* after pupils do something praiseworthy, the foreign language teacher may decide to vary these expressions and even expand them into longer statements of praise. *Su pronunciación de los 'erres' es excelente y muy española* tells the student that he has not only done something which meets with the teacher's approval but *what it is he is being commended for.* Such behaviors on the part of the teacher will act to increase the passive vocabulary of the pupils, as well as having positive affective value for them.

One goal in language learning is for learners to be able to emit specific responses, which have been shaped, in answer to certain questions, and then eventually to produce these responses at will when a variety of responses are possible. The Flanders system enables the foreign language teacher to focus in on this hoped-for transition in pupil behavior and to get a graphic picture of whether such a goal is being achieved.

The Flanders system assesses classroom climate. Certainly the atmosphere is a crucial element in the foreign language classroom, which encompasses a learning situation in which numerous errors are made by all students. In a foreign language class, inhibition and fear of participation may be experienced even by students who never feel this way in any other class, unless the teacher is highly skillful and sensitive to his own teaching behaviors and the feelings of his students. Since the climate is created by the classroom teacher, it behooves us all to be as informed as we can about the climate we are establishing in our classes.

At the end of the training in the Flanders system, the foreign language student teachers completed a questionnaire which requested their reactions to the training and to its value for foreign language teachers. All of the fourteen subjects of the study responded positively. There were four items on the questionnaire. Item one asked the student teachers to circle the number which indicated their reactions to this statement:

Item 1. I believe the study of interaction analysis applies to foreign language teaching

1	2	3	4	5	6	7	8	9

not at all   *somewhat*   *a great deal*

The mean score for the group was 7.8, indicating that the group felt the Flanders system has considerable application for the teaching of foreign language.

Question two requested that the student teachers check the extent they agreed or disagreed with the following statement:

Item 2. The study of interaction analysis should be made a require-ment for foreign language teachers.

Six of the student teachers strongly agreed with the statement. The remaining eight all agreed with it. No one chose neutral, disagree, or strongly disagree in response to item two.

Two open-ended questions were asked. Below are the questions and excerpts from a few of the responses:

Item 3. Study interaction analysis has made me realize . . .
- that I can plan the way I am going to behave in the classroom.
- what is going on in the classroom and what is successful under specific conditions.
- exactly what I am doing in front of a class both good and bad. More than that, it has made me more aware of how my students react to my behavior.
- that controlling my behavior and the behavior of my students can be done.
- what behaviors I use; what behaviors I don't use; what behaviors I should like to use and why.

Item 4. I believe the most important things the foreign language teacher can gain from knowing the Flanders system are . . .
- an understanding of how to elicit student responses and original ideas, also an understanding of student feelings.
- how to get students to contribute in class without fear.
- how to develop and use behaviors which accept, encourage, and praise the student. This system makes one consciously aware of the interaction which takes place in the classroom.
- the importance of having some tangible check system whereby he can stop and analyze some of his behaviors in the class.
- the need for more and varied encouragement and praise so as not to sound trite with merely *bien*!
- the basics of teaching no matter what the subject – that is, what areas of the matrix are useful and appropriate and under what conditions.
- how to react to student responses.
- varying teaching techniques. The Flanders system provides the teacher with some ideas as to how to do it.

Conclusions
A number of differences were found in the pre- and post-data collected in the present study. The study of interaction analysis seems to have encouraged these differences. Training the foreign language student teachers in the Flanders system appeared to be related to:
1. More positive attitudes toward teaching by the student teachers.
2. More positive attitudes by pupils toward several items which appear related to the classroom behaviors of the student teachers.

3. Less positive attitudes of the student teachers toward the cooperating teachers.
4. More indirect teaching patterns used by the student teachers.
5. More expression of the pupils' own ideas in the foreign language classes.

In answer to a primary question posed in this study, the results obtained from training foreign language student teachers in the Flanders system appear to be similar to those obtained from training teachers of the other academic disciplines: both their attitudes toward teaching and the behavior patterns the foreign language student teachers used became more positive and more indirect after training in the Flanders system.

A previous study involving other academic disciplines concluded that when both student teachers and cooperating teachers were trained in interaction analysis, reciprocally favorable attitudes resulted between them (Moskowitz 1966b). It is therefore recommended that a similar study be done in the field of foreign language in the hopes of improving these attitudes as well.

In general, teachers trained in interaction analysis become more indirect, accept more pupil ideas, and criticize less than teachers not so trained. Flanders found that teachers whose pupils had high achievement and positive attitudes were more indirect, accepted more student ideas, and used less criticism than teachers of pupils with low achievement and negative attitudes. It would seem, therefore, that training in interaction analysis is helping to produce teachers with appropriate teaching skills and that these changes are also possible in the foreign language classroom.

A number of studies have indicated that at the end of practice teaching, the attitudes of student teachers not trained in interaction analysis were more negative and their teaching behaviors became more direct.[2] That the attitudes of these foreign language student teachers and their pupils improved and that the teaching patterns of the student teachers became more positive are indeed encouraging.

As stated earlier, the second part of Moskowitz's paper was concerned with a study involving three observational systems and in-service, rather than pre-service teachers. It was particularly noteworthy for its introduction of Moskowitz's FLint system, her adaptation of Flanders' Interaction Analysis categories. It was also noteworthy, however, for its extensive use of teachers' verbal reports of the benefits they felt they had obtained from learning about systematic classroom observation and applying their learning to their

2. Hough and Amidon, Furst, Kirk, Hough and Duncan, Amidon, and others.

own classroom behaviour. Nearly two decades later it is still difficult to resist being impressed by the enthusiasm expressed by these teachers.

Part 2. A study of inservice teachers

Background

The experimental study described in the first part of this paper was conducted in the spring of 1966. During the academic year which followed (1966–67), a related study was conducted over the course of two semesters with results which were consistent with the first study (Moskowitz 1968b). Both studies indicated that after training in interaction analysis, preservice foreign language teachers made positive changes in the behaviors they used when teaching. They also reacted with enthusiasm towards the training. A question which seemed pertinent to research at this point was 'What would happen if inservice foreign language teachers were given this training?'

To help answer this question, a graduate course was offered at Temple University during the 1967 summer session. The class met for three weeks, from three to four hours a day. The course consisted of two parts: one half of the time the participants learned about observational systems for analyzing interaction in the foreign language classroom. For the other half they were exposed to multisensory foreign language curricular programs, as well as foreign language methodology. Three staff members instructed the course, with two handling the teaching of observational systems and the foreign language curriculum specialist from the Philadelphia School District teaching the methodology.

Among the twenty-eight participants in the course were teachers of French, German, Latin, Russian, Spanish, and English as a second language. There were teachers from urban, suburban, and parochial schools, with levels from FLES to senior high school represented. The teachers enrolled in the course were from Pennsylvania, New Jersey, and Delaware, ranging from those going into their first year of teaching to some with over twenty-five years of experience. In these respects, it was a heterogeneous group.

Observational systems studied in the course

Because of their potential application to the foreign language classroom, three specific observational systems were taught: The Flanders system of interaction analysis, the FLint system and the IDEI system of nonverbal communication. The Flanders system has already been described in detail. The other two systems include the categories from interaction analysis, in addition to concepts of their own.

The *Foreign Language interaction system* (FLint) is an embellishment of the Flanders system and was designed to analyze foreign language teaching (Moskowitz 1967a). The following are additional categories included in FLint: (a) *the teacher* – jokes, repeats student ideas verbatim, corrects without criticism, directs a pattern drill, criticizes student behavior, and criticizes student responses; (b) *silence*, (c) *confusion* (divided into two types: (1) enthusiastic – eager to participate, and (2) out of order); (d) *laughter*, and (e) *English*. All teacher and pupil behaviors are assumed to be spoken in the language unless an 'e' for English is coded after the category number. This means that the teacher can determine the ratio of English to foreign language statements made by both himself and the students. He can also note which behaviors were used whenever someone reverted to the native language.

In addition to the I/D ratios calculated with the Flanders system, there are Foreign Language I/D ratios, English I/D ratios, and F/E ratios (the ratio of foreign language to English) for the total lesson, the teacher, and the student. Learning the categories has been simplified by using only twelve category numbers and adding subscripts of 'a' to those numbers which have related categories.

IDEI is an instrument recently developed by Charles Galloway, noted for his work in coding and analyzing nonverbal communication. The name is derived from the initials of the major dimensions of the system: I(indirect), D(direct), E(encouraging), I(inhibiting). Galloway has introduced into the Flanders system concepts from former methods he devised for coding nonverbal communication (Galloway 1967). And so it is that the observer notes both verbal and nonverbal communication as he records the Flanders categories, subdividing them into encouraging and inhibiting acts. Some of the concepts incorporated in this system are: congruity-incongruity, personal-impersonal, responsiveness-unresponsiveness, attentive-inattentive, comfort-distress.

Experiences provided in the course
The main goal of training the teachers in observational systems was to increase their sensitivity to their own classroom behavior and its effects and influence on students. To help accomplish this purpose, each teacher was asked to make a tape recording of himself teaching one of his foreign language classes before the close of the school year. For those who pre-registered for the course too late to do this, the assignment was altered to that of gathering a few youngsters together and tape-recording themselves teaching this group a lesson in foreign language.

As the teachers were taught the three above-mentioned systems of classroom interaction, a variety of procedures were used, with lecture playing only a minor role. The instructors role-played with the group, and the participants also had opportunities for leading role-playing sessions. Built into the schedule of activities were buzz groups, skill sessions, sensitivity training, and experiencing the learning of an unfamiliar language. *Practice in developing new behaviors and analyzing their effects* was a key element in the training.

One of the tasks carried out in small groups involved deciding upon desirable sequences of behaviors which should be used in teaching different types of lessons, such as pattern drill, the discovery of a grammatical structure, a review lesson, a reading lesson, a lesson on the culture of the people. Members of each group then tried to make the various models operational by teaching brief lessons and attempting to use the behaviors decided on by the groups. After each lesson, the class described the behaviors which were actually used and these were compared with the 'ideal' behaviors for the lesson.

A set of specifically designed materials for training foreign language teachers in the Flanders system was field-tested on this group. Included was a manual of readings, relating interaction analysis to foreign language teaching, and a programed text with accompanying tapes in four foreign languages. The latter were used to train the teachers in hearing the categories in a foreign language and in coding in the target tongue (Moskowitz 1967c).

To find out more about their teaching, the teachers were asked to use the Flanders system to analyze the tapes they had made prior to taking the course. From this analysis they were to decide for themselves what changes they would like to make in the teaching patterns they used. A number of the teachers registered disappointment upon discovering they were not producing behaviors they wished to, but used instead behaviors they did not prefer.

Each teacher was then asked to prepare a ten-minute lesson in which he planned to control his behavior by increasing and/or decreasing behavior patterns of his choosing. The teachers were given the opportunity to experience micro-teaching, that is, the teaching of this brief lesson using live pupils. In teaching this lesson, the teachers were to produce behaviors which would match the 'ideal' matrix they had planned for themselves. The lessons were video-taped and played back for all to observe.

Each teacher's lesson was coded by the two staff members, one using the Flanders system and the other using FLint. Additional feedback was given by the TV pupils, who filled out a questionnaire about each lesson they were taught. The teachers built two matrices with two sets of tallies and compared their actual matrix with the model matrix and also with the lesson on audio tape which they had previously analyzed. Emphasis was placed on analyzing *what had happened* and *why* rather than solely on whether or not the model had been carried out successfully. *Using interaction systems to analyze the micro-teaching turned the experience into an objective analysis rather than an opinionated, subjective one.* Each teacher was *his own critic* and judge. The instructors did not tell the teachers which behaviors to use nor did they sit in judgment and evaluate the teaching which was done.

An interesting sidelight was the unusual cohesiveness and spirit which this group developed. Members made arrangements to keep in contact with each other and several decided to try some experimental approaches and compare the results from different schools. As sensitivity grew, it became easier to express and exchange feelings. The last day of the course several of the less-experienced teachers admitted that they had felt concern at the start of the course about being with those who were much more experienced in the field. The 'younger set' now expressed pleasure at getting to know these teachers, for this, they felt, would help them in making better adjustments with similar teachers back on the job. Spokesmen from the more experienced group stated that they felt they had learned from their juniors, and were glad to have had this chance.

Findings of the study

Five weeks after the new school year began, a questionnaire was sent to the participants to find out whether the content of the course had influenced their actual classroom teaching. Ninety-three per cent of the forms were returned. On five of the items the teachers were to circle their responses on a scale of 1–7 points. Below are the questions, a sample of the scale, and the mean responses of the group. A sample of the scales used for each item follows:

1	2	3	4	5	6	7

not at all   *somewhat*   *a great deal*

I believe learning about observational systems has . . .
(The above statement precedes items 1–4 below)

		Mean Score
1.	increased my classroom sensitivity	6.4
2.	influenced me to use more indirect behaviors	5.8
3.	improved my interaction with pupils	5.7
4.	increased my understanding of pupil perceptions	6.3
5.	I find the observational systems I learned to use apply to foreign language teaching	6.0

The mean scores for all these items were in the vicinity of the area labeled 'a great deal.' It appears that the teachers found studying observational systems had greatly influenced their perceptiveness and their interaction.

The teachers were then asked to check the responses which described their foreign language teaching during the current fall term (1967) compared with that of the last term they taught. Below are the questions and the group responses reported in percentages.

The responses in the table indicate that the teachers perceived themselves as having made a number of behavioral changes related to concepts in the systems which were studied. These changes appear to be in a positive direction, being more in keeping with the goals of language learning.

Facts and figures are informative but the open-ended question to which the teachers responded provided perhaps an even more telling tale. To summarize them would be an injustice. To select from among the many heartwarming experiences was trying. Here is the question which was asked, followed by excerpts from the very touching replies:

Since I have learned about observational systems, I find when I teach foreign language I now . . .

	More	About the same	Less
1. tend to be direct	4*	8	88
2. try to use a greater variety of behaviors	96	0	4
3. praise students	84	16	0
4. criticize students	0	4	96
5. am aware of and sensitive to student feelings	92	8	0
6. give directions	4*	60	36
7. am conscious of my nonverbal communication	84	16	0
8. use English in the class	4*	40	56
9. am conscious of nonverbal cues of students	88	12	0
10. try to correct students without intonations or words of criticism	88	12	0
11. do the talking myself during the class time	0	20	80
12. try to use student ideas which go beyond verbatim repetition	84	16	0
13. am aware of whether there is laughter in my classes	60	40	0
14. try to get divergent, open-ended student responses	88	12	0

	More	About the same	Less
15. distinguish between enthusiastic and disorderly confusion	76	24	0
16. try to get students to participate	92	8	0

* Respondent stated she changed in this direction for she taught third- and fourth-year students previously and now has first-year classes.

The following are back home classroom experiences, reactions, and applications relating to my learning about classroom interaction systems:

– After learning the Flanders system, I felt completely different as I started my teaching in September. Everything I learned during the course, I applied to my teaching, and I strongly believe it has worked just beautifully. I have spread the system among my colleagues and explained to them how categories 1, 2 and 3 work in the foreign language class. They think it is a great thing to be your own observer. My textbook has gone from one teacher to another. I strongly believe every foreign language teacher should take this course.

– I feel taking this course in educational psychology has had more far-reaching effects than I ever anticipated. Among my classes I was given a French I tenth grade group, all of whom are repeaters. The students are reluctant or slow learners. I realized this group was a keg of dynamite and a challenge and needed to be treated *à la* our course. It has really worked, I am happy to say.

– Two of the teachers in my department are aware of the Flanders system. I plan to use this in my observation of their teaching. They are quite willing to cooperate. I told my superintendent about interaction analysis. Because he feels our faculty has grown so rapidly, and it is increasingly more difficult to improve their teaching, he is making arrangements for you to speak to our faculty.

– In my advanced classes I don't use only the single word *gut*, but I now uses phrases or complete sentences to praise, i.e., *Sie haben die Worte wunderbar ausgesprochen*. I notice that my classes are more responsive and relaxed because I am more aware of my reactions and the students' reactions. Several of us who know interaction analysis have convinced our in-service planning committee to have the teachers learn more about this system.

– The children seem very surprised at the amount of praise I use. They are not used to it from previous classes. If I say *muy bien* or *sehr gut*, some pat themselves on the back and thank me very much.

– I have made a sincere effort to use indirect teaching procedures and have found that the results have meant a healthier classroom atmosphere. I try to use more student ideas, the result being that my students seem to be reacting more favorably.

– I have been accepting students' feelings and find that it really works. For example, I often remark about how the students must feel on Friday afternoon and Monday morning. The students realize I am aware of their feelings and respond more enthusiastically.

– Unexpectedly I was given a student teacher this year. My ability to use my knowledge of interaction with her has been very helpful to me. We are getting along very well together.

– I have found that it is not difficult to use a variety of behaviors in the real classroom situation. We are in a new building which is not completed. The interferences give me many opportunities to use '1's.'

– On the whole, I detect a better relationship with my pupils. The students respond willingly and oftener when I praise them for what they actually do rather than simply saying 'good' or other automatic, meaningless responses. This causes me to listen more carefully to what they are saying so that I can give a definite statement of praise or an unobtrusive correction that will not offend.

– This course should be a 'must' for all prospective teachers. I said to myself, 'If only I had this training during my early college years, I *know* I would have been a better teacher today.' It's easy to sit back and say, 'He's a good teacher,' or 'She's not too good,' but try to explain good teaching to someone, and you find yourself giving all kinds of personal opinions and unfounded reactions. Now that I know these categories and nonverbal gestures, I can very clearly see and explain why one teacher is good, mediocre, or poor.

– This year I am working with a class of third-year Spanish students who read very poorly in the target language. The first week of class there were no students who volunteered to read aloud. The students were called upon to read and all read very poorly in the target language. By praising the slightest improvement in reading and by further encouragement, I have succeeded in getting at least half of the class to the point where they want to read in class. I, the teacher, am no longer considered a judge or 'scorekeeper' but the one who shows greatest pleasure with each step of improvement.

– I notice that the kids love praise, and as a result, the class participation I get is far greater. I am *much* more sensitive to students' feelings, and I understand these feelings much more. I tried *my own* experiment in one of my classes. I made deliberate attempts at being *more* direct. After only a few weeks of school, I find that this class 'catches on' much more slowly. I intend to switch to a more indirect method now. Brother – have I learned my lesson.

– A day never passes that I don't use what I've learned about interaction analysis. Sometimes I feel that little twinge of conscience which tells me I was 'sevening' or that I passed up a 3–3 for verbatim repetition. Other times I feel good because I know I passed up the '7' and opened a discussion instead. My students show me they are aware of praise by their improved attitudes and beaming faces.

– I have initiated a less direct approach to drill patterns and directed dialogues, using the 4-8-10-8-10-8 pattern we discussed. My students realize they are talking to each other more now and seem to have a sense of accomplishment about it.

– The most significant thing I learned from our summer course was that I can regulate my behavior and the behavior of those in my classroom. I was also impressed by the variety of behaviors which can be elicited. I criticize *myself* now rather than my students when responses I want do not appear. I have also learned how to incorporate these systems in my daily and personal life, which has been very rewarding.

– Interaction analysis has helped boost my attitude toward teaching.

– One of the most significant things I've learned is to avoid criticizing. Even a simple 'No' can produce such a pitiful look on a student's face that it is more desirable to use other behaviors to indicate that he was wrong.

– I've already made another tape of my classes for comparison purposes. One teacher helped me tally my tape and became so interested in it, she made a tape of her own for us to tally. In the spring we'll try again to see if we have improved.

– I now have some very different ideas about methodology than I previously held. My main concern now is not so much the subject I teach, but rather the subjects being taught, the individuals who each day sit in those desks before me. This does not mean that I disregard the preparation of my classes. On the contrary, I am more aware of my students' needs and in planning try to foresee behaviors that would best convey my ideas and accept their ideas and feelings. I try to curtail my talking and give the students more opportunities to participate. I do not know if my pupils have noticed any change in my behavior, but several who did not show too much interest last year seem to be much more interested now.

– In supervising a new teacher, I think I have tried to be even more conscientious than usual in making sure she has supplies, equipment, etc. I am also more willing to trust her judgment, less frequently imposing my own.

– A most valuable help to me has been acceptance of 'poor behavior' or a willingness to work longer with it, not to bear a grudge, to start each day fresh, but still to demand certain limits in a pleasant, friendly but firm fashion. I cannot yet control anger at flagrantly consistent opposition, but I think my burn point is higher. On lesser infractions, I find I give students reminders without anger, almost in a joking manner.

– Becoming conscious of the almost total control a teacher has and is not usually aware of is one of the excellent things I learned.

– I find using a combination of categories one and two helps overcome timidness and leads to good performance.

– An interesting sidelight which seems to be the result of my *consciously* supportive attitude is this: I have had students *really* ask for conference time. Others have come in before school to be sure they are caught up.

– No experience I have had in teacher training comes anywhere near giving me the kind of guidance and inspiration that this course in interaction systems gave me. It is the answer to discipline problems in any walk of life. If everyone could see the value of caring for the feelings of others, what a great world it would be.

– The first thing I noticed after a few days back at teaching was how insensitive I had been before the course in interaction analysis. We form bad habits in the classroom and then lose our awareness of them.

– I got surprising results with a difficult class one Friday. It was on a miserably sticky, muggy, Delaware afternoon, cloudy and dull. This class had been saying all along 'Show us.' I was dreading facing the class and was tired by the time the period came. The first big football game of the season was the next day. Five football players and three cheer-leaders were in the class. Some of the teachers had let classes out early. Several students received their first test scores, which were low. Yet this class was one of the most successful I have ever had. What happened? I only did one thing different that I know of: I expressed a genuine understanding of their feelings, and when they laughed in a few situations which weren't exactly opportune, I laughed with them, openly and warmly, and gave them a chance to vent their feelings. All eyes were glancing at me to see my reactions. When they saw understanding, it welded the class together like glue.

Some of the teachers expressed concern about the materials they use in their classes for they felt restricted in attempting to branch out behaviorally:

– I must say, though, that it appears difficult to be direct with the _____ materials. They are so set down, but I try to alter them for more indirectness and questioning.

– I find it extremely hard to apply interaction analysis to the ____ program, for it is so highly controlled and constructed that it is quite difficult to be indirect except for discussion. Needless to say, I'm dissatisfied with this course since it is so tightly controlled. I'm doing all I can to incorporate aspects from interaction analysis.

These teachers seem to be trying to discover how to maintain their individuality and avoid the feeling of being dictated to by a set of materials.

The data and the testimonials from this 'back home' report seem to have clear indications: learning interaction systems has had decided influence on the attitudes of these teachers, as well as application for their teaching. Some people have been wondering whether knowledge of interaction analysis has meaning and application for the field of foreign language. It appears from the results of these studies that it does. It is therefore hoped that these may be first steps in the direction referred to recently by Robert L. Politzer (1966):

> The very fact that the most important goal of the language teacher is the creation of a new 'verbal behavior' on the part of the student justifies the hope that the efficiency of his teaching may also be analyzed and evaluated in terms of observable, behavioral categories.

The enthusiasm so evident in the last pages of Moskowitz's paper was itself 'infectious' in the profession at the time, although it cannot have impressed hard-line empiricists unable to accept such 'testimonials' as real data. For them it seems to have overshadowed, and caused them to neglect, all the other evidence Moskowitz had put forward in her paper for the value of systematic classroom observation as a feedback tool that facilitated behaviour change. Since that time, of course, Moskowitz has, after several more years of observational research, focused increasingly on developing humanistic techniques for language teaching (see Moskowitz 1978), a move perhaps foreshadowed in her earlier emphasis on the human responses of her in-service teacher trainees, rather than on the statistical properties of their other questionnaire responses.

When we turn to Grittner we return to the supervisor's view of the world of language teacher training. Grittner was state supervisor of foreign languages with the Wisconsin Department of Public Instruction when in 1969 he published his book 'Teaching Foreign Languages'. We have already seen, in Chapter 1, his view of methodological comparison research. It was a largely negative view in 1968, making no positive suggestions but simply calling for a 'cease-fire'. In his 1969 volume he was more constructive, looking at various ways of evaluating the instructional process and paying a considerable amount of attention to systematic classroom observation (like many others at the time, he used the term 'interaction analysis' for this). We begin with the introductory paragraph to this section of Grittner's Chapter 11.

Evaluating the instructional process through interaction analysis

One point upon which most foreign language supervisors appear to agree is that the classroom teacher of foreign languages has a badly distorted view of what he is actually accomplishing with his classroom activities. The author has visited many schools where the staff proudly claimed to have a modern audiolingual course of study. However, after visiting all teachers at all levels of instruction it was revealed that 80 per cent of the classroom work involved teacher talk, most of which was in English, and that, on those rare occasions when the students were allowed to speak, their responses were either repetitions of what the teacher had said or were responses elicited with references to written material. It is not unusual to find that all functional communication between students and teacher is carried on in English. Teachers are often astonished when a tape recording of their classroom procedures is played back and systematically analyzed, to find that their use of the target language was both minimal and uncreative and that actual student use of the language was almost nil. It should be obvious to the teacher that the complex set of skills, which are listed as objectives in the local curriculum guide, cannot possibly be developed unless the students have an opportunity to engage actively in the acquisition of those skills. Yet in all too many cases, the teacher continues to be the active performer, the students the passive listeners. Because of this lack of consistency between goal and method, a number of foreign language educators have developed a system of interaction analysis aimed at allowing the teacher to study his own behavior and that of his students in a systematic and objective manner. The insights gained by this analysis can serve as a guide to changing teacher behavior. The system of interaction analysis described here is an adaptation of the process developed by Ned Flanders (Amidon and Flanders 1962).

It is very striking that Grittner very quickly dropped his supervisor role and wrote instead about teacher self-observation, and teacher behaviour change. He then introduced Nearhoof's otherwise unpublished adaptation of Flanders' system of interaction analysis. Nearhoof's system is of interest because he, like Jarvis, saw an immediate need to distinguish between 'real' and 'other' uses of language, but he chose the now more familiar terminology of 'communicative language use' for what Jarvis labelled 'real', and made a new set of distinctions within Jarvis's 'drill' category. Also of interest in Grittner's account of Nearhoof's system is his careful attention to the procedural details, enough to enable his readers to try out the system for themselves.

The Flanders system of interaction analysis

The Flanders system of interaction analysis is particularly appropriate for the foreign language field because it is concerned primarily with verbal behavior. The assumption is that the verbal behavior of an individual, both in English and in the target language, provides a relevant sample of his total behavior vis a vis the foreign language instructional process. The various patterns of observable verbal behavior are broken down into categories. The first major division is between talk by the teacher and talk by the students. Each of these divisions can then be divided further on the basis of whether the talk involves the native or the target language. And finally, the quality of the talk can be described both with regard to the oral behavior of the teacher and of the students. Through the systematic observations of dozens of different foreign language teachers, Nearhoof has devised ten interaction categories which include all the major verbal activities commonly occurring in the foreign language classroom (Nearhoof 1969).

Interaction categories for classroom observation

With these ten categories clearly in mind, the trained observer is then able to provide a quantitative evaluation of the teaching process by assigning a number to every 3 seconds of elapsed classroom time. At the end of the observation period, these numbers can then be tabulated to determine what proportion of class time has been devoted to each category of verbal behavior. In the Nearhoof project, each teacher in the study had volunteered to record all classroom activities onto audio tape. These actual classroom activities then served as the basis for establishing and refining the interaction categories. However, this same use of audio-tape recordings (or better still, video-tape recordings) can permit the teacher to evaluate with a high degree of objectivity his own classroom performance.

For the teacher or supervisor who wishes to make use of this interaction-analysis technique, the first step is the memorization of the ten categories in association with the appropriate number. Time simply does not permit the observer to refer back to the categories while he is engaged in the process of observing and recording his observations. The categories are as follows:

1. Teacher use of the foreign language for *communication*.
   - FL used by teacher to give directions which then elicit desired pupil action.
   - FL used by teacher to discuss ideas relating to cultural contrasts, geography, history, literature, etc.
   - FL used by teacher to explain problems of structure, of sound system, of written system, or other pertinent concepts.
   - FL used by teacher to answer pupil questions.
2. Teacher use of the foreign language for *reinforcement*.
   - FL used by teacher to correct pupil errors (provides correct response or causes correct response to be elicited).
   - FL used by teacher to let student know immediately that his response has been successful.
   - FL used by teacher to shape new responses or to reshape unsuccessful responses (i.e., response is broken into smaller parts, the smaller parts are drilled, and then the full response is attempted); FL also used to give hints (i.e., paraphrase, restatement, etc.), to help pupils produce new response.
   - FL used by teacher to provide model for drills.
   - FL used by teacher to elicit response in pattern practice.
3. Teacher uses English to *clarify meaning* or provide a cue. (A few words of English used quickly and briefly by the teacher.)
4. Teacher uses English as the *functional classroom language*. (This includes the use of English by the teacher for the items of communication and reinforcement described in 1 and 2 above.)
5. Student uses foreign language for *rote response*.
   - FL used by student in mimicry-memorization drill and pattern practice.
   - FL used by one student to elicit rote response from another student.
   - FL used by students in any type of repetitive drill exercises (i.e., class repetition of a dialog, sentence, conjugation, etc.).
   - FL used by students to read from text, chalkboard, etc.
   - FL used by students for any type of exercise which requires only an automatic response.
6. Student uses foreign language *to recombine* prelearned material.
   - FL used by student to answer questions.
   - FL used by student in which he is required to recall and recombine structures (oral or written) to form an acceptable reply.

7. Student uses the foreign language *to ask a question* which he himself has originated.
8. Student (or students) uses the foreign language *spontaneously*.
- FL used by students to discuss a topic of common interest (not rote recitation of prelearned material).
- FL used by students to react freely to pictorial or other situational presentation.
9. Students use *English* for classroom communication.
10. *Noninteraction* activities (e.g., silence; confusion; organization; other language activities such as language laboratory, singing, silent reading, etc.). For specialized language-related activities which are not easily categorized, these symbols are used to identify the time interval of the activities.

   O-S – singing
   O-R – reading (silent)
   O-W – writing
   O-L – laboratory.

Procedure for categorizing teacher-pupil interaction

Best results are obtained when the observer spends several minutes orienting himself to the situation before he actually begins to categorize. He will thus develop a feeling for the total atmosphere of teacher-pupil interaction.

The observer records a category number every 3 seconds or with each change of activity. However, often during rapid question-answer sessions or when the teacher interrupts a pupil's response to correct or shape the correct response, more than one notation is required during the 3-second period. This follows the above statement regarding change of activity.

Teacher:	Tiene Ud. un libro rojo?	(2)
Pupil:	No tiene ...	(5)
Teacher:	Tengo.	(2)
Pupil:	No tengo un libro rojo.	(5)

Thus, if more than one category occurs during the 3-second interval, then all categories used in that interval are recorded. Conversely, each change in category is recorded. If no change occurs within 3 seconds, repeat the category number.

However, if a silence is long enough for a break in the interaction to be discernible, and if it occurs at a 3-second recording time, it is recorded as 0. If no change occurs within 3 seconds, repeat that category number. See description of categories for other uses of 0.

These numbers are recorded in sequence in a column, and at the end of the observation period the observer will have several long columns of numbers. It is important to keep the tempo as steady as possible, but it is even more important to be accurate. He may also wish to write down marginal notes from time to time which can be used to explain what has been happening in the classroom.

The observer stops classifying whenever the classroom activity is changed so that observing is inappropriate as, for instance, when there are various groups working on a written assignment or doing silent reading. He will usually draw a line under the recorded number, make a note of the new activity, and resume categorizing when teacher-pupil interaction continues. At all times the observer notes the kind of class activity he is observing. A shift to a new activity should also be noted.

Aids for categorizing

1. Always begin and end each observation by recording a 0.
2. If a teacher calls on a pupil for a desired response, and if this action plus an ensuing silence constitute a 3-second interval, this should be recorded as 0.
3. As stated before, during an interval when interaction observation is inappropriate (when the group is reading silently or singing in the foreign language), the observer should draw a line under the last recorded category number and indicate the time. When positive interaction recommences, again indicate the time and begin with 0. Thus, by using 20 numbers per minute, it is possible to include all classroom activity for the observation period.
4. If the teacher intermingles English and the foreign language, this should be recorded as 4.

   Teacher: Take out your books and open them *à la page deux cents trois.*
5. Drill and practice on a group basis falls in category 5, and when the drill is on an individual teacher-pupil basis, categories 2 and 5 are also used.

   Teacher: J'ai deux frères. (2)
   Class: J'ai deux frères. (5)
   Teacher: trois frères (2)
   Pupil 1: J'ai trois frères. (5)
   Teacher: Nous (2)
   Pupil 2: Nous avons trois frères. (5)
   Teacher: voitures (2)
   Pupil 3: Nous avons trois voitures. (5)

Recording data in a matrix

There is a method of recording the sequence of events in the classroom in such a way that certain facts become readily apparent. This method consists of entering the sequence of numbers into a 10-row by 10-column table which is called a *matrix* (see Table 11, [p. 92]). The generalized sequence of the teacher-pupil interaction can be examined readily in this matrix. The following example shows how an observer would classify what happens in the classroom and how the observations are recorded in the matrix. The observer has been sitting in the classroom for several minutes and has begun to get some idea of the general climate before he begins to record. The teacher begins, 'Alors, Pierre, comment allez-vous aujourd'hui?' (Observer classifies this as a 2). Pierre responds, 'Très bien, merci. Et vous?' (Observer records a 6). Teacher, 'Très bien, merci .... Jacques, quel temps fait-il?' (Observer records a sequence of two 2's). Pupil, 'Il fait beau.' (6). Teacher, 'Marie, faites-vous du russe?' (2). Pupil, 'Non, je fais du français.' (6). Teacher, 'Today we are going to complete our examination of the irregular verb *faire*. In our various structure drills and dialogues we have used only two basic sound forms of *faire: fais* (*fait*, same sound) and *faites*. Using our basic frame, *je fais du français*, we shall develop this important verb.' (Observer records a series of five 4's followed by a 0 because of a period of silence during which the teacher picks up several 3 by 5 cards for the drill session.)

Teacher:	Répétez, Je fais du français. (2)
Pupils:	Je fais du français. (5)
Teacher:	Vous faites du français. (2)
Pupils:	Vous faites du français. (5)
Teacher:	Tu fais du français. (2)
Pupils:	Tu fais du français. (5)
Teacher:	Ils font du français. (2)
Pupils:	Ils font du français. (5)

(Observer records the sequence of 2, 5 followed by a final 0.)

The observer has now classified the following sequence of numbers in this fashion:

0
2
6
2
2
6
2
6
4 in matrix sequence
4 (0,2) (2,6) (6,2) (2,2) (2,6) (6,2) (2,6)
4 (6,4) (4,4) (4,4) (4,4) (4,4) (4,0) (0,2)
4 (2,5) (5,2) (2,5) (5,2) (2,5) (5,2) (2,5) (5,0)
4 (The rapid recording of the sequence 2 and 5 results from the change of activity occurring in the three-second interval.)

0
2
5
2
5
2
5
2
5
0

Techniques for tabulating matrix data

Tabulations are now made in the matrix to represent pairs of numbers. Notice in the listing of matrix sequence that the numbers have been marked off in pairs. This first pair is 0,2; the second pair is 2,6, etc. The particular cell (see Table 11) in which the tabulation of the pair of numbers is made is determined by using the first number in the pair to indicate the *row*, and the second number in the pair for the *column*. Thus, 0,2 would be shown by a tally in the cell formed by row 0 and column 2. The second pair, 2,6, would be shown in the cell formed by row 2 and column 6, etc. Notice that each pair of numbers overlaps with the previous pair, and each number, except the first and the last, is used twice. It is for this reason that a 0 is entered as the first number and the last number in the record. Zero was chosen because it is convenient to assume that each record begins and ends with silence. This procedure also permits the total of each column to equal the total of the corresponding row.

It is convenient to check the tabulations in the matrix for accuracy by noting that there should be one less tally in the matrix than there were numbers entered in the original observation record.

In the example, we have 23 numbers and the total number of tallies in the matrix is 22. This is shown in Table 11.

Using the matrix to determine general aspects of classroom interaction

After the observer tabulates a matrix, he then has the job of developing a description of the classroom interaction. He has several ways of describing the interaction but begins by reporting the different kinds of statements in terms of percentages. The first step is computing the percentage of tallies in each of the columns. This is done by dividing each of the column totals, 1 through 0, by the total number of tallies in the matrix. This computation gives each category as a proportion of the total interaction in the observed classroom situation. A similar procedure is used to determine the

TABLE 11   Sample interaction matrix

	1	2	3	4	5	6	7	8	9	0	
1											0
2		I			IIII	III					8
3											0
4				IIII						I	5
5		III								I	4
6		II		I							3
7											0
8											0
9											0
0		II									2
Total	0	8	0	5	4	3	0	0	0	2	22

percentage of teacher activity, teacher use of FL, pupil activity, and pupil use of FL. To determine the percentage of teacher activity, divide the total of categories 1 through 4 by the matrix total. For example, in Table 12, teacher activity (columns 1–4) totals 40. Then 40 is divided by the matrix total, 100; and we find that the amount of teacher activity is 40 percent of the total amount of classroom activity. To calculate the percentage of teacher use of the FL in relation to the percentage of teacher activity, divide the total of columns 1 and 2 by the total of columns 1–4. In Table 12, teacher use of FL is 30; and by dividing 30 by the total teacher activity, 40, we find the percentage of teacher use of the FL is 75 percent. In short, teacher activity constituted 40 percent of the observation period, and the teacher used the FL 75 percent of the time he was in direct interaction.

The same procedure is employed to determine total pupil activity and pupil use of the FL. Pupil activity is recorded in columns 6

TABLE 12

Sample matrix summary

	1	2	3	4	5	6	7	8	9	0	
1											
2											
3											
4											
5											
6											
7											
8											
9											Matrix
0											Total
Column %	10	20	2	8	0	32	6	14	0	8	100
Total	10	20	2	8		32	6	14		8	

use of FL
$\frac{30}{40}$ = 75%
or 30% of total
observation period

use of FL
$\frac{52}{52}$ = 100%
or 52% of total
observation period

teacher activity
$\frac{40}{100}$ = 40%

pupil activity
$\frac{52}{100}$ = 52%

through 9, with pupil use of the FL located in columns 6, 7, and 8.

Table 13 [p. 94] is an analysis of a Spanish class. The observation period was 30 minutes. An examination of the matrix summary reveals the following information:

Total teacher activity	22.3% of observation period
Teacher use of FL	60.0% of teacher activity
Teacher use of FL	13.3% of observation period
Total pupil activity	23.5% of observation period

TABLE 13   Spanish I matrix summary (30 minutes)

	1	2	3	4	5	6	7	8	9	0	
1	0	0	0	0	0	0	0	0	1	1	
2	0	9	0	3	6	29	0	15	00	14	
3	0	0	0	0	0	0	0	0	1	1	
4	1	2	0	11	1	9	0	2	13	11	
5	1	2	0	7	219	0	0	0	0	3	
6	0	35	1	6	3	12	0	1	0	8	
7	0	0	0	0	0	0	0	0	0	0	
8	0	9	0	0	0	0	0	33	0	2	
9	0	4	0	12	0	0	0	0	0	3	
0	0	15	1	11	3	6	0	3	4	46	Matrix Total
Total	2	76	2	50	237	66	0	54	19	89	590
Column %	0.3	12.9	0.3	8.5	39.3	11.2	0	9.2	3.2	15.1	

use of FL
$\frac{78}{130} = 60\%$
or 13.3% of total observation period

use of FL
$\frac{120}{139} = 86.3\%$
or 20.4% of total observation period

teacher activity
$\frac{130}{590} = 22.3\%$

pupil activity
$\frac{139}{590} = 23.5\%$

Pupil use of FL	86.3% of pupil activity
Pupil use of FL	20.4% of observation period
Drill and practice sessions	39.3% of observation period
Interaction recorded in category 0	15.1% of observation period

Two activities constituted the major portion of interaction recorded in category 0: (1) pupils preparing themselves for language laboratory session and (2) distribution of some printed materials to the class.

Table 14 is a sample interaction form.

The reader will probably have noticed that Grittner made no attempt to justify the categories of Nearhoof's system for systematic

TABLE 14   Sample interaction form[a]

Date _____   Teacher _____

Class _____   Observer _____

School _____   Other notes _____

0	8	4									
2	8	5									
2	2	5									
0	8	5									
0	8	5									
6	8	5									
6	8	5									
2	2	5									
6	8	5									
2	8	5									
2	2	5									
2	6	5									
6	8	5									
6	8	5									
1	8	5									
1	0	5									
1	0	0									
1	4										
8	4										
8	4										
8	4										

[a] The actual length of the form is much longer. It usually provides space for 40 category numbers per column.

classroom observation. It is tempting to interpret this as evidence that the category systems were seen as self-justifying. Jarvis, Politzer, Rothfarb, and Moskowitz had all given their various but always pedagogic reasons for the categories they had chosen to work with, but Grittner apparently saw no such need. Nor is there evidence in Grittner's text that he saw the benefits of self-observation primarily in terms of consciousness-raising, a possibility we have seen alluded to in Jarvis's and Rothfarb's studies, and fully recognized and exploited in Moskowitz's work.

Four years after Grittner, in 1973, Krumm published in Europe a paper, entitled 'Interaction Analysis and Microteaching for the Training of Modern Language Teachers', that similarly chose to present Nearhoof's categories, but this time in the context of a search for a system that would meet Krumm's highly specific needs. Krumm was looking for a system that would give feedback directly and specifically relevant to a student teacher's attempts to implement a particular teaching method (in this case the 'audio-visual structural global approach'). Krumm began his paper with an analysis of the problems facing teacher trainers in his particular situation.

1. Problems of foreign language teacher training

The need for a practice-oriented reform makes itself especially felt in the training of foreign language teachers: their training has been exclusively philologically oriented up till now in German universities; neither the language abilities nor the technical qualifications have been so precisely defined, as for example the Steering Committee of the Foreign Language Program has done for the American foreign language teachers (PMLA 1955). There are three elements that constitute the professional qualifications of a modern language teacher: *language – method – instruction*.

It is only the first of these three necessary elements of teacher training, and even here more the knowledge part than the performance qualifications, that is included in the present university curriculum. Although recently the German universities have attempted to achieve a stronger professionalization by means of the institution of language centres (IFS 1971), there is still general uncertainty as to how these method skills for foreign language teaching should be transmitted. One of the most important reasons for this is that the tendencies toward educational reform, including the introduction of microteaching, have been up to the present time non-specific as regards subject or methods and are therefore difficult to apply to the reforming of the curriculum in the various subject areas. On the other hand foreign language teaching differs basically from other subjects, in that language is at the same time medium and subject of teaching.

We based our considerations about the development of teacher training courses designed specifically for foreign language teachers on the following premises:

1. The university student is at the same time a foreign language learner – this situation should provide the point of departure for his own considerations about methods of language teaching.

2. In order to enable the student to transfer the teaching skills which he is training into actual instructional processes he must be confronted with them from the outset in an instructional context.

3. If one wants to transmit teaching skills which were relevant to methods rather than elementary, non-specific ones, the decision concerning the methodological concept of language teaching in the schools must precede the decision as to the content of training. This consideration contains a special problem for the development of study units in the German teacher training: the reform of foreign language teaching in the schools is actually by no means complete. Politzer for example, could base his research on the 'Characteristics and Behaviors of the Successful Foreign Language Teacher' on the fact that the audio-lingual method is generally accepted (Politzer and Weiss 1969a). In our case, the time allotted to the spoken language, and to the literature and background culture in language teaching on the secondary level has not yet been clarified; and the methodological decisions have likewise not been made.

We have therefore limited ourselves for research and developmental purposes to courses which introduce the students to teaching one specific method, namely the audio-visual structural global approach. This is based on the fact that there is a definite methodological concept available which prescribes not only the individual teaching phases, but partially in great detail the teacher's behaviour within the various phases as well (Guberina 1965). It is therefore possible 'to describe the performance expected of a teacher in the classroom. Unless we have such performance-oriented objectives, our program may be developed in a vacuum ... and it will not likely be relevant to the task of teaching a foreign language' (Banathy 1968). A further element in the already developed teacher courses for this method provided a help for us: the fact that an attempt was made to revise the students' language learning experiences by teaching a language which was totally foreign to them according to the same audio-visual concept which they themselves as teachers would have to apply.[1]

1. Cf. Janacek 1969.

At this stage of his paper Krumm was concerned with 'performance-oriented objectives', which may now seem somewhat authoritarian in flavour, but he was at the same time trying to promote what amounted to a democratic revolution in teacher training in his country, by bringing in micro-teaching (an approach to teacher training that depended upon detailed classroom observation and feedback), and thereby replacing the old focus on *supervision* with a new focus on *self-evaluation*. Krumm continued his paper by describing first the main characteristics of the teacher training courses he was running, and then looking in detail at the observational problems involved, focusing on the selection of relevant categories.

2 The AVSG-method teacher training course

In the meantime we have conducted several teacher courses for the AVSG-method;[2] I will briefly describe them, because they form the basis for our further considerations about the development of a general training concept for modern language teachers. The main parts of the courses are:
- group preparation for teaching
- classroom teaching with a reduced number of students
- a theoretical part to which equal time is allotted.

Teaching takes place in front of real students (adults who are taught free of cost – 'German for foreigners'), so that there is only a limited possibility to repeat the same unit with new groups of students. But it would be problematic to work with paid learners or other participants of the course as 'pupils' because one cannot simulate the situation of the beginning language learner, his inability to understand. This has also consequences on the length of a lesson. While in a microteaching laboratory the lesson is reduced to 5 or 10 minutes, each lesson in our language classes lasts about 90 minutes. The situation of the trainee is facilitated by the fact that each lesson is subdivided according to the phases of the AVSG-method (e.g. phonetical correction, transfer phase), each of which is taught by another student. In this sense the procedure resembles that of Beattie and Teather (1971), even though theirs does not include a real language class and real pupils.

The group of trainees which coteaches the lesson cooperates in the preparation of it as well. A part of this *preparation* is the precise identification of the teaching behaviours (e.g. working with the filmstrip projector, types of phonetical correction or word explanation). Although the teacher cannot limit himself to one teaching skill – as is the case in the Stanford microteaching model (Allen and Ryan

2. For a detailed description see Krumm 1973.

1969) – he is nevertheless limited to one of the methodological phases within the AVSG-method and can attempt to realize this phase by using certain types of behaviour. And because each trainee will have a minimum of two teaching units he can also try to modify his behaviour in the second attempt.

The *analysis of teaching* by means of looking at the videotaped lesson therefore shall contribute to the preparation of the next lessons; though the content then will be different, the methodological phases (and problems) will remain the same. So it is possible to direct the participants' at first rather retrospective critique to the question: how can this problem be solved in another manner in the next lesson? In addition, procedures of analyzing and the connection between planning and realizing a lesson are discussed in the theoretical part of the course.

So we borrow the reduction of time (20 to 30 minutes for each trainee) and the reduction of number (about 8 to 10 students per class) from the Stanford microteaching model. We also concentrate on well-defined methodological phases (not, however, on one elementary teaching skill). But a number of problems are not yet solved; one is the difficulty to work with 'real pupils', because they are not available for language teaching purposes for several languages and in such a number that all the trainees can have more than one reteach. It is also difficult to develop teaching skills or methodological steps, for other language teaching methods with the same precision as for the AVSG-method.

In the long run therefore we try to design a combination of microteaching (in a 'laboratory-classroom'), structured teaching observation by means of some category system and actual, but facilitated teaching attempts. So the trainee will first see a teacher using certain types of behaviour, then experiment himself with this behaviour (microteaching) and finally try to practise it in the classroom still under controlled conditions, so that an evaluation is possible. This concept in some respect resembles the procedures of the 'Minicourses' developed for in-service training in the United States (Borg *et al.* 1970). The Minicourses also contain the microteaching approach: that is the training of specific teaching skills under reduced and controlled conditions and feedback given by means of videotape and evaluation schemes. But the training procedure in the Minicourses is also put into the context of educational research (the trainee has to read a handbook and see instructional films concerned with the skill he is training) and it is put into the context of real classroom situations and problems (by model tapes demonstrating the application of the teaching skills). It is in this direction that we designed a training concept for foreign language teachers which will now be discussed.

3. Teaching analysis in foreign language teaching

The point of departure in our new course model as it is shown in the diagram is constituted by the students' own language learning, which is recorded on videotape and forms the basis of a first, as yet unstructured discussion about the methodological problems in language teaching. If it is possible, special language teaching in a language with which the trainee is not familiar will be offered by selected model teachers for this purpose, so that the trainee will be able once again to place himself in the perspective of a beginning language learner. As a result of viewing these tapes the question as to the skills to be trained and to a system of categorizing the observation should emerge.

At the moment we concentrate our research on finding out categories fit to describe modern language teacher performance so that the student gets an instrument to evaluate teaching and to discriminate the skills and their connection with the underlying teaching method. Banathy's demand, that the development of a 'Design of Foreign Language Teacher Education' should depend on a precise task analysis is fully justified; he himself demonstrates as an example for the 'expected comprehension competence', what aspect a detailed description of goal-oriented teaching behaviour should have (Banathy 1968). The 'performance criteria' which he and Politzer developed (Politzer 1967), always presume an understanding of what good and bad teaching is, which does not always correspond to our own teaching and methodological situation; one can readily see that 'using visual aids' (Politzer) or 'question and answer work' (Beattie and Teather) possess extremely differing characteristics according to given teaching objectives or underlying method. We were therefore looking for an instrument that demonstrates the resulting teacher performance and teacher-student interaction when a certain method is applied. The decision as to whether the observed behaviour is correct or false, should not already be contained in the instrument of observation.[3] It seems to me at this time to be most advisable to start with the interaction analysis of Flanders and to rework his categories for the purpose of foreign language teaching (Flanders 1970, 1971). Flanders' categories are designed to illustrate teacher-student interaction stressing the distinction between directive and non-directive teacher behaviour. His 10 categories are:

Teacher   1 accepts feeling, positive or negative
        2 praises or encourages
        3 accepts or uses ideas of the student

3. Such correct or false categories may also be found in the field of modern language teacher training; cf Koehring 1970.

4 asks questions
5 lectures
6 gives directions
7 criticizes, or justifies authority
Pupil 8 student talk: response
9 student talk: spontaneously
10 silence or confusion, non-verbal activities

A first adaptation to the analysis of language teaching was made by Wragg (1970): he uses the category numbers 1 to 10 when the verbal behaviour is in the native tongue and numbers them 11 to 20 when the foreign language is applied. We found however, that the activities of the student are not discriminated well enough to demonstrate the connection between certain stimuli and specific language performances on the side of the students. So we turned to the category system that was developed by Nearhoof (1969) on the basis of interaction analysis.

Nearhoof reduces the teacher-categories to four and differentiates on the pupil's side:

Teacher 1 uses foreign language (FL) for communication
2 uses FL for reinforcement
3 uses English (mother tongue) to clarify meaning or provide a cue
4 uses English (mother tongue) as the functional classroom language
Student 5 uses FL for rote response
6 uses FL to recombine prelearned material
7 uses FL to ask a question which he himself has originated
8 uses FL spontaneously
9 uses English (mother tongue) for classroom communication
10 Noninteraction activities (silence, confusion, singing, reading/silent, laboratory a.s.o.).

At the moment I am modifying this system in order to get categories for what I could not categorize when working with this system: especially I would like to discriminate on the teacher's side between information, stimuli and narrow questions, broad questions and attempts to have the students talk to one another in the foreign language; the categories for the students seem to be satisfying after we started to use some of the Flanders' multiple coding techniques to indicate student-student interaction. I would also like to identify the use of audiovisual media by indicating which teacher activity is given to them; so if the tape recorder is giving the information or stimulus instead of marking 'V' for a teacher activity we write 'TR' under the same information or stimulus category.

I should like to emphasize once again that the development of a specific observational instrument for foreign language teaching in my opinion is necessary in order to train the student to the point that he will be able to recognize the teaching skills which are afterwards trained in isolation in the microteaching clinic. By starting with a system of analysis and applying it to videotaped classroom work the student can see the skills appearing within a teaching context and with those modifications teacher behaviour will have to undergo because of the situational components of every classroom lesson.

There is also some research evidence that the training of the student's discrimination capabilities with the help of a category system may be more important for the improvement of his teaching than the microteaching practice he will get afterwards (Wagner 1972).

It is particularly interesting to see Krumm's treatment of Politzer's ideas on 'good and bad' teaching, although Krumm appears not to have been familiar with Politzer's experimental work in the area. Krumm wisely drew attention to possible situational differences, but finally seemed to consider the problem solved when the concern was for the 'resulting teacher performance and teacher-student interaction when a certain method is applied'. Again, as for Moskowitz and Rothfarb, we have categories justified not directly in terms of language learning achievement, but in terms of *assumptions* about learner achievement. Unlike Grittner, however, Krumm was clearly concerned that each of his categories should at least be precisely motivated in terms of the method he was training his student teachers to employ. There is no sense, here, of category systems becoming self-justifying.

Finally, Krumm described the seven steps of his experimental teacher training course design.

4. Course design for foreign language teacher training

The course design we are experimenting with at the moment is illustrated by the diagram. You can identify seven steps two of which may be repeated as often as necessary (4: use of demonstration films or tapes, 5: microteaching).

Step 1 is the student's own language learning experience; the student will see videotapes of these lessons so that he becomes acquainted with the equipment and procedure of videotaping and with the situation of looking at oneself on television.

Step 2 is the teaching analysis described above, starting with the playback of the tapes from step one and then using other videotapes of various kinds.

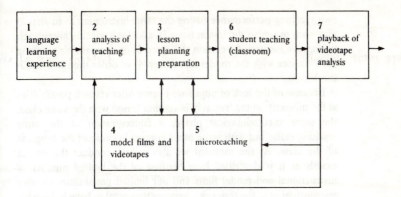

Course design for modern language teacher training

Step 3 is the lesson planning which is done within the same group of trainees that analyzed the tapes together and that will teach the class together.

Step 4 is voluntary for the students and at the moment there is not yet enough material to supply them with a variety of demonstration films or videotapes illustrating specific teaching behaviours. But because various methodological conceptions are in competition with one another it seems indispensable to demonstrate various applications and modifications of the teaching skills; since the normal teaching day includes many lulls, it seems appropriate to pick out relevant teaching sequences (that is such that constitute a specific methodological approach or teaching situation).[4] By this way it is also possible to simultaneously demonstrate the fact that there is no one teaching model but a variety of applications.[5]

Step 5 may be used if wanted by the students during their lesson planning and preparation: while preparing his part of the lesson one of the trainees may just try out some of the skills he will apply afterwards. His fellow-students will then simulate the class; usually at this stage the trainee wants to experiment with elementary skills like using the audiovisual equipment, but sometimes also more complex ones like explaining an idiom by using the foreign language and referring to the pupils' experience.

Step 6, the teaching itself, was described above: it is real classroom teaching under some reduced conditions (time, number of students, complexity of situation).

Step 7 then, the playback of the videotaped teaching practice may be the starting point for a revision cycle: the student analyzing his

4. Cf. Zitfreund 1966, von Faber 1971.
5. See Gibb 1970.

own teaching performance (using the same instrument as in step 2) may want to replan the lesson (step 3), asks for a specific microteach to improve his use of a certain skill (step 5) or compare his teaching performance with the model tapes (step 4) in order then to reteach the lesson.

Because of the lack of pupils we cannot offer reteach possibilities at the moment, so the 'reteach' is another lesson with the same class, the same methodological phase, a concentration of the same teaching skills, but with some other content because of the progress of the class. At the moment we also cannot conduct the course exactly as it is described here because of the limited number of instructional and model films and our limited possibilities to offer microteaching to the trainees whenever they want to have it. So what is described here is already tried out in various modifications and by experimenting with several steps in isolation. It is our aim at the moment to combine all these elements in order to develop a practice-centred and yet analytical training for foreign language teachers.

I consider classroom observation (by use of closed-circuit tele-vision) and teaching analysis on the one hand and microteaching on the other as related elements of a subject or method oriented training. In this course design especially the teaching analysis (provided we can develop an equivalent category system) will serve as a means of bridging the gap between theoretical studies and practical training. In addition, the course makes an important contribution, towards the acquainting of the students with technical media, which effect is highly desirable especially for foreign language teachers.

There are, nevertheless, some urgent problems to be solved in order to make our courses really contribute to the improvement of foreign language teaching:

1. As long as we do not possess a hierarchy of foreign language specific teaching skills, all our efforts may be irrelevant in some points.

2. If the teaching goal of modern language teaching is the student's ability to communicate, then it holds especially true that the teacher should hold himself back in favour of the student. One could therefore ask, whether a teacher training which is always necessarily teacher-centred is the right training form[6] or whether it would be more advisable to include some form of 'classroom simulation' where the teacher is the reacting partner.[7]

3. When one deals with foreign language teachers who are not native speakers, one will always find language as well as methodo-

6. Cf. Beattie and Teather 1971.
7. Cf. Vleck, research paper.

logical problems. Does the concentration upon the teaching behaviour allow the dismissal of the correction of language errors or is an accompanying teaching analysis as to the correctness of the use of language always indispensable? I would like to agree to the latter if there is a possibility to correct the language without bringing back to the training procedure the elements of retrospective critique and supervision which we replaced by self-evaluation and prospective replanning and reteach.

Krumm's paper represented an important step in the development of classroom observation as a feedback tool in teacher training, not because he was first to see the possibilities, but because he seems to have been the first to publish on the issue of how to incorporate systematic observation in the overall design of a teacher training course. Others must have faced the same problems, but they chose to publish accounts of their category systems rather than of their training courses. Moskowitz was something of an exception, in her 1968 paper, but when she wrote, in 1971, about 'interaction analysis' as a 'new modern language' for supervisors she did not address the issues of course design taken up by Krumm two years later.

Krumm's paper also represented an important step in that it came from Europe, not North America. He seems to have been one of the first in Europe to publish on the basis of practical experience. He himself cites Wragg's teacher training work in England, of course, which used a very simple but effective modification to Flanders' original categories (see Wragg 1970). (My own 1972 paper, by comparison, was clearly largely speculative in nature.) The dependence on work in the USA is unmistakable, and persistent.

Summary

The aim of this chapter was to show how observation 'arrived' as a feedback tool in teacher training. We started with observation as a *problem*, from the point of view of a supervisor trying to find a way of validly evaluating trainees on teaching practice. When we looked at the literature on observation as a *solution*, however, what we found was a focus away from supervision and external evaluation, and towards *self*-observation and *self*-evaluation as agents of behavioural change in teachers, both pre-service and in-service. This was seen as a move towards a more trainee-centred approach to teacher training, and was perhaps a harbinger of a more learner-centred approach to language teaching itself. In this connection one of Krumm's final comments is particularly interesting. In his last paragraph he wrote: 'One could therefore ask ... whether a teacher training which is always necessarily teacher-centred is the right training form . . .', evidence that he was already beginning to see how language teaching might usefully develop.

Krumm did not make the connection explicit, but we can note here that his comment about teacher training being teacher-centred could be related directly to the problem of finding the appropriate categories for an observation system. When Krumm was writing it seemed to be taken for granted that categories should focus on the teacher's behaviour, since that was what was to be observed principally, and certainly what was to be changed during the training process. Flanders' system, for example, consisted of ten categories, one of which was for 'silence or confusion', leaving seven for the teacher's behaviour and only two for the learners'. Moskowitz's FLint system had twenty (taking categories and subcategories together), with twelve for the teacher, three for the learners, and five more for such things as silence and two types of confusion. Nearhoof redressed the balance, with equal numbers of categories for teacher and learners, which is largely why Krumm was interested in his work. As we shall see in later chapters, classroom research slowly distanced itself from this teacher-centredness in observation systems for teacher training, and eventually began taking learner behaviour as seriously, and as exclusively, as it had once taken the behaviour of teachers. This 'distancing' also reflected a 'parting of the ways' for researchers and teacher trainers, a move I had sought to at least delay in my 1972 paper, where I had explicitly drawn attention to what seemed to me to be major common ground between the two.

At the beginning of this chapter mention was made of two aspects of the search for 'validity'. The first centred on the issue of 'objectivity', the second on the issue of knowing what matters and what does not in classroom language teaching and learning. Although the term 'objectivity' has not appeared frequently throughout the chapter, it is probably clear that behind all the observation systems described there was this major concern to be at last in a position to provide language teachers in training with incontrovertible evidence of their classroom behaviour. It also seems reasonable to suggest that this sort of objectivity was in fact achieved through the use of such category systems. But the other aspect of validity was, surely, much more important. Throughout this chapter, however, we have seen a strong move away from any attempt to validate category systems directly in terms of learner achievement. Instead there has been an appeal, at best, to previous research in general education work (as in

Moskowitz's reliance on Flanders' findings in favour of 'indirect-ness'), or to the advantages of introducing a new teaching method (as in Krumm's reliance on the improvements to be expected from the introduction of the audio-visual structural global approach in Germany). In Grittner we even saw a hint of category systems becoming self-justifying. What we did not see was any strong faith being shown in something both Jarvis and Rothfarb had hinted at in their papers, the possibility that the consciousness-raising power of self-observation might be so marked that it would not matter greatly whether or not the categories employed were causally related to learner achievement. This does seem, however, to have been the lesson of history.

In our next chapter we shall take up this last issue again, as we deal with the contemporary critique of all the language classroom observation work that took Flanders' ideas on interaction analysis as the starting point.

Follow-up activities and points for discussion

1. What sort of 'validity' do we need in teacher training? If you have any experience of self-observation using a category system, make notes from your experience, and then discuss whether or not the value of systematic classroom observation lies primarily in its 'objec-tivity', or in its attention to 'the things that really matter'.

2. Are 'testimonials' good enough? Reconsider Moskowitz's research study and decide on the status, for you, of the teachers' comments she cites in support of her claims for the effectiveness of training in interaction analysis. Can you accept them as data? If so, are they more, or less, convincing than the other forms of evidence she presents? What is their status for her, do you think? If you cannot accept them as data, is her other evidence sufficient?

(Moskowitz made further use of 'testimonials' in her 1971 Foreign Language Annals paper introducing FLint as 'a new modern language for supervisors'. If you have access to a copy you might like to consider them also. The substance of her paper is a thorough description of FLint and how it might be used in teacher supervision. As such it constitutes more of a manual for potential FLint users than the 1968 paper included here in the preceding chapter.)

3. If you have access to classroom data (via live observation, video-recordings, audio-recordings, and/or transcripts) try using Nearhoof's categories and interpretive procedures, as set out in Grittner.

Choose, if you can, data reflecting different language teaching methods, and divide into teams, each working with data from just one method.

Compare the results of each team's work and try to form an opinion on the following question: Should a category system be method specific?

(For a more recent example of a fully developed system dedicated to a particular method – the communicative approach – see Allen, Fröhlich, and Spada 1984, and/or Fröhlich, Spada and Allen 1985.)

4. Must teacher training, as Krumm seems to suggest, always be teacher-centred? If so, is this a problem? If not, what might a 'learner-centred' teacher training course look like? Is 'learner-centredness' the only alternative? Formulate your reactions in small groups and then compare results.

5. Do we have to worry about learner achievement criteria? Form two groups (A and B). When each group has prepared its response to its own group task (see below), bring the two groups together and try to outargue each other. Finally look for common ground between you.

> **Task for Group A:** make the strongest possible case *for* an approach to language classroom research that does not concern itself with learner achievement criteria.
>
> **Task for Group B:** make the strongest possible case *against* an approach to language classroom research that does not concern itself with learner achievement criteria.

3   Second thoughts

'Euphoria' is perhaps too strong a word for it, but it does seem reasonable to worry that the enthusiasm evident in the papers of the last chapter was not entirely justified. Systematic classroom observation, usually referred to simply as 'interaction analysis' at the time (following Flanders' lead) was regarded widely as a 'solution' to language teacher training problems, rather than as just another thing to try. There was general agreement that Flanders' original ten categories needed to be modified if they were to be made relevant to the language classroom, but there was very little critique of Flanders' ideas and procedures beyond that point. Rosenshine's doubts, expressed forcefully in 1970, after a decade of research, were uncharacteristic of the field:

> The verdict is not in, and is not likely to be in for some time, on the relationship between a teacher's behavior as measured by the Flanders Interaction Analysis (IA) system and pupil achievement. (1970, p. 445)

But Rosenshine was writing only about general educational research, not specifically about language teaching, and his worries do not seem to have reached the language teaching researchers and teacher trainers we have so far cited. It is also worth noting that his worries were essentially about the validity of Flanders' categories in terms of their relationship to learner achievement, not to teacher behaviour change, which was what the contributors to Chapter 2 were so excited about. We need to recall Krumm's paper in that chapter, and remind ourselves that these were the early days of the micro-teaching movement, launched by Allen and Ryan in their 1969 book. Micro-teaching offered a technology for producing behaviour change in teachers. If audiolingualism benefited in its early days from the availability of language laboratories, and from the 'advanced technology' aura they engendered, then micro-teaching benefited similarly from the availability of relatively cheap closed circuit television equipment. Now short episodes of practice teaching could be video-recorded and played back at will. Teachers could actually see themselves teaching, and so could more quickly and convincingly than ever before see the ways in which they needed to change. Combined with systematic classroom observation techniques the potential power of such a system was enormously impressive. It could be power for authoritarian control, of course, but the profession was ready for that and argued vigorously that the provision of 'objective' feedback, by videotape and/or 'interaction analysis', was essentially non-judgemental in nature, permitting teachers to see for themselves what was going on in their own classrooms, and to make their own decisions about what changes, if any, were desirable.

Bailey, however, was not convinced. (The Bailey referred to here is Leona G. Bailey, a point made to avoid potential confusion with the several other Baileys in the language teaching field.) In 1975 Bailey, a supervisor of graduate teaching assistants herself, published a considered critique of the use for feedback purposes of Flanders' Interaction Analysis system and its derivatives (principally Moskowitz's FLint system). Her critique, entitled 'An Observational Method in the Foreign Language Classroom: A Closer Look at Interaction Analysis', began with a brief statement of the importance of classroom observation, and a helpful overview of both Flanders' original system and Moskowitz's derivative one.

> The problem of accurately and reliably observing student-teacher interactions has intrigued researchers and teacher trainers for many years. Neither a colleague's personal impression nor a disgruntled former student's report is an objective judgment of a teacher's ability to teach. Thus, the importance of classroom observation is undeniable, since it is the most unbiased measure of teacher behavior and student performance available. Several classroom observation systems have been developed (Simon and Boyer 1967), ranging from the rather simple (questionnaires with such items as: Does the teacher seem well prepared today?) to the highly complex, most notably the interaction analysis system developed by Ned A. Flanders (1960a). Interaction analysis has most recently been applied to the field of foreign languages (Moskowitz 1967c) and has gained wide acceptance as an observational system (Wragg 1970a).
>
> Unfortunately the extensive use of the Flanders system has not prompted its researchers and practitioners to attempt to improve upon several major weaknesses in this observational method. Among the problems to which the user of the system must address himself are those which pertain to the basic category definitions, the ways in which observations are made and reliabilities obtained, the

significance of data taken in research studies, and the practicality of the method. Our intention, after reviewing the essentials of the system, is to point out these and other serious difficulties inherent in interaction analysis. We hope that this analysis will encourage the development of alternate ways to solve the problems which are raised.

Interaction analysis and FLint: an overview

Interaction analysis is, primarily a method of providing a feedback system to the teacher about his classroom behavior. That feedback may be given by trained observers who collect data in the classroom or, more likely, self-generated by teachers judging the value of their own teaching by listening to tapes of themselves and their students. The observers and teachers are requested to attend only to the verbal behavior present in the student-teacher interactions, since verbal behavior (the authors suggest) can be more reliably measured than nonverbal behavior.

The observations of teacher-student verbal behavior taken in the interaction analysis system must fall into one of the ten categories of behavior established by Flanders. In brief, the categories consist: of teacher talk of an indirect form (1) accepting feelings, (2) praising or encouraging, (3) accepting ideas, and (4) asking questions; or of a direct nature (5) lecturing, (6) giving directions, (7) criticizing or justifying authority. Student talk is classified as either (8) responding to teacher or (9) initiating talk. A final, multi-purpose category (10) is labelled silence or confusion.[1]

The method of observation includes recording, by three second intervals in a consecutive tally, the category number of the behavior just observed. Category numbers are repeated if the behavior, regardless of duration, calls for a different category classification. Other 'ground rules' include such items as allowing the observer to choose the category which is numerically farthest from category 5 when an observation appears to belong in two or more categories, and requiring that the observer not be influenced by his own biases or by what he assumes is the teacher's intent. There are also additional rules which the observers of interaction analysis must master before their records can show any reliability.

The raw data, collected in tally form during the course of the observations, are entered into a ten-row by ten-column matrix, from which it is possible to retrieve information regarding the sequence of events (i.e., what happened after each event) which occurred

1. For a detailed description of the ten categories, see Edmund J. Amidon and Ned A. Flanders 1967, pp. 5–11.

during the class session observed. It is also proposed that certain categories be compared with one another to yield various ratios, for example, between direct and indirect teacher behaviors or between teacher and student talk. Further, the observer can calculate the percentage of each category recorded as compared to all others (for example, during a ten-minute session 4% of the teacher's verbal behavior may be classified as category 1, 12% as category 2, etc.).

According to its proponents, the advantages of the interaction analysis observational system are numerous. Teachers, after analyzing matrices constructed of their classroom behavior, can discover and evaluate whether or not they have reached the goals they have established for their teaching. Further, teachers can identify themselves as being more or less direct, critical, receptive to ideas, questioning, etc. Moreover, teaching interns and student teachers may:

(a) air knowledge about principles of teaching and learning, (b) make use of such knowledge in a situation characterized by personal meaning, (c) get immediate feedback regarding the effects of their behavior in the classroom, and thus, (d) discover for themselves more effective patterns of teaching behavior (Amidon and Hough 1967 p. 307).

Finally, the practitioners of interaction analysis consistently agree that the Flanders system does not judge, interpret, or tell a teacher how to improve his teaching. It is simply one way of looking at teaching; only the teacher can place a value on what he does.

In the field of foreign language, the interaction analysis system has been adopted by several researchers and many teachers and teacher trainers. The most extensive work has been carried out by Gertrude Moskowitz who has also presented a system tailored to the needs of the foreign language instructor (Moskowitz 1967c).

This new system called FLint (Foreign Language interaction) is essentially the same as the Flanders method described above. FLint includes all ten categories of interaction analysis: however, it includes twelve additional categories. The observer must now be responsible for twenty-two behaviors. Most of the additional behaviors are subsets of the original categories, for example (2a) jokes, (3a) repeats student response verbatim, (5a) corrects without rejection, (6a) directs pattern drills, etc. New categories, which are used in conjunction with all the others are: (e) uses English and (n) nonverbal. The introduction of a nonverbal classification requires that observations necessarily be made 'live' or from videotapes.[2]

The FLint system makes use of a matrix, just as in the Flanders system: however, the matrix is 20×20 to account for the additional categories (English and nonverbal are recorded separately). A number of category ratios (direct to indirect teacher behaviors, etc.) are derived from this 20 × 20 matrix; as expected, these ratios are more numerous and even more complex due to the greater number of categories upon which they are based.

The purposes for which FLint was devised are quite similar to those of interaction analysis. For the supervisor or trainer of pre-service foreign language teachers, FLint will purportedly eliminate the subjectivity of the typical classroom observation and reduce the emotional overtones that personal criticism often generates. For the in-service teacher, this observational system may reveal whether he has adequately fulfilled his intentions; thus, he may become more conscious of the many dimensions of his teaching. Once the feed-back which the FLint system provides has been understood and internalized, the experience 'generally triggers the desire to explore alternatives for improvement, with the teacher becoming *his own agent for change*' (Moskowitz 1971, p. 219).

These two observational systems are parallel in their intent, methods, and rationale. Both systems aim at objective observation and recording of student-teacher interactions in a natural classroom setting.

The systems offer a categorization of classroom behaviors which the observer is trained to recognize instantaneously and record accurately. Both interaction analysis and its offshoot, FLint, hope to describe objectively to teachers a whole complex of student and teacher behaviors which occur in the teacher's classrooms, and to allow the teachers to draw their own conclusions from the data.

In her overview Bailey stressed the vital claim of non-judgementality referred to above, but as soon as she began her critique she cast doubt on the whole edifice:

> We have observed that the Flanders system relies principally on researchers' and teachers' unquestioning acceptance of and confidence in the categories of teacher and student behavior which are recorded during their observations.

What followed however was not an attack on the categories in terms of their relationship to language learning achievement, but a more 'internal' attack on the practicality of using such categories, given the

2. A complete list of the FLint categories includes: deals with feelings; praises or encourages; jokes; uses ideas of students; repeats student verbatim; asks questions; gives information; corrects without rejection; gives directions; directs pattern drills; criticizes student behavior, criticizes student response; student response, specific; student response, choral; student response, open-ended or student initiated; silence; silence-media presentation; confusion, work oriented; confusion, non-work oriented; laughter, uses English; nonverbal.

severe problems of interpretation involved, and the very limited time frame (three seconds) allowed for judgements to be made during live observations. The details of Bailey's objections are nevertheless well worth reading for anyone contemplating using what appears to be a relatively simple category system.

Re-evaluating interaction analysis and FLint

We have observed that the Flanders system relies principally on researchers' and teachers' unquestioning acceptance of and confidence in the categories of teacher and student behavior which are recorded during their observations. However, several categories must be examined with regard to their clarity and objectivity before we can accept data based upon them as being reliable.

It is immediately apparent that the first category of interaction analysis (acceptance of feelings) is open to numerous interpretations by various observers. Even the extended definition of category 1 does little to elucidate its intent. The teacher '. . . understands how the children feel, that they have the right to have these feelings' (Amidon and Flanders 1967, p. 122). Other statements that are included in this category are those '. . . that recall past feeling, refer to enjoyable or uncomfortable feelings that are present, or predict happy or sad events that will occur in the future' (ibid).

The basic notion that an observer can detect another person's 'understanding' and 'acceptance' of feelings is certainly questionable, unless the appropriate verbal behavior to be subsumed in this category is accurately and extensively spelled out. The ambiguities of this category are evident from the following example. (Numbers in parentheses refer to the categories of behavior noted on p. 111). In answer to a child's complaint, a teacher says: 'It's difficult, but you can do at least the first exercise.' If the teacher accepts the child's analysis of the difficulty of the problem, is she accepting the child's feelings (1) or the child's idea (3)? Or is she not accepting anything, but instead justifying (7) the work that must be done? Further, there are elements of encouragement (2) and giving directions (6) in this sentence which would certainly confound an observer. Under normal circumstances this sentence would be articulated in less than one second, hardly enough time to permit the observer to make a careful study of its components and to enter the results of the decision on a tally.

Category 3 (accepting ideas) also presents problems of interpretation. If a teacher responds to a student by using the child's ideas, the teacher is necessarily praising and encouraging him. Consider, for example, this teacher's statement: 'That's also a good analysis of Germany's pre-World War 1 military situation.' The student is praised (2) for his ideas, which the teacher has used (3) while giving a clarifying statement (5) about another country (Germany). Again, discrimination among the various classifications would be very difficult to make.

The first four categories of interaction analysis are labelled 'indirect teacher talk.' In the case of category 1 (asks questions), this label is misleading and appears to have been arbitrarily applied. To what extent could any classroom observer interpret the 'direct' or 'indirect' nature of asking questions? If the teacher poses programmed, narrow questions which elicit specific and predictable responses (the description given by Moskowitz (1967c, p. 7) for category 1), the student's verbal behavior would appear to be carefully and directly controlled. If the teacher provides few if any options for responding, his influence on the student must be labelled 'direct.'

The distinctions made between categories 5 (one aspect of which is correcting a student reponse without intonation or words that communicate rejection) and 7 (feedback to the students which contains criticism) are unusually subtle and would be scarcely perceptible to a classroom observer in many instances. A simple question such as 'How long did you study last night?' might be interpreted (depending on the observer) as purely informational (4), perhaps complimentary (2) or maybe highly sarcastic (7). The matter is further complicated by the fact that observers are told to classify such statements as 7 if they *feel* 'the student will probably perceive the correction as . . . . criticism' (Amidon and Flanders 1967, p. 8). To suggest that observers can decide objectively what a student does or does not 'perceive' is somewhat presumptuous. Further, if the observer happens to be the teacher himself, his decisions about whether he is critical of his students are certain to be biased.

At least one of the two student talk categories is likely to present problems of interpretation. Predictable or limited student talk (category 8) is a classification in which it is purported that the student's anticipated and expected responses are recorded. However, it would require an omniscient observer, one who had memorized all of the course material and who knew the limits of each student's repertoire to be able to decide whether any given student response was predictable or not. Thus, the only fully 'trained' observer would be the teacher, who is apt, once again, to make decisions favourable to a positive analysis of his teaching techniques.

Researchers and teacher trainers may also find it difficult to use category 10 (silence and confusion) in an effective manner. The question at issue here is not so much how to classify certain behaviors but rather why two such significantly distinct elements as silence and confusion have been grouped together. Category 10 becomes almost meaningless if one realizes this can encompass such different activities as the silence observed while the teacher looks for a piece of chalk and the pandemonium created when several angry students hurl epithets at one another. Category 10 may also be used to record confusion on the observer's part, rendering inadequate almost any interpretation of this class of behaviors.

It would thus appear that the observer of interaction analysis or FLint bears several impractical if not impossible burdens. Due to the ambiguity and multiple interpretations of most of the categories, the observer is required to make many split-second decisions while recording frequently changing behaviors. The great number of categories (twenty-two in the FLint system) which the observer is called upon to identify, judge, and record seems to be sufficient proof that the observations are probably less than accurate.

There are other problems inherent in the interaction analysis system which the observer must recognize. Of foremost concern is the necessity of making fine discriminations in the passage of time such that momentary changes in behavior can be accurately measured. In attempting to record those behaviors which last three seconds or more (in all likelihood, almost all classroom interactions are probably of this type), the observer has an apparently impossible task. Not only is he asked to observe and categorize the behavior in progress, but he must also verify the passage of time (by consulting a clock, wrist watch, or stop watch, we presume), in addition to recording the data on paper. (This important detail has not been pointed out by any of the interaction analysis researchers). The time required to perform all these tasks (seemingly simultaneously) will negate any accuracy and reliability in the data recorded.

One of the observers' 'ground rules' is particularly disconcerting to the researcher who attempts to analyze interaction analysis data. When in doubt about a classification observers are asked to choose the one farthest from category 5. Depending on how confident observers are in their own judgment, data thus recorded will be more or less weakened and thus, inaccurate. There is no guarantee that two or more observers (during reliability checks) will be unsure about the *same* behavior and therefore, by following the same rule, make identical observations.

There is a limitation peculiar to the FLint system: all classroom observers must be experts in the use of the target language. If an observer is asked to interpret statements of criticism, clarifications, confirmations, etc., he must know the foreign language involved as well as the teacher does. In an elementary or secondary school, such bilingual observers are not likely to be available. In other research settings (teacher training programs, for example), there is a serious question raised about the positive (or negative) biases of the langage expert observers (who may very well be fellow students or colleagues of the instructor being observed) who are taking classroom data.

The ambiguities of the category definitions, the problem of making rapid decisions, and the inability to overcome certain prejudices are all issues which the researcher must confront when he tries to interpret and evaluate the inter-observer reliability scores which interaction analysis and FLint users include in reports of their work. A more fundamental concern, perhaps, is the manner in which reliabilities are taken, the use of Scott's coefficient to estimate that reliability, and the interpretation given to the reliabilities thus derived.

As the name of Flanders' observational system denotes, data taken by means of interaction analysis should express teacher and student verbal interactions, or, at least, certain pairs of interactions – whether they be of the student-student, teacher-teacher, or student-teacher types. Such interactions could more simply be defined as any verbal event followed immediately by another verbal event, e.g. a category 2 (praise) followed by a category 3 (uses ideas of students) would be labelled a 2,3 interaction pair.

Data on the occurrence and frequency of interactions are derived from scanning the matrix used by the observers to summarize their tallies. One might find, for example, that a teacher had eight 2,3 interactions during an observation period. However, the reliability of such data is never established by the interaction analysis and FLint researchers. The overall reliability of all observations made (calculated by using Scott's coefficient) (Scott 1955) does not take into account these instance-by-instance interactions. Are observers A and B, for example, recording the same interaction at the same time? If not, the reliability of saying that the interaction occurred is substantially diminished. Thus, to predicate statements about a teacher's interactions on data recorded in the observer's matrix without ascertaining the reliability of such data is imprudent.

The question of how interaction analysis reliabilities are calculated is an important one which deserves some scrutiny. When a researcher wishes to assess how accurate and reliable his observer's data are, he will have two (or more) observers record data of the same classroom activities at the same time. To ascertain whether the two observers agreed that they saw and heard the same interactions at precisely the same moment, the researcher will compare the two observers' data and obtain an inter-observer reliability score (Flanders 1967a, p. 162). The most appropriate way to discover whether two observers have agreed is to compare their tallies on an item-by-item basis. Both observers should be recording exactly the same category number, (8, 6, 10, etc.) at the same moment; if so, their reliability score is 100%.

The method used by interaction analysis researchers to obtain reliability scores actually considers only summary scores of each category (during a given period of observation) rather than comparing item-by-item records. We can judge the difference in accuracy by looking at the following hypothetical tallies made by two observers observing the same class:

Observer A:

10, 6, 10, 8, 2, 4, 9, 5, 7, 6, 6, 6, 9, 10.

Observer B:

10, 6, 4, 8, 10, 6, 7, 6, 5, 6, 6, 2, 9, 9, 10.

If we use the method of estimating reliability suggested by Flanders (Scott's coefficient) for these hypothetical data, we find that the inter-observer reliability is 85%

Using an item-by-item analysis (that is, each observation made by A is compared to that made by B), we find that the two observers agreed on seven out of fifteen observations – total agreements (A) are 7, disagreements (D) are 8. The reliability is obtained by the formula: A over (A + D). Thus, the inter-observer reliability for these data is: 7 over (7 + 8) = 7/15 = 47% Thus, the observers had wide disagreement that interactions occurred at a precise moment during the observations. This aspect is totally obscured by the method of calculating reliability used by interaction analysis researchers.

There is another, even broader issue to be touched upon when making the decision about whether or not to use interaction analysis. The teacher, supervisor, or teacher trainer who wishes to observe accurately and efficiently teacher and student verbal behavior in the classroom and to communicate his findings to students or colleagues may have some serious misgivings about the practicality of interaction analysis.

First, it appears that this observational system requires as much as four to five months to master. Several interaction analysis and FLint researchers report that their student teachers have studied these systems in a semester-length graduate course. There are few in-service principals and supervisors who could afford this time investment.

Second, there are certain complexities of the systems which would militate against their effective and continued use. The categories used in interaction analysis, with their multiple interpretations and large numbers, would certainly frustrate many observers. The rapidity with which the observations must be made is particularly unnerving and likely to result in inaccurate observations.[3]

Third, the use of a matrix in which the data are recorded and the computation of numerous teacher and student verbal behavior ratios are rather burdensome and time consuming for the non-researcher. In a practical sense, a supervisor may wish to know rather basic information, such as, How much of the time does this teacher talk during a first-year Spanish class? That information is directly available from observational tallies. Although Moskowitz suggests (under certain circumstances) that one can dispense with the matrices and ratios (1971, p. 219), this would appear to be undermining the most essential contributions (according to the majority of interaction analysis researchers) of the whole system.

A final criticsm of the practicality of this method concerns the issue of whether a teacher, trained in interaction analysis, will continue to use it once he returns to his classroom. It would be very difficult for a teacher to find a trained observer in his school who could observe his class 'live.' It would be almost as troublesome for the teacher to arrange to have his class video- or audiotaped (assuming appropriate equipment is available) in order to make his own observations of his teaching. Even if data can be taken, one wonders how unbiased the teacher's self-generated recordings would be, or, if the data were highly critical of the teacher, how long he would continue to take such observations.

Bailey's next attack, even more telling in the context of the theme of this particular chapter, was on the research claiming to provide evidence for the power of Flanders' and Moskowitz's systems to promote behavioural change in teachers.

Of critical concern to teacher trainers and classroom researchers are the effects of interaction analysis on teachers who have been trained to use this method of observation. Reports of the significant changes in teacher behavior of those who have learned interaction analysis or FLint have appeared in many journals, with more or less supporting data (depending on the nature of the study). These reports merit serious consideration and examination to determine if interaction analysis and FLint are valuable observational systems and can be used as effective instruments for feedback to the teacher.

The most extensive research on the effects of foreign language teachers' learning interaction analysis has been carried out by Moskowitz, the developer of FLint. In her 1968 study, Moskowitz described research done with pre-service student teachers and in-service teachers enrolled in a graduate course in which interaction analysis was taught. Although pretest and post-test questionnaires

3. Although interaction analysis researchers mention that observations are done in three-second intervals, none of them has considered the required speed of the observation as a variable in assessing accuracy.

were administered (the nature of these questionnaires will be discussed below), there is no mention of a control group of teachers being tested. Thus, there is no basis for claiming that it was interaction analysis training that had an effect on the teachers' behavior; their verbal behavior might have changed, over time, for a number of reasons.

Further, the results of several of the tests were hardly meaningful. The mean score of the TSRT (Teaching Situation Reaction Test) on the pretest was 108; on the post-test it was 99 (the lower the score, the better the performance). Although statistically significant at the .01 level, a nine point change in test results is surely not practically valuable. The results of a second questionnaire, the FLAQ (Foreign Language Attitude Questionnaire), which is administered to students, indicated no change in the students' attitudes toward teachers who had learned interaction analysis. As a summary of these data Moskowitz indicates that 'although the attitudes of the pupils as a whole did not increase significantly, on the other hand, *they did not become less favorable*' (1968, p. 224). Surely, significant effects of research must be predicated on more substantial evidence and interpretations than the above analysis.

Other researchers have done work with control groups in attempting to measure behavioral differences between teachers trained in the use of interaction analysis and those who are not. The use of control groups and the reports of the comparative data collected do not assure, however, that significant effects have been achieved during the course of the research. An inspection of three representative studies leads to this conclusion.

In a paper entitled 'Behavioral Change in Student Teachers' (1967), Hough and Amidon report a study in which twenty pre-service teachers were taught interaction analysis in an undergraduate course on teaching methods. A control group of twenty subjects did not learn interaction analysis. Several pretests and post-tests were administered to both groups, including the TSRT, the GSRS (General Supervisory Rating Scale), and the Dogmatism Scale; these instruments are purported to relate postively to performance in student teaching.

A general criticism of the study pertains to the fact that no testing was done of either experimental or control groups to measure precisely the behavior which was to be taught in the graduate course, i.e. classroom observations of verbal behavior of teachers and students. Therefore, the primary variable of the research (whether a teacher who had learned interaction analysis could provide himself with effective feedback about his teaching) was not taken into account by the researchers.

The data presented in this paper to show the change in behavior between pretest and post-test measures indicate, in a practical sense, no improvement for the experimental group. The results on the post-test of the TSRT, for example, show that the experimental group 'improved' from a mean score of 60.70 (on the pretest) to a mean score of 56.65 (lower score indicates a positive change). Although this change was statistically significant (P < .01) it would be difficult to recommend a semester's program which produces only a 5% change in behavior. The results of other tests showed equally small changes in behavior.

Another study of the change in behavior of student teachers who were taught interaction analysis was reported by Furst (1967 pp. 315–28). The experimental group was taught a variation of interaction analysis, VICS (Verbal Interaction Category System): the control group received no such training. Several measures of both groups were taken: the TSRT test, the Dogmatism Scale, comparisons of the use of VICS by both groups, and comparison of pupil verbal behavior.

In most instances, the results of all these measures indicated no practical change and, quite often, no statistically significant difference. For example, a comparison of experimental and control groups on the TSRT given after student teaching showed no significance, statistically or otherwise. The ability of experimental and control groups to use the verbal behavior categories of VICS was approximately the same; there was no difference in ten of sixteen categories. In only two out of eight pupil verbal behavior categories could the study show a statistically significant difference between experimental and control groups.

A third study of interest to potential users of interaction analysis is the Lohman *et al.* research on the effect of pre-service training in interaction analysis on the verbal behavior of student teachers (1967). An experimental group of thirty student teachers was taught interaction analysis; the control group was not so instructed. A number of tests were administered to both groups prior to the study and chi-square tests of compatibility with regard to sex, marital status, and instructor were performed. Initially there were no significant differences on any of the measures of the groups.

The results of this study are no more encouraging than those described above. In a comparison of experimental and control groups' use of interaction analysis categories and various ratios, there are no significant differences in thirteen out of eighteen categories. In the few instances where there is a statistically significant difference, that difference is completely absent of practical meaning insofar as changing actual teaching behavior is concerned.

Perhaps the most series implication of these studies is that unsuspecting teacher trainers or supervisors may simply rely on the summary statements which are usually provided by the researchers and which furnish misleading and often inaccurate interpretations of the results. For example,

> Students trained in Flanders' interaction analysis tend to use *more* accepting behavior . . . and *more* total questioning (Furst 1967, p. 326).

> That the verbal behavior of students who were taught interaction analysis differed from those not taught this system is clear (Hough and Ober 1967, p. 313).

> . . . there was significantly more student talk . . . in classes taught by student teachers trained in the Flanders system of interaction analysis (Lohman *et al* 1967, p. 358).

are indicative of researchers' simplifications and their reliance on some statistically significant data, which, as we have noted above, are not pragmatically significant.

Finally, Bailey returned to the fundamental issue of the claimed non-judgemental nature of the categories and their use in teacher training. She was suitably sceptical.

> There is a final, perplexing issue which education researchers, teacher trainers, and supervisors must face when making a decision about whether to use such observational systems as interaction analysis and FLint. If educators are concerned with improving teaching, should they seek a feedback system whose supporters prefer not to use it as an instrument for change? The proponents of interaction analysis and FLint make no overt value judgments about the teaching behaviors which their systems measure. Yet, the questionnaire data given by teachers who have learned these systems indicate that the teachers believe that they have changed their behaviors based on these observational systems. Teachers' statements about 'improvements' they have seen in their teaching reveal that some covert attitude shaping has taken place, the researchers protest to the contrary.

> If several of the interaction analysis or FLint categories are considered to be appropriate teaching behaviors, the fact should be stated (including rationales and research findings to support such judgments). Not doing so is a disservice to the teachers who wish to learn the system so that they may improve their teaching. If observational systems such as interactional analysis and FLint are not regarded as instruments for change by their users, then learning the categories, filling in the matrices, and computing the behavior ratios becomes simply a somewhat imprecise academic exercise.

> Teachers, teacher trainers, supervisors, and education researchers who are genuinely seeking a classroom observation system which

will be effective, reliable, efficient, and practical must take into serious consideration the various problems which interaction analysis (and similar systems, such as FLint) seems to present. The lack of precision in the definitions of teacher and student verbal behavior categories, the complex and ambiguous tasks which the classroom observers must perform, the lengthy and formidable training procedures which the neophyte must undergo are perhaps the most obvious deficits of the system, without taking into account several weaknesses of the research done to evaluate interaction analysis.

We would hope that all potential and current practitioners of interaction analysis are made aware of the difficulties inherent in this classroom observation system, and that they attempt to solve these problems by redesigning the system (even by creating a method which is distinctly different) until the system becomes as credible and useful as it can be.

It is notable that in her penultimate paragraph Bailey did not reassert her doubts on the non-judgementality issue, an indication perhaps that she did not see it to be as important as it now appears. It is however intriguing to see her suggest, albeit parenthetically, that 'redesigning the system' may not suffice, and that something 'distinctly different' might be required.

It would have been possible, in this chapter, to raise many more objections to the Flanders tradition, but we have limited ourselves to the one published and contemporary critique to be found in the literature on language teaching. Enough has no doubt been done to dispel any feeling of incipient 'euphoria' (or, conversely, nausea?). In Chapter 4 we shall continue the critique, at least implicitly, by focusing on the alternatives to the Flanders tradition that were developed in the mid-seventies.

Follow-up activities and points for discussion

1. Are categories as difficult to interpret as Bailey suggested?
   a) Taking Flanders' Interaction Analysis system or Moskowitz's FLint system, assign one or two categories each to small groups.
   b) Within each group try using the assigned categories on transcript data (or any other that is available, but transcript data is probably the easiest for this purpose).
   c) Make a careful note of any interpretation problems that arise, and then classify them.

   d) Produce a report for the other groups, estimating just how damaging such interpretation problems might be to the whole enterprise.

You should find Bailey's interpretation problems a helpful starting point.

2. Can the use of a category system in the Flanders tradition be non-judgemental?

   With Bailey's doubts in mind draw up proposals for a teacher training procedure that would be truly non-judgemental in nature, using Flanders Interaction Analysis system or Moskowitz's FLint system.

   How closely do your suggestions resemble the procedures described by Moskowitz (and/or Krumm)?

3. Form two groups (A and B). When each group has prepared its response to its own group task (see below), bring the two groups together and try to outargue each other. Finally look for some common ground between you.

> **Task for Group A**: make the strongest possible case *for* a non-judgemental approach to the teaching practice element of language teacher training.
>
> **Task for Group B**: make the strongest possible case *against* a non-judgemental approach to the teaching practice element of language teacher training.

4. What's so special about language teaching? Language teaching is obviously different in that it has language both as medium and as content. Is that all, though, or are there other reasons why language teaching should pose special problems for systematic classroom observation and for teaching practice supervision?

5. Moskowitz's bold and innovative 1976 *Foreign Language Annals* (9/2, pp. 135–157) paper on 'The Classroom Interaction of Outstanding Foreign Language Teachers' proposes detailed findings it would be valuable to review in the light of the interpretation problems raised by Bailey. Can we trust them? If not, why not?

4 First alternatives to Flanders

Introduction

At the beginning of the previous chapter we saw how Rosenshine had injected a strong note of caution into the debate, but it was telling that his objections were not, fundamentally, about either the principles or the procedures of systematic classroom observation in the Flanders tradition. What Rosenshine was objecting to was what he reasonably saw as premature enthusiasm for and uncritical acceptance of Flanders' claim to have found reliable and significant relationships between teacher behaviour and learner achievement. Even Bailey's strong critique of the Flanders tradition did not lead her to do more than parenthetically suggest that something 'distinctly different' might be necessary.

Rosenshine was writing as a researcher, and Bailey as a teacher supervisor, Rosenshine in 1970, Bailey in 1975. Between those two dates at least one 'distinctly different' alternative was being developed, by someone who was both researcher and language teacher trainer. This was Fanselow, who took his inspiration from the pioneering work of Bellack and associates at Teachers College, Columbia University (Bellack *et al.* 1966 – four years before Rosenshine's paper was published). Two other alternatives to Flanders were also soon to appear on the language scene, one based on Barnes' work in England, and one based, though loosely, on the Californian work on conversational analysis. In both cases there was a significant shift of focus away from Bailey's concern for teacher training and supervision, and towards Rosenshine's concern for research. But it was for research now freed both from the constraint to pursue directly the interest represented by Rosenshine in the relationship between teacher behaviour and learner achievement, and from the constraint to pursue so exclusively the interest in teacher behaviour represented by Bailey.

In this chapter we shall look in turn at these three alternatives to the Flanders tradition.

1 The Bellack perspective on classroom interaction

Bellack had led a team working on the nature of language use in the classroom. Their immediate concern was not with devising an efficient technology for teacher training, nor even with establishing direct relationships between teaching styles and student learning. They were trying to understand how the classroom worked as a learning environment, by studying how language was used to structure that environment. Unlike Flanders, who saw classroom interaction in terms of a limited set of teaching acts, crucially relatable to a distinction between relatively authoritarian and relatively democratic teaching styles, and thus to more or less effective instruction, they saw classroom interaction more as a social 'game', bound by convention, and consisting of an implicitly agreed set of 'moves' by all participants, rather than a set of teaching 'acts'.

In Britain Sinclair led a team which took Bellack's ideas, among others, as their starting point first for a similar study of classroom language use (published in 1972 under the title *The English Used by Teachers and Pupils*), and then for a directly 'theoretical' contribution to the field of discourse analysis (published by Sinclair and Coulthard in 1975 under the title *Towards an Analysis of Discourse*). Like Bellack's team, they were not concerned with teacher training, particularly, nor with language teaching rather than any other sort. They were not even trying to treat teaching as special. They only worked out their ideas on discourse analysis in the classroom context because they expected that particular context to be relatively amenable to research. Apart from its other qualities, then, their work is interesting here because it represents research that is certainly 'distinctly different', both in content and in aims, from work in the Flanders tradition. But it was research that could not meet Bailey's needs, because the system of analysis it produced was altogether too complex, and too time-consuming to use, for ordinary teacher training purposes, and of course it made no attempt to respond to the special needs of language teachers. In short, it was research work that was leading the field away from immediate practical concerns and towards more theoretical ones. As such it was a retreat that implicitly criticized the Flanders tradition for claiming to have found 'answers' long before anyone had really demonstrated that they understood even the background to the questions. More positively, it is no doubt best seen as a sort of retreat from practical concerns, not through a thoughtless lack of interest in them, but through this increasing realization that *understanding* had to be given first priority.

Fanselow took up a somewhat different position in the way he built on the foundations of Bellack's work. Fanselow personally combined the roles of language teacher trainer and researcher, and saw the issues very differently from the British team. His interpretation was that what the field most needed was a common language with which to talk about language teaching. For him the field encompassed not only researchers, supervisors, and teachers, but also employers, students, and salespeople, all of whom needed to be able to talk to each other intelligibly about language teaching and learning. This is a refreshingly different perspective, and one which constituted something of a rearguard action against the seemingly inexorable tendency of the field to divide rather than unite. He was looking for unity in another sense as well, since he, like the British team in this particular respect, saw no reason in principle or practice to analyse classroom discourse any differently from discourse in any other settings.

Fanselow's paper, 'Beyond *Rashomon* – Conceptualizing and Describing the Teaching Act', was published in 1977, several years after the bulk of the work had been done and put into practice, both for teacher training and for research purposes. It concentrated on presenting Fanselow's FOCUS observation system in enough detail for the paper to constitute almost a user's manual. It is presented here in its entirely, complete with abstract and appendices.

> When teachers, supervisors, employers, students or salespeople discuss the same lessons, texts, tests, methods and schools of language teaching, they often sound like the characters in the Japanese movie, *Rashomon* – they each give contradictory and equivocal accounts of the same events or items. To classify the communications people send and receive in both teaching and non-teaching settings so that we can move beyond *Rashomon*, and give similar accounts of the same events, an instrument has been developed called FOCUS, an acronym for Foci for Observing Communications Used in Settings. The language of FOCUS is technical: composed of operationally defined terms that are non-judgmental.
>
> One purpose of the article is to teach the five characteristics of communications that are noted with FOCUS, provide a rationale for each and suggest applications of the instrument for teachers, teacher trainers, supervisors and researchers. Another purpose is to argue that the teaching act is not a mystery that defies precise and rational description and that we can learn a great deal about how to teach by analyzing descriptions that show how practicing teachers and their students communicate both in the classroom and outside the classroom at parties, on the job and at home.

In *The Silent Language*, Edward Hall (1959) describes three types of learning: formal, informal and technical. Formal instruction is prescriptive, outlining what should and should not be done and judging the degree of approximation to a model. Informal instruction depends on models presented for imitation. Technical instruction depends on an explicit description and classification of what is to be learned, conveyed in a vocabulary of operationally defined terms; it is non-judgmental.

To illustrate these three types of learning, Hall uses the example of skiing. In a village where all have to ski to get around, children learn to ski mainly by watching their parents – informal learning. Weekend skiers in the same village learn mainly by being admonished with judgments and prescriptions as they ski – formal learning. One learns skiing technically through explicit labels. These labels are based on a description, classification and analysis of the patterned behaviors of skiers and are non-judgmental.

Though all three types of learning exist in various proportions in all learning situations, formal and informal learning dominate the practica in the pre-service and in-service education of most second language teachers. Some programs are entirely formal, relying solely on injunction. In other programs, judgments and prescriptions (formal) are presented along with demonstration lessons or micro lessons (informal). We have all heard these admonitions: 'Your pace was good, but you have to be more attentive to those in the back' or 'I think my voice sounds off, and I have to get some of that weight off' or 'Be sure not to ever write an error on the blackboard, but give a lot of praise.' The philosophy of many teacher educators, supervisors and employers seems to be that teachers will get the hang of teaching if they teach, look at enough classes and listen to enough admonitions.

Few seem to believe that teachers will get the hang of linguistics. Perhaps this is why technical teaching in most second language teacher education programs has for the most part been reserved for various aspects of linguistics, the technical language used to describe the content second language teachers are expected to teach. Thus, most second language teachers have been exposed to the technical language of phonology, morphology, and syntax and some even know the technical language of sociolinguistics and psycholinguistics. The terms used in these technical languages have precise meanings that receive wide consent.

No technical language exists to designate the teaching behavior in second language learning settings. The vocabulary used to discuss language teaching, textbooks and tests is composed of such words as *drill, reinforcement, mechanical, communicate, pace, audio-lingual, situational reinforcement*, words that are ill-defined and inconsistently used. We have phonemes and morphemes but no *teachemes*.[1]

The lack of a technical language to discuss the informal teaching done in demonstration lessons and micro-teaching and the formal teaching that occurs when we judge and critique a lesson we have seen leads to a situation analogous to one in the Japanese movie *Rashomon*, where four people give contradictory and equivocal accounts and interpretations of an event they have all witnessed. Like the characters in the movie, second language teachers and supervisors, when pressed to defend their accounts, interpretations, and judgments after a lesson, highlight behaviors, exercises, and communications that support their point of view, even though such items may be infrequent and even incidental to the central event.

Without a common unit of analysis or operationally defined words that are part of an overall shared concept, each viewer is bound to see events through his own perceptions and preconceived notions. Consequently, the words he uses to describe each teaching act will often have meanings that do not coincide with the meanings attached to them by another viewer. As a result, technical instruction is impossible, and these types of discussion can lead to little more than the advocacy of one particular theory over another or to the superiority of one type of exercise over another. Without technical language one cannot develop a description of what teachers and students actually do, compare lessons, methods or different 'schools' of language teaching or see the relationship between what was done and the teacher's intentions. Nor can one see the extent to which classroom behaviors reflect a theory of language teaching or measure the effect on learning of particular communications.

In my view, we need a technical language for the teaching act[2] equal to the technical language used to teach content. To this end, I have developed a conceptual framework and set of terms for classifying, creating and evaluating communications in a range of settings. This system is called FOCUS, an acronym for Foci for Observing Communications Used in Settings. In this system, communications both inside and outside the classroom are seen as a series of patterned events in which two or more people use

1. I first heard this term from Professor Austerlitz, Department of Linguistics, Columbia University, during a discussion of my research on the teaching act.
2. The term 'teaching act' must be broader when discussing language teaching than when discussing other types of teaching. Studying the teaching act of the language teacher must include study of how we communicate in non-teaching settings as well as teaching settings since part of our job is to teach our students how to communicate outside of the classroom, in non-teaching settings.

mediums such as speech, gestures, noise, or writing to evaluate, interpret and in other ways communicate separate areas of content such as the meaning of words, personal feelings, or classroom procedure, for one of four pedagogical purposes: structuring, soliciting, responding, and reacting. Therefore, FOCUS distinguishes five characteristics of communications: the source, the medium, the use, the content and the pedagogical purpose.

Though I do not have a technical language to code the settings in which communications are made I do note the setting and some details of it since the setting has such a strong effect on determining patterns of characteristics of communications. A bar produces patterns impossible in most teaching settings, and a confessional calls forth communications that could never be made in a toll booth. The word *setting* in the acronym FOCUS highlights the importance of noting the setting in which communications take place.

I note the pedagogical purpose of communications in FOCUS because this characteristic determines the basic unit of analysis, the move (Bellack *et al.* 1966). Communications that set the stage for subsequent behavior and exercises or self-directed activities such as reading silently or cleaning up a classroom on one's own without being told are structuring moves. Those communications that set tasks or ask questions are considered soliciting moves. Communications that modify previous moves, rate them or are called forth by previous moves are reacting moves. Both context and source are crucial in determining move boundaries and move types.[3]

Names of schools of language teaching, types of skills developed and names of techniques and methods have been used as basic units of analysis in previous discussions of language teaching. Thus, one hears of the audio-lingual methods as opposed to the silent way, situational reinforcement and its similarity to the direct method or the relationship between grammar-translation and counselling-learning. In some discussions the interaction between the development of one of the four traditional skills and favorite techniques or methods receives attention. One hears how helpful games can be in the development of reading skills, the utility of songs in developing speaking skills and the advantages of dialogs in fostering face to face language skills, etc.

Using such large units for analysis – the school, the skill, the method – can obscure a great deal. Three teachers may consider themselves members of School 1, practitioners of Method A and believers in the need to develop oral skills before any others. Yet, one teacher shakes students' hands after many correct responses; another never comments about student performance. A third

3. For a guide to learning the moves see Carol Rubin, *Self-Instructional Materials for Learning Bellack's Moves.*

comments only after a good student's response and does not react to poor students at all, whether their responses are correct or not correct. In addition, one of the three teachers who believes in the same school periodically explains the rationale for the method used at the beginning of class while the other two never do; they begin each class with greetings and personal remarks. Since teachers of the same school may use different behaviors, a smaller unit of analysis than the school is necessary. And if either the preparation for the setting of tasks or feedback gave any effect on learning it makes sense to use structuring and reacting moves as basic units of analysis rather than schools, skills or types of methods. Since tasks are set and performed or questions are asked and answered in classes no matter what school, method or skill is purportedly involved, it makes sense to use soliciting and responding moves as basic units of analysis as well.

Though the move is defined as a combination having one of four pedagogical purposes it can be used to classify communications in non-teaching settings as well, since we ask and answer questions, comment on what others do and perform self-directed activities in all settings. Thus, we can employ the same basic unit to classify communications both inside and outside of classrooms. As a result, precise comparisons can be made between teaching and non-teaching settings. Since the move has been used in scores of studies of classes other than those in which language is taught, comparisons between patterns of moves in history, science, math and second language classes can also be made.

Categories developed in studies of the functions of language have not been used as the basic unit of analysis both because they usually refer to a series of communications and because deciding between them required more inference than deciding between move types. Halliday's classification of the purposes for which we communicate, for example, is helpful in interpreting data discovered by analyzing the characteristics we note (Halliday 1973). But the categories do not allow for as precise a tabulation as we are interested in.

Simply making tallies of the pedagogical purposes of communications is not as instructive as tallying the source of each communication along with the purpose. In the latter, we can tell the proportion of moves made by each person in a setting. One believer in Method A may make 100% of the soliciting moves in the class; another may encourage student solicits. If half of the reacting moves are performed by students in one class and only a few in another class this difference in source must be shown. When the solicit 'Shut up!' is made by a student to a teacher it has a very different meaning than when made by the teacher to a student.

Precise descriptions of these distinctions are not possible using the usual units of analysis such as the school, method or skill.

The boxes in the two columns below are just like items in a substitution table; any box in Column 1 can combine with any box in Column 2.

Two Characteristics of Communications in Settings

Column 1 Source*

*Column 1 Source**
Who communicates?

teacher   t

textbook   b

informant   i

student   s

group of students   g

class   c

Column 2 Move Type

Column 2 Move Type
What is the pedagogical purpose
of the communication?

to structure   str

to solicit   sol

to respond   res

to react   rea

* In a non-teaching setting, the sources would of course be different; any abbreviations can be used. On a quiz show an m could be used for the master of ceremonies and a g for guests; in a sandbox c_1 could stand for one child and c_2 for another.

Using the boxes to note these two characteristics of communication in a conversation has often revealed a pattern of two sources reacting about an equal number of times in my observations. However, in some conversations one source structures constantly and the other person only has a chance to react. In a classroom, the teacher structures, solicits and reacts while the students only respond, while in a tutoring session and in group work in classrooms the students also solicit and react. Of course in a classroom setting without discipline students also react and solicit. The setting in which communications take place has a great effect on determining the patterns of sources and moves. Thus, altering the settings in which language instruction takes place can itself radically change the pattern of behavior that goes on. And altering the patterns of these two characteristics of communication in a class, at a cocktail party or in any other setting will greatly alter the nature of interaction in these settings.

Of course, two classes may show a very similar frequency,

sequence and combination of moves and sources and yet be very different. Three teachers may each communicate 200 soliciting moves by setting 200 tasks or asking 200 questions. But if the solicit in one class requires the oral repetition of a word, in another the copying of a word from the blackboard and in still another the phonetic transcription of words, these differences must be noted. Therefore, with FOCUS, in addition to noting the source and pedagogical purpose of communications we note the mediums the moves contain.

Though some might object to McLuhan's famous dictum that the medium is the message, most would agree that a major difference between many communications is that the messages are communicated in different mediums. Showing a picture of an avocado, holding up a real avocado, writing the word *avocado* in phonetic script or uttering *avocado* in soliciting moves all may bring an image of a pear-shaped food into the minds of those who know the object and its name. But the transcribed words bring no image to the mind of those unfamiliar with phonetic script. And the real avocado may communicate something of the texture and actual size of the avocado in a way the picture does not. In the same way, one may wish to present one's personal displeasure in a reacting move with a comment, a grunt or an agonized look. The comment would communicate displeasure only if the audience understood the words, and the agonized look would communicate only if it were seen. Edmund Carpenter contends that Mendel's theories of genetics were ignored for thirty-five years because they were presented originally in print without visual illustrations (1974). Thus, in FOCUS one reason I note the type of medium is because I assume that different mediums communicating the same content provide different kinds and amounts of information.

I also note the type of medium used because a great range of mediums is used frequently both in teaching and non-teaching settings. When a teacher reacts to an error in tense by putting his right thumb up over his shoulder as if he were hitching a ride and the student reacts by saying 'Oh, past!' gesture and speech are both used. Likewise, in a non-teaching setting, a flower given to one's date before dinner communicates just as 'How are you?' does. It seems unreasonable to note and classify communications made in speech and ignore those made with other types of mediums such as gestures and flowers.

Noting mediums in moves also provides insight into *how* messages are communicated. The solicit, 'Pick up the book,' can mean either 'Please pick up the book; nothing is wrong; we just want the book on the desk' or 'Pick up the book; you are clumsy; you should not have dropped it' depending on the tone of voice used. In FOCUS, the tone of voice and spoken words are considered two separate mediums. In 'Pick up the book' the words are the same whether one is being neutral or showing displeasure. The tone of voice communicates an extra message. People make evaluations with their tone of voice, their looks and their movements even though the words they utter may simply be stating a fact or giving a command. 'It's not what he said, but how he said it that bothered me' and 'Her words said "no" while her eyes said "yes"' are two familiar communications that reflect the crucial importance of examining more than the medium of the spoken word alone.

For ease of discussion, the mediums used to communicate content in moves are categorized as linguistic, non-linguistic and para-linguistic. Communications expressed with words, produced by the vocal cords and tongue, or written representations of such communications, constitute linguistic mediums. Communications that are made with instruments or with parts of the body used as an instrument and things made from tools or produced artistically, mechanically, or naturally such as pictures, objects and music are classified non-linguistic. Communications expressed by the body without vocal cords and tongue such as gestures, movement and touch constitute para-linguistic mediums, referred to by some as body language.

On a lower level of analysis, these three major categories are further split into three sub-categories. Mediums that appeal primarily to the ear such as spoken words, intonation, noise, music, and laughing are coded as aural. Those that appeal primarily to the eye such as printed words, phonetic transcriptions, pictures, diagrams, and gestures are coded as visual. Those that appeal to more than one sense or other senses such as touching, distance, dancing, movement, and clothing are classified 'other.' Looking at a videotape with the sound off clearly highlights the visual mediums. Listening to an audio recording of conversations or a teaching session clearly highlights aural mediums. Categories of the mediums along with examples are shown in the Tables in Appendix I.

This categorization of mediums is more helpful than a two-way division between verbal and non-verbal seen in much of the literature because this classification allows us to show differences between mediums that are critical in second language settings. We usually do not teach students to draw in language class yet we do teach them gestures. If we did not separate non-linguistic from para-linguistic we would code a class learning gestures and a class learning to draw in the same way since both drawing and gesturing would be considered non-verbal. It is important to show whether students are learning how to communicate with linguistic mediums such as words, para-linguistic mediums such as body language or non-linguistic mediums such as drawings. It is also important to distinguish between aural mediums such as spoken words, music, tone of voice and visual mediums such as print, drawings, and maps because these distinctions show us whether students are developing receptive or productive skills.

Our substitution table now has three columns. The four move types now interact not only with the six major sources but also with the three major categories of mediums and three sub-categories of each. Noting the mediums used in moves by different sources greatly expands the power of FOCUS. Six sources combining with four move types may produce at least twenty-four distinct groupings. When six sources combine with four move types and three categories of mediums many more distinct combinations are possible. Within each category of medium there are three sub-categories; aural, written, and other, and in each at least ten separate types of mediums are possible. The number of permutations possible when noting just these three characteristics is thus extremely large.

Attention to the mediums used to communicate moves not only reveals a great deal about how different people communicate; it also reveals a great number of moves that would not ordinarily be noticed because they are communicated in mediums we frequently fail to note, such as distance, movement, background noise and other non-linguistic and para-linguistic mediums that appear in some cases to the eyes and ears and in other cases to senses other than the eyes or ears such as touch and feeling.

Similar patterns of sources, moves and mediums in separate lessons do not mean the lessons are the same. A lesson on tense, intonation, adjective word order, the classification of snakes or students' views on religion will develop mastery of different areas of content. Teacher and student moves that communicate personal feelings must be coded differently from moves that communicate the theme of *Last Tango in Paris* or procedures for a fire drill. Likewise, at a party the topic of a conversation might be personal feelings about a film or a description of the way the film was made. Therefore, with FOCUS, in addition to noting the source, pedagogical purpose, and mediums I note the content the moves contain.

I employ four major categories of content. If some aspect of the target language is being communicated as an area of study – as information set apart and being studied, tested, or practiced – the content is labeled *language*. The content in the solicit 'Give me a match' would be considered language if it were communicated to test one's understanding of the words *give* or *match* or to practice the pronunciation of the final sound in *match* for example. Language is divided into subcategories representing seven systems developed in second language classes: contextual, grammatical, literary, meaning, mechanics of writing, sound, speech production. Categories of content along with examples are shown in the Tables in Appendix I.

If one said 'Give me a match' because one really needed to light a cigar, the content would be coded *life*. Expressing formulas such as greetings, reflections from the imagination, personal feelings or personal information or general knowledge such as historical dates, prices of cars or issues such as inflation are all examples of communications that would be considered to have content of *life*.

The third category of content, *procedure*, is employed when mediums are used to communicate information in one of these sub-categories: administration, classroom social behavior, language teaching procedure, teaching and learning rationale. The calling of the roll, disciplining of students, directions to manipulate language, explanations of the reasons particular exercises are being done are all examples of communications that would be classified as *procedure*.

When mediums communicate information that cannot be classified as language, life or procedure the content is coded *subject matter*, the fourth category of content. Thus if anyone communicates a skill such as knitting, wine tasting, bridge or cooking, or a school subject such as history, biology or mathematics, or a survival skill such as how to cash a check or read a lease, the content is classified as *subject matter*.

For decades, language teachers have been saying that if history teachers and science teachers do not help teach language the students will suffer. During the same decades, many language teachers in Africa and perhaps other areas were saying that the way to teach language was to teach history, science, crafts and other subjects limited to particular subject matter classes; language and subject matter in the same language were taught hand in hand. Today, this idea is being applied in some classes in the United States and being discussed under the label *Language for Special or Specific Purposes*. The category *subject matter* is designed to show teaching of this type.

Each category has sub-categories and each sub-category divisions. The level of category of content one employs depends on the needs one has. If one wants to compare a number of settings to see the extent to which each category is communicated, then only the four major categories need be used. If one is interested in determining the areas of language most frequently communicated in a series of lessons, then the sub-categories shown in the Tables in Appendix I would be employed. If the entire lesson is devoted to a sub-category such as the sound system, then the divisions of the sound system would be called for. In this case, either the usual linguistic divisions of the sound system could be employed or those listed in the Tables in Appendix I.

A central characteristic noted with FOCUS is the *use*. The *use* shows how the mediums are used to communicate content. To determine the category of use, the first question is whether the mediums communicate any content. In receptive activities such as silent reading, listening exercises, feeling, tasting or smelling things to sense their texture, flavor or scent, a person is trying to make sense out of content another person communicated; the receiver is not communicating content; the sender is. These receptive activities are coded *attend* (1).

To distinguish between different categories of productive activities we first ask whether the mediums communicate comments about content or content itself. When speech, print, pictures or other mediums are used to comment on something else we code the communications *characterize* (2). If speech, print, pictures or other mediums are used to present content itself rather than a comment on content or an item, we code the communication *present* (3). In a game of bridge, a player can bid 'one heart,' 'one spade' or 'two clubs'; since these statements do not literally mean he has one heart, one spade or two clubs but rather are labels indicating an approximate number of points and number of hearts, spades or clubs, the player is communicating a message about his hand; therefore, these communications would be coded *characterize* (2). If a player were allowed to say 'I have five hearts: the ace, queen, jack, ten and nine, etc.' rather than the label 'one heart' he would be communicating messages that would be coded *present* (3). Activities such as indicating whether communications are the same or different, incorrect or correct or true or false, defining words by giving their attributes, indicating how many syllables a word has or giving categorical labels are all coded *characterize* (2). Giving directions and asking questions, identifying objects, giving antonyms and synonyms, reading orally, writing dictations, and communicating content of life or subject matter directly are all coded *present* (3). This distinction has of course been made by others. Most recently, Smith, in a discussion of cognitive interrelations, makes the distinction. The category *present* (3) represents what he calls an 'is a ("izza") relationship' (1975:21). An example would be 'Fred is a teacher.' The category *characterize* (2) represents what he discussed as a 'has' relationship or an 'is' relationship without the 'a.' Examples would be 'Fred has long hair' and 'Fred is young.'

If the communications do not fit into the categories *attend* (1), *characterize* (2), or *present* (3), we ask whether the communications give an explanation or make an inference. If they do, we code the communications *relate* (4). Generalizations, giving reasons for behavior, speculating, and making inferences are activities that are coded *relate* (4). As Long has shown, further classification of this type of communication can be useful (Long *et al.* 1976).

If the communications do not fit any of these four categories, we assume speech, print, etc. are simply being used to re-present communications another has made in the same medium. If they are used in this way we code them *re-present* (5). Copying, imitating, paraphrasing, making substitutions in sentences, and changing the word order in sentences are all examples of the category *re-present* (5). Detailed definitions of these major categories of use as well as the sub-categories, together with examples, are presented in Appendix I and II.

This categorization of uses means that in my conceptualization there are basically only five major kinds of structuring, soliciting, responding and reacting moves possible. Variation in these major kinds of structuring, soliciting, responding and reacting moves comes either from their source, alteration in the mediums and content or in the information given in the surrounding moves. Thus, Class 1 and Class 2 may both respond with the use *present* 80% of the time. But in Class 1, the medium used in the responses is print while in Class 2 it is speech. And in Class 1, the content is language while in Class 2 it is speech. And in Class 1, the content is language while in Class 2 it is life. Furthermore, the solicits in Class 1 are communicated with realia while in Class 2 they are presented with speech. The reactions in both Class 1 and Class 2 are all in the sub-category of characterize called *evaluate*. But in Class 1 the evaluations are communicated with gestures while in Class 2 the teacher shakes students' hands so the medium is touch. Finally, when errors are made in Class 1 the teacher consistently uses the sub-category of characterize called *label* in solicits that follow the error, e.g., 'Use the past tense.' In Class 2, the teacher never uses the category *label* after errors, simply saying 'Again,' but students say the answers. Therefore, the information given after incorrect responses is very different in both classes. In fact, one reason that so many comparison of methods studies have not found many differences in learning in classes exposed to different methods may be simply because the supposedly different methods in fact required the same types of responses from students. Students supposedly exposed to different methods may have been doing mostly the same types of things; and students supposedly exposed to the same method may have been doing different things.

Heretofore, this categorization has not been employed to describe and compare communications in classrooms and other settings. Rather, communications have been called *mechanical, meaningful, skill getting, pseudo-communicative, communicative,* etc. These distinctions fail to take into account different mental operations demanded by different communications. Saying a word has three syllables, or is a noun, or is different from another word, or is incorrect, or giving it a definition or stating a rule, or inferring or recalling or repeating – all require different mental operations.

Two groups – one in a bar and another in a classroom – may

spend hours exchanging data about a sport using gestures, laughing and passing score cards around – extremely communicative activity! But if one group is using metaphors to describe some team members, making generalizations about why the team is so active, evaluating each other's generalizations and classifying the attributes of each player, and the other group is simply describing the games they have seen, the communicative activity in each group is very different. It seems as important to note that the participants in each group are using mediums in vastly different ways that reflect different mental operations as to note that the communications in both groups are meaningful or communicative.

Words such as *mechanical, meaningful,* etc. not only fail to account for different types of mental operations, they also require a high degree of inference. Many are similar to items in rating scales that contain comments such as these: conversation was interesting; teacher was well prepared; teacher achieved goal. Each person's interpretation of *interesting* or *meaningful* is different. Because a technical language such as FOCUS has operationally defined terms it does not require the high degree of inference that words such as *meaningful* do. Without the use of technical terms, descriptions of communications in and out of classes will invariably include global, imprecise language requiring high inference and leading to varying and often contradictory versions of the same events.

In addition to requiring high inference, words such as *meaningful* and *interesting* are loaded; the words themselves have good and bad connotations. If asked to choose, most would no doubt like to teach a class or participate in a conversation that was meaningful and interesting rather than meaningless or uninteresting. Words such as *meaningful* and *interesting* are in themselves judgmental as well as descriptive. Judgments mean someone's ego is involved and this can interfere with perception. At the conclusion of a conference on teacher education, a participant related St. Paul's comment on self-perception to the use of a technical language in teacher education.

> ... St. Paul said, 'Ye shall be compared to a man beholding his own countenance in a glass, for he beheld himself and went his way, and presently forgot what manner of man he was.' This is what happened to these student teachers. They saw themselves on television teaching ... saw what little they did right. Then, they turned the projector off and they went back to the classroom, and, whatever they did had nothing to do with what they saw of themselves, as they did not know how to perceive themselves. A language of teacher behavior provides a vocabulary for self-perception for the teacher (Burkhart 1969, p. 63).

A recent book on tennis contains the same theme: Step 1 in learning is to 'observe non-judgmentally, existing behavior ... awareness of what *is*, without judgment ... is the best precondition for change' (Gallwey 1974, p. 80).

The use of high inference words that themselves are judgmental is a characteristic of formal instruction. While formal instruction contributes to the *Rashomon* effect technical instruction moves beyond the *Rashomon* effect. In technical instruction the 'headsets,' egos and preoccupations of the participant/observers filter perception much less; and contradictory versions of the same event, caused in part by the use of terms requiring high inference are decreased. While interpretations and evaluations of the effects of events may still differ after a description in which technical terms are used, at least the participants will be discussing the events themselves with precise operationally defined terms that are not judgmental.

The basic elements of FOCUS are shown below in Table 1. Though the number of characteristics of communication noted with FOCUS is only five – source, pedagogical purpose, medium, use, content – and the number of major categories of each characteristic is always less than six – just as 103 chemical elements combine to form thousands of compounds, the 12 tone system can produce jazz, rock and roll or classical music, and the differences in the point and manner of articulation can describe most sounds – a cross-categorization of the categories of characteristics noted with FOCUS can be used to describe the existing variety of communications both in second language learning settings and elsewhere. Different frequencies, combinations and sequences of the basic elements of FOCUS can clearly illustrate both similarities and differences of communications made by two children in a sandbox, two teachers presenting the same lesson in *Lado English*, two students being taught by a tape recorder, two history teachers teaching in Hungarian, and most other combinations of settings, sources and targets one could conjure up.

This conceptualization and these labels can be employed both in lesson planning and research at many levels. For example, a teacher might decide to see the extent to which the students understand polite and impolite gestures. To meet this aim, the teacher could include solicits in a lesson plan which required students to respond using gestures to present content in the subcategory of language called the contextual system. Or, the teacher could perform the gestures in his solicits and require the students to characterize them by using speech to evaluate them in their responses.

As a research instrument, FOCUS can be employed to analyze communications on many different levels and with varying degrees

TABLE 1   Five characteristics of communications in settings

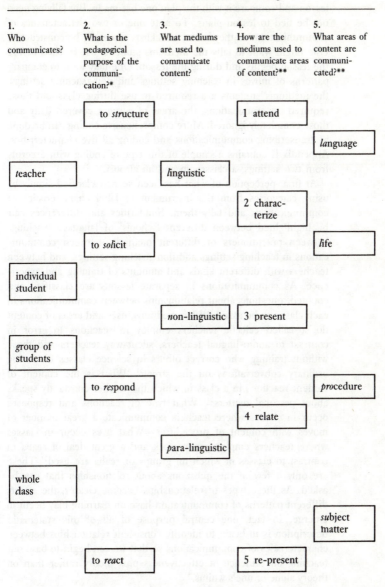

1. Who communicates?	2. What is the pedagogical purpose of the communication?*	3. What mediums are used to communicate content?	4. How are the mediums used to communicate areas of content?**	5. What areas of content are communicated?**
	to *structure*		1 attend	
				language
teacher		*linguistic*		
			2 characterize	
	to *solicit*			*life*
individual student				
		non-linguistic	3 present	
group of students				
	to *respond*			*procedure*
			4 relate	
		para-linguistic		
whole class				
				subject matter
	to *react*		5 re-present	

---

* These four pedagogical purposes are from Bellack.
** The uses and areas of content are presented alphabetically rather than in any hierarchical order.

of comprehensiveness. It is a simple matter to listen to a tape of a lesson and compare it with the plan one has made. But tallying need not be tied to lesson plans. To note one or two characteristics of communications as they occur, checklists can easily be constructed. One might want to tally the mediums students use in class before the lesson begins and during the lesson. One may want to compare patterns of moves in teaching settings and non-teaching settings, the mediums students are required to use during class and those required on examinations, the areas of content covered daily and those completely ignored. More comprehensive coding can be done by transcribing communications and coding all five characteristics; Appendix II contains a sample of this type of coding with excerpts from two settings: a classroom and an airport.

At first, perception of what has been seen is clarified simply by using categories from the instrument to label characteristics of communications and tally them. Similarities and differences can be highlighted between different 'schools' of language teaching, between practitioners of different methods, between communications in teaching settings and non-teaching settings, and between teachers with different kinds and amounts of training and experience. As communications in separate lessons are classified and counted, questions about relationships between communications in each class can be asked. 'What mediums, uses and areas of content do so-called eclectic teachers employ in reactions to error in contrast to audio-lingual teachers, silent-way teachers and those without training who correct others in science classes or during ordinary conversations on the street?' 'What is the content of student reactions in a class in which the teacher constantly speaks about personal matters?' 'What type of reactions and responses occur in classes where teachers communicate a great number of moves with content of procedure?' 'What uses occur in classes where teachers employ group work and a great deal of realia in contrast to classes in which no groups or realia are used?' These are only a few of the questions about relationships that can be asked. As these types of relationships become clearer, the effects different patterns of communication have on learning may begin to emerge. In fact, one central purpose of all of this systematic description is to begin to identify consistent relationships between characteristics of communications so that we can begin to base our teaching on evidence of effectiveness plus theory rather than on theory alone or one's whims.[4]

---

4. For those who are totally repelled by this idea of classifying and quantifying such a human activity as teaching in this way, I suggest you read *Zen and the Art of Motorcycle Maintenance*. The author's discussion of the school of reason and the romantic school provide insight into the problem of classifying and quantifying.

Without a conceptual framework to which we may attach our descriptions of teacher-learner behaviors, we cannot as clearly discern the relationship between pedagogical intention and learning response. Nor can we adequately integrate desired modifications into our teaching. Suggestions from others, detailed notes in lesson plans, specific behaviors to be employed, patterns of communications in teaching and non-teaching settings – all can be better understood, remembered, and mastered when placed within the broad conceptual framework provided by FOCUS.

The Competency Based Teacher Education Movement encourages the type of precise, systematic, and non-judgmental study of the teaching act and its effects that FOCUS can provide. The CBTE movement believes that if teachers can see the range of teacher behaviors possible, use the behaviors consciously and measure their effects on learning, teachers may expand the repertoire of their behaviors both in subject matter classes (Bellack *et al.* 1966; Flanders 1970; Hoetker and Ahlbrand 1969) and in second language classes (Fanselow 1977; Gamta 1976; Long *et al.* 1976 [this volume, pp. 153–170]; Moskowitz 1976; Naiman *et al.* 1975, Rwakyaka 1976). Since another tenet of CBTE requires that teacher trainers must study the degree to which the training program they execute aids in the expansion of teacher behaviors (Elam 1971), future research studies should be able to tell us the extent to which the use of technical instruction in the teaching act alters what almost seems to have become a ritual for many teachers.

For too long, we have sought technical information only from psychologists, linguists and researchers who did comparison of methods studies. Or we have sought formal and informal instruction from authors of methods books, advocates of particular 'schools' or sets of tests or materials. To be sure, these sources have been helpful and ought not to be discarded. They can be supplemented however, by instruments such as FOCUS which (1) permit us to develop technical information about what we practicing language teachers and our students actually do both in classrooms and other settings, (2) help us examine the effects different communications have on learning; and (3) enable us to translate the suggestions and theories from linguists, advocates of particular theories and others into precise objectives.

Just as observing and playing a game of chess is more valuable if one understands that the game is limited to various combinations of moves of 32 chess pieces in distinct ways over 64 squares, and just as a physical examination makes more sense if the doctor does it with a conceptual framework and with technical terms based on a classification his colleagues share, so observing of teaching in second language classes and other settings is more valuable if it is seen conceptually and is discussed with operationally defined terms.

Appendix I Tables 2 and 3

TABLE 2 Five characteristics of communications in settings

1. Who communicates?	2. What is the pedagogical purpose of the communication?*	3. What mediums are used to communicate content?	4. How are the mediums used to communicate areas of content?**	5. What areas of content are communicated?**
teacher	to structure	linguistic	1 attend	language systems
		aural	2 characterize	contextual
		visual	21 differentiate	grammatical
			22 evaluate	literary
		ideogram	23 examine	meaning
		transcribed	24 illustrate	mechanics of writing
		written	25 label	sound segmental supra-segmental
individual student	to solicit	other	3 present	speech production
		non-linguistic	31 call words	unclassified

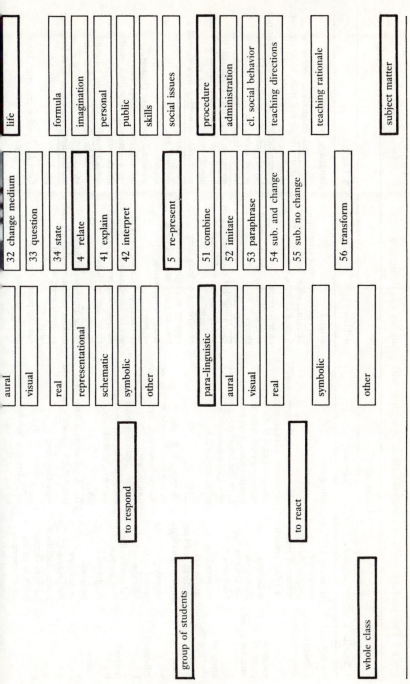

		life
aural	32 change medium	formula
visual	33 question	imagination
	34 state	personal
real	4 relate	public
representational	41 explain	skills
schematic	42 interpret	social issues
symbolic		
other	5 re-present	procedure
		administration
para-linguistic	51 combine	cl. social behavior
aural	52 imitate	teaching directions
visual	53 paraphrase	
real	54 sub. and change	
	55 sub. no change	teaching rationale
symbolic		
	56 transform	
other		subject matter

to respond

to react

group of students

whole class

* These four pedagogical purposes are from Bellack.
** The uses and areas of content are presented alphabetically.

TABLE 3: Five characteristics of communications in settings with examples and definitions

1 Source	2 Pedagogical purpose*	Messages** 3 Mediums	4 Uses	5 Content
teacher t	**structuring** moves str prepare for the setting of tasks or other activities	**linguistic** aural fillers, individual letters, words, sentences, sounds, syllables, etc. (Add an s if the supra-segmentals are used to communicate a separate message as in the lengthening of vowels or rising intonation in repetitions, etc.)	**attend** not communicating content – listening, silent reading, tasting, feeling objects, etc.	**language systems** contextual: collocation, connotation, culture, detail and main idea, register, situation, etc. grammatical: function words, sentence forms, inflections, reduced forms, word, order, etc.
individual student s_1 to s_n	**soliciting** moves sol set tasks or ask questions	visual *ideogram:* \$, #, etc. *transcribed:* phonetic writing of fillers, intonation, stress, words, sounds, etc.	**characterize** communicating about content or things	literary: imagery, mood, style, etc. meaning: figurative, grammatical, historical, humorous, idiomatic, ironic, literal, etc.
assigned group of students g_1 to g_n	**responding** moves res perform tasks or answer questions	*written:* printed written individual letters, words, commas, periods, etc.	**differentiate** indicating that communications are the same or different	mechanics of writing: how to hold a pen, making capitals, punctuation, spelling, etc. sound:
group of students ss_1 to ss_n	**reacting** moves rea reflexive communications that are not requested	other Braille; drawing a letter or stress mark on one's hand, etc.	**evaluate** prescribing or indicating comms. are right or wrong or true or false; ans. yes/no & either/or questions	*segmental:* consonant clusters, syllabification, sounds, etc. *supra-segmental:* intonation, rhythm, stress, etc.
class c	**bearing** moves bea unconscious communications such as jiggling one's keys; the environment or situation one is	**non-linguistic** aural bell, clapping, humming, music, noise, tapping, etc.	**examine** counting or locating parts of words; emphasizing; diagramming sentences; infor. about size or shape	speech production: your tongue should be up; the voice box vibrates, etc. unclassified: many aspects of language
informant i			**illustrate** giving attributes of items, making judgments that are not explicitly good or bad	**life**
textbook b			**label** naming parts of speech or groups of items	formula: genuine greetings, leave-taking, etc.
visitor v				

visual

real: food, live things, objects, people, speech organs, voice box, working things, etc.
representational: cartoon, picture, puppet, sketch, etc.
schematic: diagram, erasing, line showing space, map, underlining, etc.
symbolic: rod representating a house, etc.

other

clothing, furniture, temperature, etc.

para-linguistic

aural

crying, laughing, silence, tone of voice, volume, etc.

visual

real: color, faces, gazing, gesture, movement, posture, etc.
symbolic: gesture for summer, etc.

other

dance, distance, touch, etc.

---

present

communicating content itself
call words
change medium
question
state

relate

relating communications about content and content itself
explain
making generalizations, giving rules or reasons; explicitly relating, etc.
interpret
making inferences, generating new patterns, implicitly relating, etc.

re-present

communicating content another has just, communicated in the same medium with or without change.
combining
imitating
paraphrasing
substituting with changes
substituting without changes
transforming

---

imagination: what would happen if ...?, etc.
personal: feelings, information, etc.
public: general knowledge about persons, places, things, aesthetics, religion, etc.
skills: cooking, studying, track, typing, etc.
social issues: population, prejudice, etc.

procedure

administration: calling roll; phoney greetings; checking questions – do you follow?; transition – OK, Uhm; query – repeating with rising intonation, etc.
classroom social behavior: discipline, etc.
teaching directions: setting tasks, communicating instructional information, etc.
teaching rationale: support for a method or procedure, etc.

subject matter

school subjects: biology, math, *not* language, etc.
survival skills: how to budget, understanding a lease, etc.

unspecified

---

* from Bellack
** The term message refers to the combination of medium, use and content.

Developments in teaching, as in any field, come from those who have conceptualized their discipline and possess shared terms to describe their craft. Conceptualization strengthens the basic elements and combines them in new ways, thereby increasing control and expanding options. Teachers and students who, through heightened understanding, can create new combinations of sources, pedagogical purposes, mediums, uses, and areas of content will produce totally different and more varied patterns of communications in a range of settings. Much like chess masters, poets, artists, or scientists who have created new and original patterns in their respective fields because they have attached intricacy of detail to simplicity of concept, teachers, too, may now seek the creative, innovative and effective, confident that the teaching act is no longer a mystery that defies precise and rational control.

Appendix II   Communications coded with focus[1]

Setting: *An intermediate language classroom; students are seated in rows. Here are some excerpts from lessons:*	Source	Pedagogical purpose	Medium	Use	Content
1. Read this passage silently.	t	sol	la[+]	pres:state	language+life
Was Truman from Texas?			lv		
No, Missouri.					
What about Eisenhower?					
He was from Texas.					
(Student reads passage silently.)	s	res	lv	attend	language+life
2. What part of speech is *from*?	t	sol	la	pres:ques[+]	language:gram.
A preposition.	s	res	la	char:label	language:gram.
(Teacher shakes student's hand.)	t	rea	po	char:evaluate[3]	language:gram.
3. Is *about* a preposition too?	s	sol	la	pres:ques[+]	language:gram
Yes.	t	res	la	char:label	language:gram.
Good question – glad you ask questions.				char:evaluate[3]	
	t	rea	la	char:evaluate	procedure
4. Where was Johnson from?	s	sol	la	pres:ques	life
Texas.	t	res	la	pres:state	life

Setting: *An intermediate language classroom; students are seated in rows. Here are some excerpts from lessons:*	Five characteristics of communications				
	Source	Pedagogical purpose	Medium	Use	Content
5. How many syllables in Eisenhower?	t	sol	la	pres:ques	language:sound
Four.	s	res	la	char:examine	language:sound
6. Does Truman have two?	s	sol	la	pres:ques$^+$ char:examine	language:sound
Yes.	t	res	la	char:evaluate[3]	language:sound
7. We'll do some vocabulary work now.	t	str	la	pres:state	procedure$^+$
8. Say something about this. (Holds up an old, torn plastic raincoat.)	t	sol	la$^+$ nvl	pres:state	language:mean.
It's for the water.	s$_1$	res	la	char:illustrate	language:mean.
It's ugly.	s$_2$	res	la	char:illustrate	language:mean.
I like it.	s$_3$	res	la	char:evaluate	language:mean.
It is just like mine.	s$_4$	res	la	char:differentiate	life
Feel this. (Gives student a candle.)	t	sol	la$^+$ nvl	pres:state	language:mean.
(Student feels candle.)	s	res	nvl	attend	language:mean.
Is it rough or smooth?	t	sol	la$^+$ nvl	pres:state$^+$ contrast	language:mean.
Smooth.	s	res	la	char:evaluate[3]	language:mean
(Shakes head up and down.)	t	rea	pv	char:evaluate	language:mean.

[1] Practice coding of excerpts from lessons, texts, tests and conversations is needed to master FOCUS in much the same way that a great deal of transcription practice is needed before serious phonetic work can be done.

[2] Of course since there is a direction in the solicit the content of procedure is presented also. However, as a convention we do not code procedural content in solicits.

[3] An alternate way to code these responses, and all others, is to show what is given in the solicit on the response line. Here are three of the responses coded the alternate way.

3 s res la evaluate language: grammar (la pres:ques+char:label)

6 t res la evaluate language: sound (la pres:ques+char:examine)

8 s res la evaluate language: meaning (la pres:state+contrast+nvl pres:state)

Setting: *An airport – first at the ticket counter, then at customs and finally on a plane*	Source	Pedagogical purpose	Medium	Use	Content
Five characteristics of communications					
1. How much is a ticket to Chicago?	s[1]	sol	la	pres:ques	life
$120.00.	t[1]	res	la	pres:state	life
That's rather high.	s	rea	la	char:illustrate	life
It's gone up because of the price of fuel, the increased wages for pilots and higher fees at all the airports.	t	rea	la	relate:explain	life
Please book me on the next flight. (after checking)	s	sol	la	pres:ques	procedure
I've booked you on the 3 o'clock.	t	res	la	pres:state	procedure
Thank you. (and smiles in a friendly way)	s	rea	la⁺ pv	pres:state char:evaluate	life:formula
2. How long have you been in Montreal?	t[1]	sol	la	pres:ques	procedure[2]
For three days.	s[1]	res	la	pres:state	procedure
Why were you here?	t	sol	la	pres:ques	procedure
To visit some friends.	s	res	la	pres:state	procedure
Please open your bags.	t	sol	la	pres:ques	procedure
(opens bags)	s	res	pv⁺ nvl	pres:state	procedure
(looks through the bags and checks with his hands the contents of some bags)	t	rea	pv⁺ nvl	attend	procedure
You have to pay duty on these shoes.	t	sol	la	char:evaluate	procedure
That's stupid!	s	rea	la⁺ pa	char:evaluate	life
Go over to the collection booth.	t	sol	la	pres:ques	procedure
It's to the left of Avis.			la	char:examine	procedure
(points to the collection booth)			pv	char:examine	procedure
(goes over to the collection booth)	s	res	pv	pres:state	procedure

Setting: *An airport – first at the ticket counter, then at customs and finally on a plane*	Five characteristics of communications				
	Source	Pedagogical purpose	Medium	Use	Content
3. Welcome aboard.	t[1]	rea	la	pres:state	life:formula
(passenger goes to seat)	s[1]	str	pv	pres:state	procedure
This is the captain speaking. We will be taking off soon – right on schedule. We will be flying at 35,000 feet. The weather is clear all the way and the ceiling in the Chicago area is high. Enjoy the flight.	t	str	la	pres:state	procedure+ life:formula
(one passenger to another) They all sound the same.	s	rea	la	char:differentiate	life
Would you like a cocktail or a soft drink? (pointing to both on the cart)	t	sol	la+ nvl	pres:ques pres:state	life
A cocktail.	s	res	la	char:evaluate	life
(Steward begins to fill glass with ice)	s	str	nvl	pres:state	procedure
Light on the ice though.	t	rea	la	char:illustrate	life
(Here the roles are switched; the steward is serving the passenger and the passenger is coded as t.)					

[1] We use the letter t for the knower or the one in charge and an s for the learner or the person being served or directed.

[2] The content of these same questions if asked over dinner by a friend would be coded *life*. But in the setting of the customs area the content is *procedure*. The official is only interested in whether you did or did not do something that was not allowed by the rules. Here is a good example of how crucial the setting is in determining the meaning of communications.

Several points remain to be made. Firstly, concerning the issue of system complexity, FOCUS is clearly a highly complex system, infinitely more complex even than Moskowitz's FLint system, which Bailey had judged as unreasonably elaborate for practical observation purposes. Fanselow's approach to this problem was the ingenious one of suggesting that only a small part of the system need be used at any one time, a point made by the acronym FOCUS itself. Fanselow could also, in the mid-seventies, rely on the ever increasing availability of video-recording equipment to obviate the need for any system to be easily usable for real-time observations. Secondly, concerning the issue of non-judgementality, Fanselow could hope to have gone a long way towards meeting Bailey's objections, since he had devised a system for all settings, for all sorts of participants, and could not therefore have built into his system pedagogic prejudices about preferred behaviour. It is worth noting, perhaps, that he specifically referred to the non-judgemental aspect when relating his work to the concerns of the Competency Based Teacher Education Movement. Thirdly, in devising a system based on Bellack's work on *language* use in the classroom, Fanselow's categories, though intended to be universal in application, could be argued to have a better chance than Flanders' linguistically naive categories to be able to represent the undoubted complexities of the language classroom.

To summarize, Fanselow's sophisticated alternative to Flanders tried to bridge the gap between teacher trainers and researchers by providing something of practical value to everybody, in any field. Our next paper is much less ambitious, but it does try to evaluate the usefulness of a variety of systems, and to propose an alternative of its own.

2 The Barnes perspective

Like Bellack, Barnes was not concerned with language teaching particularly, but he was concerned with language use in the class-room, and particularly with language use, for learning purposes, among learners. He published an influential collection of papers on the subject in England in 1969, under the title *Language, the Learner, and the School*. Barnes was not proposing a particular system of analysis, however, nor a particular theory of discourse. He focused instead on the problem of convincing teachers that if they looked carefully enough at what their learners were saying to each other they would find it both impressive and instructive. His work was neither directed at language teachers nor generally well known among them, but Long saw its relevance to his own interest in the operation of group work in the language classroom (an interest he was to return to almost a decade later from a more theoretical perspective – see Long and Porter 1985). Long and his colleagues in Mexico in 1976 set out to explore language learner behaviour in small groups. The word 'explore' is their term, and it is well chosen. They were not trying, in the methodological comparisons tradition, to prove that group work was 'best', nor were they trying to change teacher behaviour. They simply wanted to know if the sorts of claims then being made about group work would stand up to close inspection. They started their paper 'Doing Things with Words – Verbal Interaction in Lockstep and Small Group Classroom Situations' with a statement of the general pedagogic issue.

Anyone concerned with the teaching of English to speakers of other languages will be familiar with the frustration felt by practicing teachers at the apparent inability of their students to transfer knowledge of the target language to situations outside language classrooms. Parallels exist between this problem and the linguistic/communicative competence distinction (Paulston 1975; Allwright 1976; Long 1975). Briefly, most English language programmes and the students who enroll in them have as their (explicit or implicit) aim the acquisition by learners of communicative competence; yet most teachers and textbooks concentrate mainly or exclusively upon grammatical and phonological accuracy in English. (This is not to say that linguistic competence will be unnecessary, simply that it will be insufficient). The problem may be seen, therefore, not as one of lack of transfer, but lack of opportunity to develop inside the classroom some of the skills that will be required outside it.

It has been argued that two obstacles in the way of acquisition by learners of communicative competence are (1) reliance on certain kinds of exercise and drill material, and (2) the most traditional form of classroom organization – the lockstep (Long 1975). Re the first, the majority of textbooks still present the target language in terms of grammatical structures made 'meaningful' by their being 'situationalized.' Widdowson (1972) has pointed out the sterility of an approach which focuses attention on language forms, and ignores ways in which these forms are appropriately used to realize communicative acts, such as commentary, generalization and hypothesis. Manipulation of structures in drills and exercises results typically in the production by students of unrelated grammatically correct *sentences* in a communicative vacuum. In two recent papers, Allwright (1976) and Phillips and Shettlesworth (1976) have gone so far as to doubt the feasibility of eliciting in the classroom the kind of discourse learners will encounter in their target situations so long as the bases of classroom language production are materials originally written for language teaching.

Re classroom organization, it has been suggested that lockstep work sets severe restraints on discourse potential. It is believed to do so through its denial to students of certain options as to roles they may take up and, hence, of the variety of uses to which they may put language – the things, that is, they may do with words. It is claimed that the quality of verbal interaction possible between teacher and student, and student and student, is influenced adversely by such factors as (1) the pressure teachers feel to maintain a rapid pace during student oral work in order to avoid boredom among the learners, and (2) the pressures students feel as a result of what Barnes (1973, p. 19) calls the 'audience effect,' i.e. the inhibitions resulting from having to speak 'publically' in front of a large group of fellow students and the dominating figure of the teacher. One of the results of the pressure on teachers is a tendency for them to limit individual student production to isolated sentences; the audience effect creates in students a need to provide the short, polished 'finished article' in the form of a grammatically correct sentence in which generally truth value and almost always adequacy and appropriacy are hardly considered either by student or teacher.

By way of contrast, small group work, appropriately organized, is believed to provide students with an intimate setting in which the above inhibitions disappear, and in which what Barnes (ibid.) calls 'exploratory' talk may occur. Barnes writes:

> An intimate group allows us to be relatively inexplicit and incoherent, to change direction in the middle of a sentence, to be uncertain and self-contradictory. What we say may not amount to much, but our confidence in our friends allows us to take the first groping steps towards sorting out our thoughts and feelings by putting them into words. I shall call this sort of talk 'exploratory' (1973, p. 19).

Roles open to students are more varied, the very absence of the teacher automatically delegating to them responsibilities, which result in language use of kinds not open to them in lockstep work.

It was to explore the validity of some of these claims in the context of a large-scale special purpose foreign language teaching operation that a study was carried out by members of the Foreign Language Department of the Universidad Autónoma Metropolitana, at its Xochimilco campus in Mexico City. Specifically it was hoped to establish something of the nature of the differences, if any, between the quantity and quality of student language production in classroom learning organized on (1) a lockstep, and (2) a small group basis. By 'quality' was meant not the number of errors or correct language forms produced, but the varieties of things students *did* with language under the two conditions, i.e. what communicative acts of one kind or another they performed with the language they produced. Determining this, it was realized, might usefully involve the application of different systems for the analysis of classroom language, and thereby provide some insights into the potential for this type of research of some of those observational and analytic procedures. As will soon become apparent, it was in fact, the problems of analysis which came to occupy the greater part of the researchers' time and interest.

Of particular interest here is their realization that it might be useful to apply a variety of systematic observational systems. This represented a significant move away from the field's apparent confidence in any one system to suffice for all sorts of data for all purposes, and was of course directly contrary to Fanselow's intentions in producing FOCUS. Theirs seems to have been one of the first studies to attempt to let data and precise observational purposes dictate the terms of the analysis. Others, like Jarvis, Politzer, Nearhoof, and Moskowitz, had devised categories to reflect quite narrowly methodological considerations, while Fanselow had adopted the more abstractly conceptual approach of Bellack in his attempt to be thoroughly comprehensive. Long *et al.* wanted first and foremost an insightful way of exploring their data, and that meant a data- and purposes-driven approach to the analysis. Theirs is an example of the descriptive side of the 'prescriptive/descriptive' distinction, where 'description' did not mean simply painting a representational picture, but something altogether more interesting, because it was motivated by a desire to *understand* classroom interaction.

The next part of their paper described their study and then the various analytical systems they applied to their data. They started with Bellack, moved through Moskowitz's FLint to Fanselow's FOCUS, and then turned to Barnes for help before devising their own 'embryonic' system.

The study

For the purposes of the study, decisions were taken re the task to be carried out in the lockstep and small group situations and as to the nature of the grouping to be used. It seemed relatively unchallenging to compare student language production in anything approaching a 'regimented' drill-type lockstep class with that produced by an unsupervised small group of students. While many important differences would undoubtedly have shown up in a comparison of the language produced in the two conditions, this type of lockstep activity, we knew, was not typical of teachers working in our Department and would anyway have been difficult to replicate in the small group, given the obvious lack of 'teaching' experiences of the students. Secondly, the value of small group work would be tested much more rigorously if the learning task in the lockstep situation were designed to facilitate production of the same kind of communicative use of language as was thought more feasible 'out of lockstep.' With respect to the nature of the grouping it was decided to contrast lockstep work with the most 'extreme' small group attainable, namely the pair. This was because classes at Xochimilco are rarely larger than fifteen students (quite a *small* group in many teaching situations, of course), and removing groups of (say) five students would have left only a 'large small group' in the lockstep conditions. It was also decided to group students according to their own expressed preferences due to the belief that it is the ability to work with chosen classmates which provides the intimacy upon which student confidence in small group work is based (Long 1975, 1976).

Method

Over a two-week period sound recordings were made of four lessons at the intermediate level in which teachers and students discussed the similarities and differences between man and other animals. Specifically, students were asked whether they thought man was fundamentally different from other animals, and were provided with a handout (see Appendix) on which were listed some of the factors they might consider during the discussion. Instructions to teachers prior to the recordings were phrased in such a way as to avoid indicating any particular role *they* should adopt, focusing instead on what it was required that the *students* do (discuss) during the period to be recorded. It was hoped thereby not to influence the degree to which they, the teachers, 'led' or 'organized' the ensuing verbal interaction. Questions from the four teachers relating in any way to their teaching roles were, quite simply, evaded. They were asked to handle the lesson in any way they liked, but not to use group work.

Sound recordings were made of a total of forty minutes per class. During the first ten minutes teachers taught lockstep. At the end of this first period students were asked to choose a partner with whom they would like to work should they be chosen to do so. A pair of students was then chosen at random, and these students went into a room adjoining the main classroom for the second period of ten minutes. They were recorded 'continuing the discussion' while the teacher was recorded doing the same with the remaining students, still functioning as one group. At the end of the second period of ten minutes the pair rejoined the full class for a final ten minute recording of a lockstep continuation of the same discussion. The tapes were transcribed, and our subsequent analysis used the original recordings or transcriptions of them, as appropriate.

Analysis of the data – (1) the application of existing coding systems.

Two existing classroom interaction analysis coding systems were applied to parts of our data. The first, Bellack's system, (Bellack *et al.* 1966) was used to code the four types of pedagogical moves which occur in the classroom. These are: Structuring, Soliciting, Reacting and Responding. The structuring move as defined by Bellack is an initiatory move; it sets the context for classroom behaviour by launching or halting – excluding interaction between teacher and pupil. An example of the move is utterance 74.

74 T: For example, uh you have a chimpanzee in a labyrinth. OK? And suppose . . . this labyrinth has a rule that you've got to turn right always. If you turn left, it's no good. OK? You've got to turn right to find the food . . . We will think that all labyrinths, labyrinths in general . . .

The soliciting move is designed to elicit a verbal response, to encourage persons addressed to attend to something or to elicit a physical response. All questions are solicitations, as are commands, imperatives and requests. The responding moves bear a reciprocal relation to soliciting moves and occur only in relation to them. Utterances 104 and 105 are examples of a soliciting move followed by a responding move:

104 T: Do you know anything about elephants?
105 S: They are big.

These utterances are followed by two reacting moves. The students and teacher laugh, and following this the teacher says: 'They say they have a very good memory.' Thus, a reacting move is occasioned by a structuring, soliciting, responding or a prior reacting move, but is not directly elicited by them.

Using Bellack's system to record the types of frequency of moves and the sequence in which they occurred enabled us to calculate the percentage of student moves made during the class period and the distribution of the student responses among the four categories. It was found that, in Group I, during the 30 minute segment of lockstep teaching, students made 183 moves out of a total of 262, i.e. they made 69.8 per cent of the total number of moves. Further analysis of the frequencies of types of moves made by the students showed that 0.5 per cent of the student moves were structuring moves (20 moves), 33.3 per cent were responding moves (61 moves) and 55.2 per cent were reacting moves (101 moves). The percentage of student moves in Group I was much higher than in the classes studied by Bellack, where the median percentage of student moves in all classes was 38.2. This presumably reflects the teacher's style, the task and teaching situation.

The second instrument used was the Moskowitz system, (Moskowitz 1976), which is an adaptation of the Flanders system of Interaction Analysis for the foreign language classroom (Flanders 1970). The Moskowitz system consists of twelve categories; seven designate teacher behaviour, two are for student behaviour, and the last three are for silence, confusion and laughter. All student utterances are coded as category 8, Student talk – specific, or category 9, Student talk – open-ended or initiated.

One important type of information concerning student participation which can be obtained from this system is the amount of total student participation and the degree to which this participation is controlled by the teacher. For example, performing a matrix analysis on the data from Group I showed that student talk accounted for 51.8% of the total talk, and that 74.7% of the total student talk was coded as category 9, open-ended or initiated utterances. Again, as with the high incidence of student moves, the high incidence of category 9 also presumably reflects the type of task and the language teaching situation as well as the teacher's style.

Discussion – the development of an embryonic category system
Because there are only two categories in the Moskowitz system which describe student utterances, there are limitations on the type of information which can be obtained concerning the quality of student utterances in terms, e.g., of their rhetorical functions. This is a characteristic of several other systems of analysis for foreign language classrooms (e.g. Wragg 1971; Nearhoof 1969 [this volume Chapter 2]; Jarvis 1968 [this volume Chapter 1]). The limitation is more pronounced when dealing with student-student interaction. Consider the following series of student utterances from the middle ten minute period of lockstep work in group one:

110 SS: History.
111 T: History. How?
112 S4: To write.
113 S5: Yeah, we have monuments, we have some authors, we have –
114 S2: Films.
115 S1: Communications.
116 S5: – some some different things that that make us remember what happened.
117 S1: We we can communicate each other, yeah? And ...
118 S4: Yes, that's that's how the other uh characteristics come in in communication to use the other language.
119 S1: Mm hum.

Student participation in the above fragment would be coded 9-10-9-10, etc. using Moskowitz's system even though elements of the interaction are quite different in terms of the types of thing students are *doing* with the utterances they produce. In this sequence there are examples of students agreeing, providing information and inducing. If this had been teacher-student interaction, it would have been possible to differentiate and code the teacher utterances as agreeing or accepting ideas (categories 2 and 3) and providing information (category 5). However, no such provision for differentiating student responses of this type exists in the present system.

A third system for interaction analysis, developed by John Fanselow, called FOCUS (Foci for Observing Communications Used in Settings) [this volume, pp. 127–151], gives us more detailed information about student behaviour because categories can be applied to both teacher and student and must be coded accordingly. FOCUS also provides more detailed categories for types of student utterances. For example, under the heading of *use*, student performance of the following types of utterances can be coded:

> Uses
> attend
>
> characterize
> differentiate
> evaluate
> examine
> illustrate
> label
>
> present
>
> relate
> explain
> interpret
>
> re-present
> combine
> repeat
> substitute
> transform

(From Fanselow 1976)

Fanselow writes, '. . . if we accept the fact that one goal of language learning is to be able to use mediums in a variety of ways – as humans do in ordinary discourse – then the way mediums are used becomes an important characteristic of communications to note.' (ibid. 3). However, the two subcategories of relate – explain and interpret – are rather broad. Other types of relationships exist such as induce, deduce, hypothesize, etc. It might be useful to show these. In addition, although Fanselow does deal with communicative functions such as differentiate or explain, he does so primarily to describe the continuity of discourse; many of the categories are too big to discern whether the students' knowledge of the language allows them to cope with a wider and finer range of communicative functions or enables them to organize them coherently in logical terms. For example, 'explain' may include a variety of rhetorical acts at a lower level.

Because we were interested in what *acts* our students were performing when they spoke within the context of the flow of discourse, because, that is, we wanted additional information to that we could obtain by applying the systems known to us for analysing verbal interaction in foreign language classrooms, we looked to two other attempts at analysing verbal interaction in educational settings, those of Sinclair's team at Birmingham, and Barnes and Todd at Leeds. Both studied discourse in so-called 'content' subjects. The Birmingham research has produced a tentative model for discourse (Sinclair and Coulthard 1975) as well as a system for analysing teacher-directed classroom interaction. The latter has been applied successfully, but the authors note:

> (W)hat it cannot handle, and of course was not designed to handle, is pupil/pupil interaction in project work, discussion groups, or the playground. (ibid. 6).

The work at Leeds, which had grown out of an earlier small-scale study (Barnes 1969), had as its underlying purpose:

> to examine the relationship between short-term, small-scale aspects of the social interaction of small groups and the cognitive strategies generated in the course of the interaction. ... Small groups were chosen in order to obtain as much information as possible about the learning strategies of children in the absence of a teacher. (Barnes and Todd 1975)

Subjects were thirteen-year-old children of average intelligence, and the investigators particularly wanted to establish the ways in which they used strategies in dialogue which encouraged or impeded hypothetico-deductive thinking. They were interested, in other words, in a setting in which children *talk to learn*, whereas we wanted to know what facilities small group interaction provided for students to talk to *learn to speak*, i.e. to learn how to *use* a foreign language.

Accordingly, while interested in trying out Barnes and Todd's categories in the foreign language setting, we took over only those which intuitively seemed appropriate to our needs, basically ones grouped by them under 'logical process' and 'social skills.' Even then, categories found under 'social skills' in our embryonic system, such as 'student competes for the floor' (category S1), 'student interrupts' (S2) or 'student contradicts' (S4), which come straight from Barnes and Todd's work, interested us as ends in themselves rather than means to an end. For example, the worker in foreign language teaching will want to recognize use of an interrupting strategy when he sees one, but will not be interested in what is being gained by its use in terms of learning, other than language learning.

The following are our categories used in the second analysis of our data.

Embryonic Category System (ECS)

1. *Pedagogical moves*

P.1. Student initiates discussion.

P.2. Student focuses discussion.

P.3. Student summarizes and completes a sequence/ends discussion or section of discussion.

P.4. Student moves conversation on to a new topic.

P.5. Student qualifies another person's contribution.

P.6. Student implicity accepts a qualification.

P.7. Student extends a previous contribution of his own or of others.

P.8. Student reformulates own or other's previous assertion.

P.9. Student expresses understanding.

P.10. Student provides an example.

P.11. Student uses evidence to challenge an assertion.

P.12. Student asks for information.

P.13. Student asks for information about the target language.

P.14. Student gives information on request.

P.15. Student gives information about the target language.

P.16 Student asks for clarification.

P.17. Student clarifies.

2. *Social skills*

S.1. Student competes for the floor.

S.2. Student interrupts.

S.3. Student completes other's unfinished utterance.

S.4. Student contradicts.

S.5. Student invites participation by other students.

S.6. Student explicity expresses agreement.

S.7. Student makes explicit reference to other's contribution.

S.8. Student encourages other.

S.9. Student explicitly supports other's assertion with evidence.

S.10. Student jokes.

S.11. Student avoids discussion.

S.12. Student repeats.

S.13. Student confirms.

3. *Rhetorical acts*
R.1.   Student predicts.
R.2.   Student hypothesizes.
R.3.   Student makes an observation.
R.4.   Student deduces.
R.5.   Student induces.
R.6.   Student states generalization.
R.7.   Student defines.
R.8.   Student negates.
R.9.   Student expresses cause and effect relationship.
R.10.   Student exemplifies.
R.11.   Student identifies.
R.12.   Student categorizes.
R.13.   Student classifies.
R.14.   Student concludes.
.
.
.

X Confusion/inaudible tape.

The dots under 'rhetorical acts' are there to recognize that this list is far from complete; acts listed so far are simply those we found we needed to categorize things in this area which students did in the lessons we analysed.

Before illustrating the application of the categories in ECS, it is important to note that, while we have spoken of adopting some of Barnes and Todd's categories, they in fact abandoned their original plan to attempt to categorize in this way. They did so firstly because utterances in free-flowing talk often realize more than one kind of act at the same time. Secondly, 'meanings' are frequently constructed over quite lengthy *cycles* of utterances, which are difficult to isolate and dependent on:

> the interaction between utterances, and the speaker-hearer's intentions for, and interpretation, of these utterances. (ibid. 16–17)

Thirdly, meanings hidden in the interaction, which it is the purpose of discourse analysis to reveal, are fluid and changing, and may have one value for a participant during the interaction and another in the observer's intuitive interpretation of them during subsequent analysis of that interaction. Fourthly, it was difficult to ascertain whether linguistic features which tended to appear in stretches of discourse where what Barnes and Todd call 'knowledge-making' seemed to be occurring were really playing an important role in that knowledge-making.

While recognizing as very real the difficulties of which Barnes and Todd write, we have persevered with our attempts at categorization for a variety of reasons. Firstly, as they implicitly recognize, it is possible to code individual utterances more than once. Secondly, we believe it may prove possible to pin down the larger 'meaningful' cycles, at least insofar as meanings explicitly or implicitly stated in the discourse are concerned, as we discuss below. Thirdly, in the foreign language setting we are not, as we said earlier, necessarily interested in tying linguistic features to the learning of 'content', but rather with evidence of the existence of those features in the students' foreign language repertoire and their use in the performance of speech acts. Fourthly, an ability to categorize data is useful for many research and most teacher-training applications of whatever category instrument we might develop.

For the purpose of exemplifying the application of our system to the data we will now look (in an excerpt from transcript 1), at a stretch of continuous discourse produced by a pair of students working in the absence of a teacher. The pair began like this:

Transcript I

234 S3: OK. So what do you think about
creativity?   P1,S5.

235 S9: Uh well I think like Fanny (S7),/but
I think it the same because um I
think have ability to to mind and do
things . . .   P14,S7/P5.

236 S3: Um I {   } do you agree what
uh about the creatures have
creativity?   P16,S5.

237 S9: Uh no. Last uh course I was uh six
uh course seven BEFAS* six . . .   S11.

238 S3: Mm hum.   S8.

239 S9: and we don't uh we don't see that.   S11.

240 S3: Yes,/I don't think the creatures have
creativity/because if they would have
creativity, they all the they will
changing his his way to do the   S1/R2/R1/
things,/and they every year are doing
the same the same the same./So I
don't think it's creativity./And the   R3/R14/
man all the years and even all day he
is changing his way to act and his   R3/P4,S5.
way to build and everything and um
um . . . Do you think the agriculture
is a chara- a main characteristic?

241 S9: Um. Yes./ Because um the animals
don't um um the animals um don't
change the the environment of the
earth um . . .   P14/P10,R3.

242 S3: Here we have the problem. What
        what we understand what is the
        meaning of agriculture?/It's only like
        the man does that he takes he . . .
        little things and put general, no, like
        {   } can,/ or it's uh agriculture   P2/R2/R2
        can be well an animal c- uh who
        practice ag-agriculture can be an   R14/P14,S5.
        animal that goes over the trees and
        to eat? . . ./I think these of the
        animals wouldn't agriculture./ Do you
        think it's agriculture?
243 S9: Um no, I don't./Um what um what's
        agriculture for you?   P14, S6/P16,S5.
244 S3: Agriculture?/I think it's um a special
        manner to 'sembrar'**?   S12/P14,R7
245 S9: {   }   X.
246 S3: a special manner to 'sembrar' and
        after that that we can have this
        {   } but not in a natural way uh
        not uh not in a in a natural way this   P7, R7/P10,R3.
        . . ./the man does the man does that
        the there will be vegetables and
        fruits in his {   } not not like in
        the mountains.
247 S9: And uh or artificial by artificial
        ways . . .   P9,S13.
248 S3: Um, yes.   S13.

* BEFAS = acronym for *Basic English for Academic Study*. This course is
          used at the elementary and early intermediate levels by students
          at our University's Xochimilco campus.
** sembrar = Spanish for 'sow'.

Intervention 234 shows student 3 simultaneously initiating the
discussion and inviting participation by her partner. The utterance
is, therefore, coded twice, as P1,S5. Communication 235 is an
example of a student giving information when requested to do so,
making explicit reference to another's contribution (intervention 51
on the complete transcript), followed by a qualification of the ideas
expressed in that contribution, and so is coded as P14, S7/P5. Two
category levels referring to the same utterance are separated by a
comma; P1, S5. Where different parts of an intervention realize
different acts of various kinds, those acts are coded in sequence,
and the category labels separated by a diagonal stroke: P5/S7.
Communication 236 has student 3 asking for clarification of student
9's previous contribution, and is again simultaneously an invitation
for her partner to participate. It is coded as P16,S5. In 237 student

9 somewhat desperately attempts to explain why she is having difficulty contributing namely because she has only recently been promoted from a lower-level course. Her intervention is coded as S11, student avoids discussion. At 238 her partner encourages her with a commiserating 'Mm hum', and is coded S8, student encourages. And so on.

Analysis of the data – (2) the application of ECS

At the time of writing ECS has been applied to the middle ten minute periods of lockstep work in two of our classes and to the two corresponding ten minute periods of pairwork. Coding of each transcript was carried out by the four members of the investigating team working as a group to reach consensus. Modifications to categories were made and new ones added as and when this was found necessary in order to handle the data.

Talk by each of twenty-six students in the data analysed was coded under pedagogical moves, social skills and rhetorical acts and quantified in two sections, talk produced in the lockstep and small group conditions. For each student scores were then computed of totals of pedagogical moves, social skills, rhetorical acts and total moves (the sum of the first three scores), and the same was done for the *variety* of pedagogical moves, social skills, rhetorical acts and the sum of these. In either the lockstep or small group condition, for example, Student X may have realized 12 pedagogical moves in ten minutes of class time, including 6 different types of moves, 12 social skills, including 7 different types of skills, and 11 rhetorical acts, including 5 different types of acts altogether. Thus, eight scores for each student were available for the final statistical analysis.

The Kolmogorov-Smirnov test for two samples was applied, using the formula for approximation to chi-squared developed by Goodman (1954). It was found that the *quantities* of pedagogical moves, social skills, rhetorical acts and total numbers of moves performed by students working in the small group condition were significantly higher ($p < .01$, $p < .05$, $p < .05$ and $p < .01$ respectively) than those by students in the lockstep condition. *Variety* of pedagogical moves and social skills and the total varieties of moves were also significantly greater (all at the $p < .01$ level) in the small group condition. The variety of rhetorical acts performed by students in the small group condition was also greater than that in the lockstep condition, but the difference was just short of significant at the .05 level.

Their account leaves the reader in no doubt about the problems and the pitfalls of the struggle to find categories capable of doing justice to the complexities of the data. Here we find the same sort of concern for interpretation problems as we found in Bailey. In fact their work neatly reinforced Bailey's concerns about 'interaction analysis', especially when we consider that Long *et al.* had not been operating under the three second time constraint characteristic of the Flanders tradition, but had had infinitely replayable sound recordings to work from.

Long *et al.* ended their paper with a judiciously cautious and brief statement of their preliminary findings, and then a much more substantial further discussion of their 'Embryonic Category System'.

Discussion – (a) the experimental findings

Nothing conclusive can be stated on the basis of the findings so far, given that they reflect analyses of only a part of the data. However, a clear trend in the results is emerging which, if continued, will provide strong support for our initial hypotheses as to the positive effects on quantity and quality of language production of having students work in small groups as opposed to a lockstep classroom setting. The greater *quantity* of acts of different kinds performed by students in the small group condition is presumably partly a function of greater opportunity, i.e. of the greater number of turns available to the members of a small group for speaking, and, hence, for doing something to move the discourse on. Nevertheless, this advantage in terms of language practice possible is something we often forget as teachers. So many language-learning activities carried out by teacher-led classes of students could just as easily be performed by students working in small groups, with greater opportunity for each individual to practice rather than merely to observe.

More interesting is the preliminary finding that students working on the same discussion task and the language going with it do a significantly greater *variety* of things with language when working with one other student than with a 'large' group of fellow students and with their teacher leading the discussion. It is worth emphasizing the fact that these results were obtained under conditions not at all favorable to our ideas, i.e. with a smaller than usual number of students (eleven) in the lockstep condition, during work on a task and with materials calculated to lead to a wider variety of communicative language used than that found in many standard EFL texts, and with discussion led by teachers who, based on our experience of observing and training foreign language teachers, we would judge to be unusually 'non-interfering' (see Long and Castaños 1976) and non-authoritarian, i.e. not of the type who tend to dominate the leading and structuring of classroom discussion. Despite these 'unfavorable' lockstep climates (unfavorable from the point of view of our experiments, that is), students working in the absence of their teacher in a group of two engaged in language practice which was more varied in communicative values as measured along at least two dimensions. Assuming the later analyses confirm our present results, it will remain to be established, among other factors, whether these findings hold good in larger small groups, with students at beginning and advanced levels of proficiency in the target language and over different types of learning tasks, and whether language practice with something approaching the characteristics of that found in the small group condition can be achieved in large groups of students without the teacher's presence or in small groups with the teacher present.

Discussion – (b) ECS

At this point a discussion of some of the Embryonic Category System's obvious limitations is appropriate. Firstly, while we are more confident about the information being provided by the categories in our 'pedagogical moves' and 'social skills' list, we are under no illusions as to the worth of our 'rhetorical acts.' Our analysis at this level is undoubtedly extremely superficial. Indeed, by atomizing the data and attaching one label to one or more utterances, as exemplified in the above examples of coding, we are in danger of losing the hidden meanings over *cycles* in the discourse of which Barnes and Todd warn. For example, we code the utterance:

... and they every year are doing the same the same the same ... in intervention 240, as a student making an observation (R3), yet it is clear that in doing so she is also starting a generalization. Furthermore, taken together, it and several of the utterances in 240 combine to exemplify other 'macro' rhetorical acts not coded by us. In other words, intervention 240 as a whole is more than the sum of the 'parts' we distinguished. Instead of the simple one-to-one coding we have described, intervention 240 could be analysed something as follows:

Having already decided that they are going to micro-classify according to + or − creativity:

234: *OK. So what do you think about creativity?*

the pair of students now divided the problem into two parts: 'the creatures,' and 'the man.' Next, the analysis of the first part, 'the creatures,' is introduced by advancing the conclusion, in the form of a hypothesis, that creatures are − creative.

'I don't think the creatures have creativity.'

The hypothesis is now proved:

'I don't think the creatures have creativity because . . .,'

and the conclusion confirmed:

'So *I don't think it's creativity.'*

The proof has 3 steps:

1. Animals can only be + or − creative.
2. Animals are not + creative.
3. Therefore, they are − creative.

These steps are carried out in the following way:

The hypothesis that animals are − creative is restated as animals having creativity, i.e. that they are + creative (2). Step (1) is performed implicitly by the order of the starting and reformulating of the hypothesis. The proof that animals are not + creative is carried out not by providing direct evidence but by showing the logical implications of the hypothesis:

'because if they would have creativity, they all the they will changing his his way to do the things.'

and then comparing these against evidence,

'. . . *and* . . .'

making the comparison, with the evidence being provided in the form of the observation:

'. . . *(and) they every year are doing the same the same the same.'*

The analysis of the second part of the problem is done in a similar way, except that all the steps that bar 'comparison against evidence' are ellipted:

'*And the man*' (comparison introduced)

'*all the years and even all day he is changing his way to act and his way to build and everything* . . .'

The students are, of course, working on the assumption that creativity has already been defined as 'the ability to change things.' For this reason, during the statement of the implications and the comparison of the evidence, no new opinions as to the meaning of creativity are introduced; the existing information, only, is processed. If new opinions had been introduced, the analysis would have been more complex. The establishing of the two categories, + and − creative, is implicit and probably suggested by the materials (see Appendix), as was mentioned earlier.

In summary, our categories capture 'micro' rhetorical acts. At a succession of ever higher levels intervention 240 shows students in the pair using the foreign language to perform several of them (predicting, stating a generalization, etc.) in the setting up of hypotheses for the purpose of classifying man and other animals into a set of previously established categories. In order to pick up this sort of information work is needed establishing some sort of *hierarchy* or identifying other relationships among rhetorical acts. (See Castaños 1976.)

Some other obvious weaknesses of our embryonic system are that as yet its categories have not been operationally defined, and it lacks finiteness, exhaustiveness and objectivity. Operational definitions for the categories should not prove too great a problem; there are borderline cases, of course, but our experience at coding so far suggests there are no serious cases of overlap. Finiteness is the biggest problem: how many rhetorical acts are there? The question of exhaustiveness is related to this; accounting for all the data does not mean much unless one knows both that the categories are not netting different species of fish, or missing bigger fish altogether through constituting too fine a mesh. As for objectivity, like all systems for analysing classroom interaction, our categories are subjective, and classification of language into them intuitive. One may reasonably suppose that a teacher's or student's coughing is not important and so does not justify having a category to record it, but where does one draw the line? What most present systems need is work correlating incidence of the behaviors they categorize – whatever kind of behaviors they may be – with student learning.

This last point is one among several which have led Gage (1963) and, more recently, Neujahr (1972), among others, to criticize the proliferation and lack of productivity of category systems of this kind, and of the research done with them. With our embryonic system we risk adding to the confusion. However, if communicative competence is accepted as talking about the realizing of rhetorical acts in situated discourse, then we think we are at least taking a step in a direction which has been largely ignored in the past. We feel we need something like this to get at the features of verbal interaction in foreign language classrooms which are relevant to our students' communicative needs outside them.

Appendix

Man and other animals – same or different?
Man's abilities are great and varied. Some people find it difficult to accept that he is an animal – a member of the species, *homo sapiens*. Even if he is an animal, some people say he is completely different from other animals.

Consider the following list. Are they characteristic of man, of other animals, or both?
intelligence
complex thinking
creativity
bipedal locomotion and upright posture*
the ability to learn from experience
communication – the use of language – to regulate social behavior
the use of tools**

the building of shelters***
the practice of agriculture
distinguishing between love and sex
the use of education
the use of symbols
job specialization
the use of money as a system of exchange
the possession of emotions
thinking about past and future actions
the ability to control the environment
the ability to adapt to the environment

Do you think man is fundamentally different from other animals?

* *upright posture = una postura vertical*
** *tools = herramientas*
*** *shelters = refugios*

Long *et al.*'s struggle with their data presents a strong contrast to the previous research studies in this volume. It also presents further evidence of the wisdom of the retreat from immediate practical concerns for the sake of concentrating on the task of trying to develop an understanding of classroom interaction.

Two points remain to be made before we move on to this chapter's third alternative to Flanders. Firstly, Long *et al.* drew attention to a problem not so far mentioned in this volume, that category systems seemed to be proliferating beyond the bounds of reason. Fanselow had tried to 'stop the rot' by devising an all-purpose system, but it seems reasonable to suggest now that Long *et al.*'s study demonstrated clearly that a lot more thought needed to be put into category systems if they were to become at all adequate to researchers' purposes. Using old-established systems just to avoid the proliferation problem was not a viable strategy. Secondly, Long *et al.*, having broken new ground in their concern for analytical adequacy, and thus for a priority on understanding, reminded their readers in their penultimate paragraph that they too were concerned ultimately with learner achievement. The retreat was to be, in principle and in practice (see Long's subsequent work), a temporary one.

It has perhaps struck the reader that several of the papers in this volume have been 'progress' reports rather than 'final' ones. It does seem to have been characteristic of the times that such interim reports were considered publishable, presumably because of their news value as 'hot off the press' items. It seems also to have been characteristic of the times that rarely were these progress reports followed up by publication of the final ones, if such were ever produced, an indication perhaps of the speed, not to say haste, with which the field was moving.

3 The 'conversational analysis' perspective

While Fanselow had been building on Bellack's perception of classroom interaction as a game with pre-determined 'moves', and Long had been building on Barnes' perception of it more as a negotiation of a learning event, the ethnomethodologists had been laying the foundations for another alternative to Flanders in their work on the analysis of conversation. They looked at conversational interaction as 'socially constructed', by participants following a complex set of 'rules' of which they were not themselves aware, to accomplish something remarkably orderly. Unlike the Sinclair team, who had chosen to look at classroom interaction because it promised to be amenable to research, the ethnomethodologists chose to look at conversational interaction for the very different reason that it was something very complex that had hitherto been taken for granted, not only by researchers, but also, and perhaps more importantly, by participants. Very conscious of the problems of interpretation posed by other approaches, the ethnomethodologists began with what might have appeared to be less problematic, the organization of the distribution of talk in conversation. In 1974 Sacks, Schegloff, and Jefferson published their very influential paper 'A Simplest Systematics for the Organisation of Turn-Taking in Conversation'. Also in 1974, Mehan published 'Accomplishing Classroom Lessons', which showed how the ethnomethodological view of interaction could be applied to instruction. My own work at the time, prompted by Mehan's example but concerned more with turn-taking, started as had Long *et al.*'s with a pedagogic issue, the distribution of classroom talk. Having begun to investigate the treatment of error in oral work (Allwright 1975, see Chapter 5 this volume) I had somewhat rapidly moved on (in the manner described at the end of the previous section) because that investigation, combined with the insights culled from Mehan, had forced me to the conclusion that whatever happened in the classroom was indeed a co-production, and therefore that it no longer made sense to look at classroom interaction as if it was only the teacher's behaviour that mattered (a crude over-simplification of the Flanders tradition, but not grossly unfair to it). I was therefore interested in how learners accomplished their half of the business of distributing talk, especially in a situation where the teacher was dedicated to managing that distribution as evenly as possible across the class participants. I was also intrigued by the possibilities, similarly suggested by Mehan, of looking in detail at a few learners, rather than following the Flanders tradition of treating learners as an undifferentiated mass. My paper, 'Turns, Topics and Tasks: Patterns of Participation in Language Learning and Teaching' (published in 1980), began with a brief introduction to such ideas and to my overall conceptualization of classroom language instruction.

> Learners are interesting, at least as interesting as teachers, because they are the people who do whatever learning gets done, whether it is because of or in spite of the teacher. We have studied teachers, though, because teachers are commonly held responsible for 'producing learning.' This makes sense, clearly, when we consider the time, effort, and money we spend training people to teach. But it also seems sensible to suggest that, since it is learners who do the learning, we should take a close look at what the learners actually do. Curiously the case-study approach, so central to the methodological baggage of first and second language acquisition researchers, has not, typically, been thought sensible for learners in class. The result is that what we know about second language acquisition is perhaps of limited relevance to language teaching and classroom learning. Of course, classroom language learning has been studied, and sometimes with explicit reference to individual differences among learners (Chastain 1969; Politzer 1970a). Also, a considerable research effort has been devoted to isolating the key characteristics of 'good' learners (see Rubin 1975; Naiman *et al.* 1977). But case studies of the classroom behavior of particular learners do seem to have been neglected. This paper aims to establish the potential fruitfulness of the case-study approach as applied to the language classroom. It will put such an approach in the context of a general conceptual framework for language teaching and learning in classrooms, and show how this framework can be developed into a system for the analysis of recorded classroom data, which can then be used for the isolation of 'interesting' subjects for a detailed case study. In this way the resulting case studies will fit into a much wider research program for investigating language teaching and learning.
>
> The central concern here is the nature of any particular learner's participation in whatever happens in the classroom. For many years teachers have been urged to secure the active participation of all learners at all times, in the belief that this is a key variable. More recently the term 'involvement' has perhaps seemed more appropriate as writers have stressed the personal investment that characterizes a 'good' receptive learning situation (Stevick 1976;

see also Jakobovits and Gordon 1974). Clearly a simple approach to the notion of 'active participation' will no longer suffice. It is not a straightforward quantitative matter, but a highly complex qualitative one. Nevertheless, as I shall hope to show, it is amenable, in the early stages of a case-study analysis, to a quantitative approach. We assume, of course, that learners are not wholly under the control of the teacher, that they have some freedom concerning the nature and extent of their participation in class. Teachers may have definite plans for any particular learner, but learners are in some sort of bargaining position. In short, the management of participation, by teachers and by learners, is a negotiated process, and potentially a crucially important one. Given a teacher with the declared aim of securing an even distribution of participation, some learners will negotiate for more than their 'fair' share, others for 'less', some consciously, some unconsciously. The situation is well summed up in Mehan's (1974) phrase 'accomplishing classroom lessons.'

Such classroom negotiations, however, are not just about the amount of public work any one learner is prepared to perform. They are directly or indirectly concerned, potentially at least, with all aspects of the management of learning. To understand the process of participation, therefore, we need a framework for the understanding of the whole of language teaching and learning. It is to this general conceptual background that we now turn.

A macro-analysis of language teaching and learning[1]

At an extreme level of generality, what happens in language classrooms can be described in terms of three basic elements:
1. *Samples*, instances of the target language, in isolation or in use.
2. *Guidance*, instances of communication concerning the nature of the target language.
3. *Management activities*, aimed at ensuring the profitable occurrence of (1) and (2).

These are not mutually exclusive elements, because any instances of 'guidance' or 'management activities' provided in the target language simultaneously provide samples of that language. Another point to make at this early stage is that this three-element analysis does not distinguish between teachers and learners. All may provide samples, offer guidance, and contribute to the management of the occurrence of samples and guidance.

1. The macro-analysis will be described as briefly as possible, and the interested reader is therefore referred to an earlier paper (Allwright 1975b) for a fuller discussion.

These three elements are held to vary in themselves, and in relation to each other, in four ways:

A. Their *relative proportion* (most easily measured in terms of time, but not necessarily *best* measured in that way).

B. Their *distribution* between teacher and learners, and among the individual learners.

C. Their *sequencing*.

D. The *language* used, in terms of *target* or *other*.

Already this macro-analysis suggests a substantial research program. The present research is just a first step. It is concerned with all three elements but focuses on point B of their interrelationship. The three elements themselves clearly invite further analysis, and what follows is only a rough sketch to suggest the general background involved.

Samples of the target language are clearly essential to language learning but not sufficient in themselves (unless they simultaneously constitute guidance, of course). For example, one would not, as a beginner, expect to learn very much of a language merely from listening to monologues on the radio. A further point to be made about 'samples' is that only some will be intended, by their producers, as 'models' of the target language, but that any may be so interpreted by any other participant or participants. This point becomes particularly important for research on the treatment of error (Allwright 1975a [this volume Chapter 5]).

Guidance is also a clearly essential element, though again not sufficient (although of course guidance *in* the target language will necessarily provide samples *of* it). Guidance is a conveniently vague term but analysable into three imaginably distinct categories.

G1. The realm of rules and explanations, at any linguistic level, of talking about the language, its system, and its use.

G2. The realm of hints and cues rather than rules or explanations, of activities (like pointing to a word on the blackboard, at one extreme, to setting up a pattern drill at the other) that draw attention to criterial features of the target language. This is the realm of procedures to aid induction, in contrast to G1's emphasis on 'telling' and deduction.

G3. The realm of quality judgments, straightforward 'knowledge of results' (e.g., 'Fine,' 'Good,' 'Better,' 'Not quite').

Again the point should be made that it is not only the teacher who may provide 'guidance' although traditionally this is seen to be exclusively the teacher's business.

Management activities are perhaps not even necessary, let alone sufficient, for language learning, given the success first language acquirers are agreed to have, usually, with no one managing the business for them. It could be argued that, in fact, this is a misguided view of informal language acquisition, but in any case it seems clear that, in a classroom situation, someone needs to do something to ensure the occurrence of 'samples' and of 'guidance.' This is what distinguishes formal from informal learning situations, and it would be foolish, no doubt, to try to ignore that distinction.[2]

The question arises: 'How can an analysis at such a level of generality be made operational as the way into a case-study approach to language learning?' To answer this question, we move to the idea of a turn-taking analysis of language classes. This will clearly relate to the problem of the distribution of the three elements between teacher and learners, and among the individual learners.

The conceptualization outlined above had the status in my own thinking of a 'way of looking at' instruction rather than a theory about it. As such it remained, with subsequent modifications (see Allwright 1984), broadly helpful. It was intended to break with the Flanders tradition partly by having nothing to say about teacher effectiveness, and by instead motivating research aimed at 'illuminating' classroom language instruction, at throwing light on the innumerable puzzles that beset teachers thoughtful about what they are doing. My paper continued with my own first attempt at a workable system of analysis for turn taking.

A turn-taking analysis of classroom behavior

The number of systems produced for the analysis of classroom behavior is embarrassingly large, and any proposal to add to that number should be treated with caution if not with downright skepticism, but turn-taking studies are still in their infancy (still at the embryonic stage with respect to language classroom research), and the following system is therefore presented with some confidence that it is not entirely superfluous.[3]

The following analytical categories have been found useful and usable to date:

1. *Turn getting*
1. *Accept*   Respond to a personal solicit.

2. The question of the nature and degree of teacher control over the occurrence of 'samples' and of 'guidance' is clearly a quite separate issue. (See Allwright 1976.)
3. Other systems may record the information necessary for a turn-taking analysis, but typically they treat the learners as if they were just one person, and in any case offer too indirect a route to turn taking to be methodologically attractive.

2. *Steal*   Respond to a personal solicit made to another.
3. *Take*   Respond to a general solicit (e.g. a question addressed to the whole class).
4. *Take*   Take an unsolicited turn, when a turn is available – 'discourse maintenance.'
5. *Make*   Make an unsolicited turn, during the current speaker's turn, without intent to gain the floor (e.g. comments that indicate one is paying attention).
6. *Make*   Start a turn, during that of the current speaker, with intent to gain the flow (i.e. interrupt, make a takeover bid).
7. *Make*   Take a wholly private turn, at any point in the discourse (e.g. a private rehearsal, for pronunciation practice, of a word spoken by the teacher).
0. *Miss*   Fail to respond to a personal solicit, within whatever time is allowed by the interlocutor(s).[4]

2. *Turn giving*
    Symbol
    –   Fade out and/or give way to an interruption.
    Ø   Make a turn available without making either a personal or a general solicit (e.g. by simply concluding one's utterance with the appropriate terminal intonation markers).
    P   Make a personal solicit (i.e. nominate the next speaker).
    G   Make a general solicit.

These categories are clearly of the high-inference type, which means in practice that the principles of coding are difficult, if not impossible, to specify operationally. The above specifications are only a very weak representation of some underlying criteria that cannot yet be satisfactorily described, and certainly not within the limits of the present paper. The main defense of the use of such high-inference categories must be that, if they are tolerably workable, they capture things that are interesting; whereas low-inference categories, though easy to use and talk about, are liable to capture only uninteresting trivia.

A further point about the categories is that they are equally applicable to verbal and to nonverbal behavior, it being clear, and important to remember, that a turn can, and often will, be taken with a nod of the head and disposed of equally silently but no less explicitly.

The final introductory point to be made is that, like the macro-

4. For a brief discussion of the difficulties surrounding this category, see Allwright 1975a.

analysis already described, there is no attempt to differentiate a priori between the behavior of the teacher and that of the learners. Any differences will therefore emerge from the analysis, rather than be built into it from the outset. This point is important enough for classroom research, where it seems best not to take teacher/learner differences for granted, but crucial for any wider application of the turn-taking analytical system.

It is perhaps worth drawing attention to the discussion in the above extract of my choice of 'high-inference' categories. This constituted an implicit criticism of the Flanders tradition, again, where the requirements of real time coding, inter alia, had prompted the use of what were intended to be relatively easily observable categories (although Bailey had already pointed out that in fact they were not so easily observable at all).

Another point to draw attention to is the deliberate avoidance, in my turn-taking categories, of any built-in distinction between teacher and learners. This was an extremely important departure from the Flanders tradition, and was common to all three of the alternatives presented in this chapter. It was an essential feature of any system designed to be applicable to any and every setting, of course, but it was also motivated by a desire to avoid bringing our pedagogic assumptions to the data, and thus to let the data speak for itself, to tell us whether or not teachers behaved significantly differently from learners.

The next part of the paper described the application of these turn-taking categories to some classroom data. It focused on comparing teacher and learner behaviour in general, and on isolating just one learner for further, more detailed, study.

The turn-taking analysis applied to a university-level ESL class

Two parallel UCLA low-level (33A in the UCLA system) ESL classes were regularly audiotaped for two of their twenty hours of instruction each week for ten weeks.

Table 1 shows a purely numerical summary of turn getting for just one class hour, in the earliest weeks of the course.

The first comment to make concerns the large number of turns unidentified either as to participant or as to turn-getting type or both. Even with the full cooperation of the teacher involved, this seems an inevitable problem with audio-only data, and data collection should preferably be on videotape. Many of the problems of identification occur when several participants respond simultaneously, though not in chorus, to a general solicit. This again seems inevitable, and improved data collection will help but will not remove the problem entirely.

TABLE 1   Turn getting

Turn-getting category	Participant												Totals
	T	S1	S2	S3	S4	S5	S6	S7	S8	S9	S10	S?	
1	18	3	18	8	5	4	7	2	1	3	5	1	75
2	1	—	3	3	—	—	—	—	—	1	—	2	10
3	—	—	6	4	2	2	1	—	—	5	1	38	59
4	160	—	14	6	—	3	—	2	1	6	1	36	229
5	7	1	1	3	1	—	2	—	—	1	—	7	23
6	12	—	1	—	—	—	—	—	—	—	—	—	13
7	—	—	—	1	—	—	—	—	—	—	—	1	2
0	—	—	1	—	—	—	—	—	—	—	—	—	1
?	6	—	3	—	—	1	—	—	—	—	2	62	74
Totals	204	4	47	25	8	10	10	4	2	16	9	147	486

S? = unidentified speaker   ?= uncategorizable turn type

In terms of the categories of the analysis the most striking finding is the preponderance of 4's – discourse maintenance in the absence of a solicit. As one might expect, the great majority of 4's are attributed to the teacher, who has a vastly disproportionate number of turns overall compared with the other participants. The teacher also does almost all the interrupting, and is even among those guilty of turn stealing. Of course, one of the reasons the teacher's figures are so high is the fact that her voice, as a native speaker, was distinctive, and we have probably identified all but a very few of her contributions. The voice of S2 (a student from the USSR, whom we shall call Igor) was not so distinctive, and yet he also has a wholly disproportionate share of the identified turns. This is the starting point for the case-study approach, where one learner stands out as of particular interest. S1 did have a quite distinctive voice, and we are confident that the four turns attributed to her represent fairly the full extent of her participation. She is of interest, also, although the sparseness of the data will make the interpretation problematic.

Table 2 presents the findings of the turn-giving analysis applied to the same class hour.

TABLE 2 Turn giving

Turn-giving category	Participant												
	T	S1	S2	S3	S4	S5	S6	S7	S8	S9	S10	S?	Totals
—	5	—	5	2	1	1	—	—	1	3	—	7	25
Ø	80	4	34	19	7	7	9	4	1	10	8	71	254
P	76	—	8	3	—	1	1	—	—	3	1	2	95
G	75	—	—	—	—	—	—	—	—	—	—	—	75
?	3	—	—	1	—	1	—	—	—	—	—	67	72
Totals	239	4	47	25	8	10	10	4	2	16	9	147	521

The discrepancy between the grand totals of the two tables (486 versus 521) is entirely attributable to the teacher's habit of performing a personal solicit by a set of semantically related (but not perfectly synonymous) questions, rather than by a single one. These were coded separately as solicits, because they could have permitted the respondent to claim as many turns as it took to answer all of them separately or the teacher to insist on a set of separate answers. Learners did not take up this option, however, and did not get punished for it; so it seemed unreasonable to code their unitary responses alongside a series of 'Misses' (0's) to cover the technically unanswered questions. The result is anomalous figures in the tables.

We now see that S2, Igor, seems to follow the general pattern for learners, by disposing of most of his turns without making a solicit of any kind. We can also see that the teacher's turn giving differs radically from that of the learners, in that, as one might expect, it includes a great many solicits addressed to the whole class, almost as many as are addressed to individuals, instead of an overwhelming preponderance of unmarked turn giving. In fact the distribution for the teacher is remarkable even for the central Ø, P, and G categories.

A point that emerges if we compare the two tables is that all the personal solicits from learners, with just one exception, are to the teacher. The exception is, predictably perhaps, to Igor, from his neighbor, but he misses it, and the teacher steals the turn. A picture is built up, then, of a class hour perhaps conversational in tone, given the overwhelming incidence of category 4 and the preponderance of unmarked turn giving, but nevertheless a class hour that was very much teacher-centered in terms of discourse management at least, and a class hour to which one student seems to have made a quite disproportionate contribution.

The turn-taking analyses permit us to test out a whole set of preliminary hypotheses about Igor's participation:

1. *The teacher called on him most? (Category 1)*
   The evidence is certainly consistent with this hypothesis, given that Igor is recorded as having been asked by the teacher to contribute no fewer than eighteen times, as often as the teacher, in fact, and twice as often as any other learner, and only one other learner is recorded as getting more than eighteen turns in any way.

2. *He stole most turns? (Category 2)*
   The evidence is not so convincing, given that stealing was rare, and that Igor's three 'steals' (the largest number for any individual, including the teacher) is equaled by S3.

3. *He responded most frequently to general solicits? (Category 3)*
   The evidence is again consistent with the hypothesis, but not very convincing, for a variety of reasons. First, the numbers are again quite modest. Second, his six responses are rivaled by the five of another student. More important, perhaps, is the problem that, given their nature, responses to general solicits were difficult to identify as to speaker, and so these numbers are relatively unreliable.

4. *He did most discourse maintenance? (Category 4)*
   The evidence here is much more convincing, since Igor's 14 is again (as for category 1) twice that of the nearest other learner (but not to be compared with teacher's 160).

5. *He made the most 'concurrent' comments? (Category 5)*
   Here the evidence is against the hypothesis, because Igor's 1 is exceeded by two other learners as well as by the teacher, but the overall numbers are low.

6. *He interrupted most? (Category 6)*
   Igor is the only learner recorded as having interrupted at all, but his 1 is to be seen against the teacher's 12.

7. *He spoke most to himself? (Category 7)*
   This is a particularly high inference category, especially when one is working from audiotape. Only one 7 was in fact coded, and that not for Igor, so that the evidence is not consistent with the hypothesis.

8. *He missed turns least often? (Category 0)*
   The evidence is numerically weak, given only one 0 is recorded,

but that 0 was attributed to Igor, and so the hypothesis is certainly not confirmed.

9. *He made most solicits? (Categories P and G of turn giving)*

The evidence under this heading would be relevant, if one accepted that asking others to contribute increases the likelihood of oneself being asked subsequently. The rationale for this might be different in different situations, but, in friendly conversation, for example, one might expect that behavior that suggests an interest in others' contributions is indeed likely to bring a reciprocal interest. Whatever the interpretation, the evidence again differentiates Igor clearly from the other learners, with eight recorded solicits (again twice as many as any other learner).

This analysis at the relatively crude level of turn taking enables us to see that Igor's behavior is to be interpreted in terms of a radical departure from the norm only in quantitative terms. The *pattern* of his participation is reasonably similar to that of other learners, but there is more of it under almost all headings. Igor did not get more than his share by stealing from others very often or by interrupting. He got it by being asked more often, by responding more frequently to general solicits, and by taking advantage more often of opportunities for discourse maintenance.

The teacher's behavior, we see, is relatable to that of the learners (although it could be argued that this is simply a product of the crudity of the analysis so far), but distinguished again quantitatively, in the most obvious way, given that the teacher is credited with just under 42 percent of all recorded turns (including those not identified either as to speaker or as to turn type). It is also clear from the tables that the teacher does not respond to any general solicits because only the teacher makes them.

To return to Igor, it is probably obvious that the turn-taking analysis has permitted a descriptive statement of this learner's participation, but hardly an explanatory one. We still have no idea as to *why* Igor should have contributed so frequently, although we do know *how* it happened, in crude terms. To get nearer to an explanatory account, we need to move back to the macro-analysis outlined above, from which a topic analysis has been developed.

Of particular interest in the above extract is the drawing of a distinction between 'description' and 'explanation'. While Long *et al.* had been struggling with the problem of even *representing* their data adequately, the focus here was on trying to *account* for data, to understand why it was as it was. That meant going beyond turn taking into even more problematic areas.

A topic analysis of classroom turn-taking behavior

One might expect that turn-taking behavior would be sensibly related to topic, such that some learners might work for a larger share of contributions where the language is being systematically practiced, others when it is being discussed, and others when it is being used to discuss, or do, something else entirely. Learners' behavior might be expected to vary from lesson to lesson, but one would not be surprised, perhaps, to see regularities emerge in a longitudinal study. A topic analysis, therefore might offer the beginnings of an explanatory account for turn-taking behavior.

The macro-analysis presented above, however, is not operational as it stands. To make it operational, at least in part, is a matter of dealing as rationally as possible with the problem of overlap. Guidance may simultaneously provide samples, as may management activities, and so on. This captures an important point about language classrooms, but poses difficulties for a workable analytical system. The following categories of the topic analysis represent a working compromise, therefore.

M instances of the target language intended primarily (if not exclusively) as 'models' (hence the M). The most obvious example would be something said by the teacher, to be imitated by a learner. The learner's reply, if an imitation, would also be coded M.

I instances of communication concerned primarily (if not exclusively) with information (hence the I) about the target language and/or about instances of it (i.e. M's).

P instances of communication concerned primarily (if not exclusively) with pedagogical/procedural matters.

O any other (O) use of language or nonverbal communication (e.g. to discuss traffic problems in the target language for conversation practice).

Category M focuses on samples as models and ignores all other samples. Category I focuses on information about the target language and might be thought to be isomorphic with guidance, but category I does not capture the guidance implicit in the teacher's choice and presentation of model utterances, for example, although it does capture the guidance involved explicitly when model utterances are evaluated in public. Category P also represents a subset, but of management activities. We have so far found it useful to code as instances of P only the most clear examples, where the teacher is concentrating on setting a complex task for out-of-class work, or giving instructions about what exercise will be next. This has meant ignoring the important point, if we accept the view of the language class as a continuing process of negotiation, that virtually everything that everybody does has a 'management activities' aspect. The final category, O, may be seen as a completely new item, one that is not represented at all in the macro-analysis. But devising a workable analytical system means operating at a different level, and here category O serves as a necessary subcategory for further instances of samples of the target language. It is not just a 'ragbag.'

The topic analysis applied to the university-level ESL class

The topic analysis is to be applied twice – once to the turn getting and once to the turn giving. In both cases the number of codings may be different from that of the turns themselves, since each turn may involve any number of topics, and possibly more than one entry under any one topic heading (e.g. a model, followed by something about the pedagogy, followed by another model). Table 3 shows the distribution of topics for turn getting, globally and by participant (this does not include turns consisting solely of a solicit – they are entered only under turn giving).

TABLE 3   Turn getting by topic

Topic	Participant													
	T	S1	S2	S3	S4	S5	S6	S7	S8	S9	S10	S?	All S's	Totals
M	19	3	4	5	4	—	7	3	2	—	5	33	66	85
I	29	—	1	—	—	—	2	—	—	—	—	11	14	43
P	43	2	—	5	—	3	1	—	—	1	—	—	12	55
O	65	—	36	11	5	7	1	3	—	13	4	37	117	182
?	5	—	—	3	—	1	—	—	—	—	—	1	60	65	70
Totals	161	5	41	24	9	11	11	6	2	14	10	141	274	435

These figures support the description of this class hour as conversational in tone, given the fact that category O accounts for 182 out of 435 codings, more than twice the figure for any of the other categories. For the learners, using a turn to present a model is the next most frequent category, with 66; I and P are relatively infrequent, with 14 and 12 codings, respectively. For the teacher the picture is somewhat different since, as one might perhaps expect, P is the second most frequent category, followed by I and M. For convenience Table 4 shows these figures in percentages but with one column for Igor (S2) and another for all learners taken together (including S2).

TABLE 4   Turn getting (percentages)

| | Participant | | | |
Topic	T	S2	All S's	T and S's
M	11.8	9.8	24.1	19.5
I	18.0	2.4	5.1	9.9
P	26.7	0.0	4.4	12.6
O	40.4	87.8	42.7	41.8
?	3.1	0.0	23.7	16.2
Totals	100.0	100.0	100.0	100.0%

Now we can see that there is a strong similarity between teacher and learners for category O, but there are considerable differences in all other categories. As one might expect, the learners average a higher proportion of 'modelling' and a lower proportion of talking about the target language. No real surprises then, but does this analysis throw any new light on Igor's behavior? His figure for entries in category O, 87.8 percent, is more than double the average for all learners (42.7 percent), indicating that Igor (though not only Igor – see S5 and S9 in Table 3) was probably more interested in contributing whenever the topic got away from the target language or the pedagogy itself. It could be, of course, that Igor's category O figures have been largely produced by what the solicits he received demanded of him. To investigate this possibility we need a topic analysis of turn giving. Table 5 gives the raw figures, as did Table 3 for turn getting.

TABLE 5   Turn giving by topic

| | Participant | | | | | | | | | | | | | |
Topic	T	S1	S2	S3	S4	S5	S6	S7	S8	S9	S10	S?	All S's	Totals
M	26	—	—	—	—	—	—	—	—	—	—	—	—	26
I	19	—	1	—	—	—	—	—	—	1	1	—	3	22
P	31	—	2	1	—	—	1	—	—	—	—	1	5	36
O	89	—	5	2	—	1	—	—	—	2	—	1	11	100
?	4	—	—	—	—	—	—	—	—	—	—	—	—	4
Totals	169	—	8	3	—	1	1	—	—	3	1	2	19	188

These raw figures show how Igor stands out in absolute numerical terms, among the learners, as a user of solicits in category O.

Table 6 presents the results in percentages, as did Table 4.

TABLE 6 Turn giving (percentages)

Topic	Participant			
	T	S2	All S's	T and S's
M	15.4	—	—	13.8
I	11.2	12.5	15.8	11.7
P	18.3	25.0	26.3	19.2
O	52.7	62.5	57.9	53.2
?	2.4	—	—	2.1
Totals	100.0	100.0	100.0	100.0%

We can now see that, apart from category M, there is a remarkable similarity between teacher and learners, and that Igor, although a greater user of solicits, is only marginally more prone than the others to use them in category O. We do not yet know, however, the nature of the solicits to Igor; we only know that he favored the O category when making them. Table 7 shows what topics were coded for the solicits made to Igor and the topics involved in his responses.

TABLE 7 Solicits to Igor, responses by Igor, resolicits to Igor by topic

Topic of solicits	Number of solicits	Igor's response topic					Resolicit topic					Zero response
		M	I	P	O	?	M	I	P	O	?	
M	2	2	1	—	—	—	—	—	—	—	—	—
I	—	—	—	—	—	—	—	—	—	—	—	—
P	2	—	—	—	—	—	—	1	1	—	—	—
O	15	—	—	—	13	—	—	—	—	1	—	1
?	—	—	—	—	—	—	—	—	—	—	—	—
Totals	19	2	1	—	13	—	—	1	1	1	—	1

From this we see that 13 of Igor's 36 category O turns in the turn-getting analysis can be attributed directly to solicits in that category, although it should be noted that he is capable of responding in a category that does not match that of the solicit and does so twice. The one zero response is for when S3 made the solicit to Igor, and the teacher stole the turn, as already mentioned.

This topic analysis has given us a more detailed picture of Igor's participation in this class hour but has hardly produced an explanation of it. There are still too many questions so far untouched. For example, is there any evidence that Igor's participation is really under the control of the teacher? Does the teacher attempt to cut short his contributions, or apparently prolong them? And we still know nothing about the quality of Igor's contributions, in terms of efficient communication. Does he contribute so much because he is good at communicating, or because he is willing but not good, and therefore has to engage in lengthy 'repairs'? And we know nothing about the potential productivity of his contributions, in terms of language learning, either for Igor himself or for the other members of the class.

To even begin to consider such questions we need to move to our third-level task analysis, where Igor's contributions can be studied in terms of the tasks involved. This means also looking at the structure of the episodes in which Igor makes his contributions, and thus we finally move to text analysis, where the audio recording, as transcribed, is the 'text.'

Task analysis

'Task analysis' is perhaps not the best term for what follows, because it implies a study of the internal structure of tasks, whereas what is of prime interest here is the interactive aspect of tasks: how what people do in discourse sets a task for other participants (see Fanselow 1977, for this task-setting view of classroom behavior); how simply stopping sets a task, implicitly, for someone to do some 'discourse maintenance,' for example; also, how setting a task often involves making a personal solicit but how the receiver of such a solicit can choose either to accept or to reject the turn itself, and in the case of 'accept,' to choose separately to accept or reject the task involved.

Methodologically this sort of analysis is particularly problematic. At present it does not appear to be profitable to attempt to produce an analytical category system and continue with the counting found appropriate at the level of turn taking and topic analyses. It seems likely to be more profitable to concentrate on the detailed study of manageably brief episodes of classroom (and preferably other) discourse.

Even for this we must distinguish tasks at at least three levels. First, there are tasks at the level of turn taking itself. For example, when a speaker concludes without allocating the next turn, all the other participants face the task of deciding whether or not to accept the task of maintaining the discourse. Second, there are tasks at the level of topic management. By this, we mean the sort of problem involved, for a participant, in deciding whether to pursue a topic or to attempt to switch topic (go from I to M, in technical terms; or, quite separately, go from 'traffic' to 'vehicle design'). The third level of the task analysis is perhaps best appreciated in terms of 'cognitive tasks' or 'operations.' If I ask someone to answer a question, but the person counters by asking me the same question (e.g. 'How do you spell "claim"?' – 'How do *you* spell "claim"?'), then that person has completed the task at the level of turn taking, has not tried to switch topic category (in the 'technical' sense), and has stayed within the subject-matter area of the spelling of 'claim,' but has used the turn to counter the specific task involved, rather than to perform the operation requested.

For present purposes such issues in task analysis can probably best be illustrated by returning to Igor and looking in detail at a relatively extended episode which involves no fewer than 13 of his 47 turns, including 9 of the 18 solicits he received from the teacher. Only one page of transcript is involved, but it deserves extensive analysis because of the light it throws on Igor's contribution to this one class hour.

Text analysis of an episode of classroom interaction

The transcript is presented first, followed by a line-by-line analysis. Indentation is used in the transcript to indicate the point at which an overlapping utterance was begun. SS is the symbol used to refer to simultaneous (but not choral, and therefore often untranscribable) contributions from several participants. xx in the text indicates the presence of something, probably a phrase, that it has not been possible to transcribe.

Transcript extract

    T Yeah. Or to make an accusation. OK. You say he he did, he killed that man, OK. You claim that, but you, if you can't prove it, it's only a claim. Yeah?

165 S2 It's to say something louder?

    T No. That would be *exclaim*. To to make shout, say something louds, it's exclaim.

    S2 He claims . . .

    T   Yeah.

170 S2 I think they'd better produce electric machine for car to use.

    T For, for to to end the pollution problem?

    S2   Yeah.

    S2 Yeah.

    T Yeah. OK. what does this mean? 'Get to'? Uh.

175 SS xx
      T OK. It says the group has been trying to get the govern-
         ment, the city government, to help uhm draw special lanes,
         lanes like this [draws on board] on the street. OK. These
         are for cars. These are for bikes... [pointing to
         blackboard]
180 S2 You know, in Moscow they reproduce all all cab.
      T Uhm?
    S2 They reproduced all cabs xx.
      T They produce?
    S2 *Re*produce
185   T D'you mean uh they they use old cabs, old taxis?
    S2 No, no, no. They reproduced all A L L cabs.
      T All the cabs?
    S2 Yeah, all the cabs for electric (electric you know) electric
         points.
190   T Cab. Oh you mean they made the cabs in down in down-
         town areas uh uh use electric uh motors?
    S2   Yeah, no downtown, all cabs in Moscow.
      T   Where?
    S2 In Moscow.
195   T Oh. And it's successful?
    S2 Yeah.
      T OK. Uhm. Just a second, Igor. Let's what does this mean?
         If you get someone to do something. Uhm.

Analysis

164 The teacher is performing a specific cognitive task in the I
     category – explaining what 'claim' means. Igor (nonverbally)
     requests permission to contribute. The teacher accepts,
     thereby giving Igor the discourse task of taking a turn, but
     leaving the topic and task itself unspecified (albeit implied).

165 Igor accepts the opportunity to take a turn, remains within the
     I category for topic, and uses his turn to set an I category
     cognitive task for the teacher.

166 The teacher accepts the turn, the topic, and the task,
     producing a G3 response followed by a G1 response (i.e.,
     simple evaluation followed by verbal explanation). The teacher
     then simply stops, leaving the 'turn taking' or discourse task
     of maintaining the discourse to a class member.

168 Igor takes this task upon himself and uses it to start to present
     a model utterance involving the vocabulary item under
     discussion. He therefore changes topic category (to M)
     without 'changing the subject.'

169 The teacher does not wait for the implied evaluation task to
     be made explicit but instead interrupts Igor with a positive G3

evaluation and then stops, leaving a discourse maintenance task.

170 Igor again takes the turn, but uses it to change the topic category from I to O, by giving his opinion with respect to the problem raised by the reading about traffic in the textbook for the course. Notice that this is in some sense *not* 'changing the subject,' since Igor is not going beyond the boundary of the ostensible subject matter (or carrier topic) of the lesson so far.

171 The teacher takes the discourse maintenance task as Igor stops, and faces a problem now. Strictly speaking Igor has left no task except that at the level of turn taking (the problem of leaving someone else to maintain the discourse) but a basic 'rule' of discourse is that successive turns shall be topically relevant to each other. He has just changed the topic category from I to O (albeit within the same subject at a 'global' level), and the teacher must decide whether or not to accept the change. To reject it might suggest an unwillingness to allow real communication to flourish in the classroom, while to accept it means a disruption of the lesson plan, which might be resented by other learners and might even lessen their confidence in her ability to control events. In fact, the teacher accepts the change of topic category and sets a further task for Igor by suggesting how his contribution might fit into the general argument, and requesting confirmation from Igor.

172, Igor confirms, while the teacher is still talking, and again after
173 she stops, but minimally ('Yeah'). Igor therefore shows no special interest in pursuing either the topic or the sequence of turns, given that he could have used the opportunity to develop his earlier statement, or to change topic, or 'subject,' again.

174 The teacher takes the opportunity to dispose of the topic, or 'subject,' again.

176 After an indistinct set of what seem to be attempts by several learners to cope with the I task, the teacher sets herself the task of a lengthy provision of G2 type help, involving drawing on the blackboard.

180 Igor takes advantage of the teacher's silence to raise again the category O topic he had previously left undeveloped. Again he fails to set a specific cognitive task, however.

181 The teacher, again faced with a bid to change the course of the lesson, again accepts the topic change and could be said to be encouraging Igor because she again prolongs rather than cuts off (notice the only time she has cut him off so far was when he was producing a model utterance). This time, however, she simply asks for clarification, and so we cannot

discount the possibility that she is not aware of the suggested topic change.

182   Igor accepts the turn and the clarification task. He does not attempt to elaborate or develop his topic, however. He simply repeats it in a revised form and stops.

183   The teacher takes the discourse maintenance task and uses the turn to continue her attempt to repair, since Igor's statement is still not comprehensible to her, apparently. She thus gives Igor another opportunity to contribute, but specifically asks him to evaluate her attempted limitation of one two-word part of his revised statement.

184   Igor accepts the turn, the topic and the task, but narrows the repair down to one word, to which he gives exaggerated stress. Again he leaves it at that, without elaborating on the topic or setting any new task explicitly.

185   The teacher takes the discourse maintenance task and uses the turn to propose a paraphrase for Igor's confirmation.

186   Igor accepts the turn, the topic, and the task but has to disconfirm because the teacher's paraphrase has revealed a further misunderstanding. He attempts to repair this by repeating the relevant utterance with a spelling out of the key word. Still he makes no attempt to elaborate the topic or set a new task.

187   The teacher takes the discourse maintenance task again, and still apparently feels a need to continue the repair work. For this she requests confirmation for a repeat of Igor's last phrase (slightly amended to include the definite article).

188   Igor accepts the turn, the topic, and the task, but this time he does take the opportunity to develop the topic (now that basic understanding has been achieved). He still stops without specifying a task, however.

190   The teacher takes the discourse maintenance task upon herself again, and now feels confident enough to request confirmation for a full paraphrase of Igor's original statement. Notice that this implies a total acceptance of Igor's original topic change, and constitutes a sharing of responsibility for classroom discourse.

192   Igor anticipates her solicit, confirms in general, but corrects an illegitimate inference that was in the teacher's paraphrase.

193   The teacher interrupts to repair again with a new solicit, having apparently failed to catch one word.

194   Igor accepts the turn, the topic and the task, but makes no attempt to use the opportunity to elaborate or set a new task.

195   The teacher takes the discourse maintenance task, when Igor stops, and uses it to ask a supplementary question that stays

within the same topic category but starts a new angle on the subject.

196 Igor accepts the turn and the task, but produces a minimal response ('Yeah'), further evidence, perhaps, of a lack of any inclination to pursue and develop the topic.

197 The teacher takes the discourse maintenance task left when Igor stops, and uses it to acknowledge his previous response, but minimally ('OK'), and then uses the opportunity to explicitly break free from Igor, turn back to the whole class and 'get . . . to.' This whole episode has to be understood in relation to the problem, in language teaching and learning, that 'content' and 'medium' are in a sense interchangeable. The ostensible content of 'traffic problems' is the medium whereby target language samples are produced. These can then be treated as the lesson content, from a purely linguistic point of view. At any moment, then, there are two potential topics: the content of verbal interaction, and the medium itself. Normally the teacher keeps the two apart without obvious difficulty, but Igor does not respect these boundaries and thus, in this sense, poses a discourse management problem for the teacher.

After this episode, Igor disappears from the transcript for forty lines. When he next appears it is just for one word, in category M.

Comments on the text analysis

From such a close study we can obtain a different sort of picture of Igor's behavior, though one still centrally based on the three levels of turns, topics and tasks. We now see, for example, that Igor is quite capable of negotiating successfully for a change of topic category (not just of topic), but we also see that, at least on this occasion (the longest episode continuously involving Igor in this particular transcript), Igor's success in getting turns one after the other seems to depend more on an inability to make himself understood than on any ability to develop a topic. In fact he misses many opportunities to elaborate, and when all the repairs on the original proposition have been done, he lets the topic go in spite of the fact that the teacher invites development by introducing a new angle. We see a teacher patiently fostering real communication, although it means digressing from the vocabulary work on her plan, and a learner apparently keen to establish the digression, but not following it through to a particularly satisfying conclusion. From a study of the remainder of this transcript it seems that Igor's success at turn getting is indeed largely due to a lack, rather than an abundance, of communicative competence. Learners with few turns tend not to attempt to change topic category in the middle of an exercise, but what they do do they do relatively neatly and efficiently, thus avoiding lengthy repair sequences and all the extra turns they bring.

It is clearly difficult, and no doubt unwise even to try, to decide whether or not Igor's extra participation in the class is a 'good thing' from the point of view of his language development and, equally important for the teacher, of that of the other members of the class. His preference for category O topics may seem unlikely to be linguistically productive and his willingness to 'disrupt' the lesson plan may also be worrying, but it could also be argued that real attempts at real communication (whatever one takes that to mean) are in the last resort the most productive events for language learners. A curious sidelight on this last point is given by the observation that perhaps communication attempts like Igor's are more productive for the 'audience' than for those who make them. The teacher ranked Igor first for verbal fluency at the beginning of the ten-week course, first for 'willingness to volunteer contributions,' and first for 'frequency of contributions' throughout the course. S1, a girl from Iran, who had only four turns during the class hour discussed here, was ranked eighth (out of ten) for verbal fluency at entry, eighth for frequency of contributions throughout the course, and ninth for willingness to volunteer contributions, but first for progress. Perhaps every class should have an 'Igor,' but more for their sake than for his.

Summary and conclusions

This paper has attempted to make out a convincing case for the potential fruitfulness of a research program based on a fundamentally simple macro-analysis of language teaching and learning, developed, so far, into somewhat more complex analyses at the level of turns, topics, and tasks. This research has been illustrated with detailed reference to just one class hour, and to just one individual learner. Such a limited focus was necessitated by the interim nature of the research report, but it also offered an illustration of an important feature of the research program – the adoption of a case-study approach within the coherent framework offered by the macro-analysis and the analyses of turns, topics, and tasks.

A further intention of the paper has been to establish a case for studying learners in class, with a view to gaining insights into how classrooms 'work,' and how learners contribute to their own and to each other's learning.

Only the most tentative conclusions are at present permissible, except the one that further research is needed, which can always be stated confidently. The main conclusion to propose is that language learners in class are not only interesting, which we knew already, but also amenable to systematic study at a variety of levels of delicacy within an overall conceptual framework of considerable generality. That was perhaps not so obvious, if we are to judge from the lack of previous studies to draw on. A further conclusion to propose is that the relatively novel foci for analysis ('turns, topics, and tasks') have so far justified the special attention now being given them. In addition perhaps it can also be claimed that the adoption of a framework that makes no a priori distinction between teacher and learners has also so far proved justified.

Finally, perhaps the best excuse for a work-in-progress paper at this early stage is that if it encourages others to begin pursuing the same lines of enquiry, or to share their experiences if they have already begun, then progress will not be quite as painfully slow as it might otherwise have been.

Resorting to a detailed text analysis amounted in itself to an admission of the inadequacy of category analyses to offer a sufficiently illuminating account of the data, but how illuminating the text analysis itself is must be left to the individual reader. Of particular interest here is that this alternative to the Flanders tradition does appear to have been the first to attempt both to describe and to account for individual learner behaviour in a language class. As such it fitted into the quite independent development of research into learner behaviour (launched by Rubin in 1975, and followed up by the Ontario team of Naiman *et al.* in their 1978 publication) which itself developed into explorations of the concept of 'learner training'. A related line of enquiry worth mentioning in this connection is that of diary studies (see, for example, Bailey 1983), also dedicated to exploring learner behaviour, but going to the extreme of eliminating the direct observational component altogether in favour of obtaining instead learners' diary accounts of their experiences. Such approaches to classroom language learning research have been generically and usefully labelled 'mentalistic' (see Cohen and Hosenfeld 1981), which distinguishes them neatly from the observational tradition with which this volume is concerned. Together they constitute an important challenge (elaborated and argued cogently in Breen 1985) to the very notion, implicit throughout this volume, but to be reconsidered in Chapter 6, that classroom language learning could ever be adequately investigated by purely observational techniques.

One final point to mention before moving on is the connection between my work in the mid-seventies and that of Seliger (see Chapter 5). Like Seliger, I was interested in the possibility that there might be a positive relationship between learners' active participation in classroom interaction and their linguistic progress (such a relationship was after all commonly assumed by teachers and materials designers), but my case study cast doubt on Seliger's positive findings and this contributed significantly to the shift of focus in my later work towards trying to comprehend just how it is that learners get whatever they do get from classroom language lessons (see Allwright 1984).

Summary

This chapter started by announcing the existence of three 'alternatives' to the Flanders tradition, but in retrospect it might appear that it was perhaps only Fanselow's contribution that deserved that label, since only Fanselow had at all in mind the most common application of observational systems familiar from the Flanders tradition – the provision of feedback in teacher training. This would be an unhelpfully narrow interpretation, however. The three 'alternatives' presented in this chapter are best seen as offering three 'distinctly different' perspectives on the whole field of classroom language learning and teaching, challenging the old priorities and suggesting new ones. As such they did not need to even attempt to meet Bailey's objections to the Flanders tradition, although Fanselow's FOCUS did offer an ingenious answer to some of them. Long *et al.*'s contribution simply reinforced Bailey's points about interpreting categories, and my own work went so far as to suggest that the data could not be adequately accounted for by a category system analysis at all.

This volume started in Chapter 1 with a focus on the role of classroom observation in research, and the attention shifted to its role in teacher training in Chapters 2 and 3. With Chapter 4 we have documented a return to research as the first priority, but it is by no means the same sort of research as was dealt with in Chapter 1. By the mid-seventies the 'prescriptive/descriptive' debate seems largely to have been won by the 'descriptivists', with 'prescription' not necessarily abandoned but certainly postponed indefinitely, and 'description' now interpreted more interestingly to indicate 'exploratory and explanatory' investigations rather than simply descriptive ones.

There was a problem however. Observational research in the language classroom had as its unifying force simply the wish to understand classroom language learning and teaching, and the belief that such an understanding could best be sought by looking in detail at what happened in classroom language lessons. This gave the field a location and a general procedure for research, but no particular guidance as to what to look *for* in the language classroom. There was no 'theory', within the research paradigm itself, to motivate predictions that observations could test, or at least throw some much needed light on. There were only more or less fascinating puzzles for researchers to play with, as exemplified in Long's interest in what happened when language learners were left in small groups, and my own in how learners contributed to the management of the distribution of talk. (My 'macro-analysis', it should be recalled, was intended to provide a framework for research, and as such it has continued to prove useful, but not to lead to precise predictions.)

The field of second language acquisition, with its own origins also in the late sixties (see, for example, Corder 1967), had no explicit theory either, but it did offer a framework developed expressly for the purpose of understanding the processes of language learning (to use the term 'learning' non-technically for the moment). As such it was the obvious place for classroom researchers to go to in their search for more precise motivation. In Chapter 5 we shall look at some of the earliest classroom observation studies motivated in this way by research in second language acquisition.

Follow-up activities and points for discussion

1. Did Fanselow solve Bailey's problems? In small groups of no more than two or three people:
   a) take Fanselow's first sample of coded data,
   b) cover Fanselow's own suggested codings,
   c) work out your own application of FOCUS, without consulting the original codings,
   d) compare codings between groups,
   e) check your codings with the original.
Finally, consider whether or not Fanselow succeeded in overcoming the problems of interpretation, and others, described by Bailey.

(Had Fanselow already solved the problems in 1974? Fanselow's Foreign Language Annals paper on the 'treatment of error in oral work' was based on earlier work (reported at the Denver TESOL Convention in 1974) that used 16 'low-inference' categories. If you have access to a copy of that paper, study the 16 categories to see if you find that they appear likely to minimize interpretation problems.)

2. Do research and teacher training really make such different demands on an observation system? Draw up a short list of possible uses of an observation system, and then, separately for each putative use, outline the design criteria applicable for an observation system to be workable and useful. Chart the results, plotting uses against design criteria.

Does the charting operation reflect a broad division between research and teacher training uses, as the contributions to this chapter would have led us to expect?

3. Apply the categories of Long *et al.*'s 'Embryonic Category System' to the transcript extract in Allwright 1980. Assess the extent to which such an analysis of this data could serve to throw light on the questions addressed in Allwright's paper. Would it be more, or less, illuminating than the three stage procedure adopted by Allwright?

4. Who needs category systems? Allwright's paper suggests that close textual analysis is essential even after two category systems have been applied. It could be argued, however, that close textual analysis was all that was ever necessary in the first place. Could this be true? Take some classroom data (a page or two should be enough) and collectively decide what is interesting about it – what research question it can be used to address. Then divide into two groups for the following tasks:

> *Group A:*   select the category system most appropriate to the research question already determined and apply it to the data. Prepare a report directly responding to the research question.
> *Group B:*   study the data more as if it were an extract from a novel. Read and re-read it in the light of the agreed research question, then prepare a report directly responding to the research question.

Finally, present your reports to each other and try to reach consensus on the relative merits of category systems and text analysis.

5 Classroom observation and second language acquisition

It was suggested at the end of the last chapter that classroom observation was a procedure looking for a purpose, a purpose it could hope to find in studies of the processes of second language acquisition. In this chapter we will look at three examples of observation-based classroooom research that took as their starting point not so much immediate pedagogic problems as concepts, problems, even hypotheses, arising directly out of work in second language acquisition. In the mid-seventies second language acquisition researchers were moving on from their earlier preoccupation with error analysis. Schumann was developing his ideas on the possible similarities between second language acquisition and the pidginization process. Krashen was developing his 'monitor theory'. In short, the time had come in second language acquisition studies when people were thinking more generally in terms of possible ways of 'explaining' second language acquisition phenomena, after a decade of research aimed rather at discovering what the basic phenomena of the field were and how they could be described. The parallels with classroom language learning research are obvious and interesting, and all the more interesting because there had been remarkably little contact between the two research fields *until* the mid-seventies.

It was in the best traditions of interdisciplinary work that the first example of classroom observation research taking its fundamental ideas from studies in second language acquisition should choose to take ideas that were themselves in the process of receding from centre stage. Such was the case for my own 1975 work on the treatment of errors in oral work. The initial idea came in fact from Fanselow's 1974 treatment of the topic at the Denver TESOL Convention (published 1977), but the background thinking for the paper itself came from second language acquisition work on error analysis. We start Chapter 5 with this common interest in learners' errors and what happens to them in language classes. The next concept to be taken over from second language acquisition work into observational research was 'input', and more specifically the concept of teacher talk as input. For that we turn to Gaies' 1977 study. Finally, for this chapter, we have classroom observation work on a third area of common interest between researchers in the field of second language acquisition and researchers in the field of classroom language pedagogy – the role of interaction (already introduced in Chapter 4 via my own work on turn taking in the language classroom). For an observational study of classroom interaction we turn to Seliger's work, also published in 1977.

1 Learners' errors

Fanselow's interest in what happened to errors in the language classroom came from his pedagogic interest in knowing how to help teachers in training with practical and helpful ideas for how they should best treat their learners' errors. My own, as explained above, came more from an interest in the treatment of an error as an event in a learner's life, something to be comprehended and learned from as part of the whole process of second language acquisition (still not using the term to distinguish it from 'learning', or from 'development'), although there is no doubt that I came at it initially from an interest in the treatment of learner error as a potential crisis point in a teacher's classroom life.

My paper, 'Problems in the Study of the Language Teacher's Treatment of Learner Error' (1975a), began with some reasons why it made good sense to be interested in studying errors in the language classroom.

> It seems common now to read that errors are crucial to language learners (see Dulay and Burt 1974) because learners learn, it is argued, by forming hypotheses about the target language and by testing their hypotheses to destruction. It is clear from studies of rule-learning by hypothesis formation and testing (see Wason 1971) that negative instances are far more informative than positive instances and therefore error-making (the creation of negative instances) would appear crucial to language learning.
>
> It is equally clear from such research that subjects tend to prefer creating positive instances, even though such a procedure is incapable of permitting the elimination of alternative hypotheses. Without going so far as Braine (1971) who doubts the general validity of a hypothesis-testing model for language acquisition, we can concede that what is important, probably, is not that the learner deliberately creates negative instances as the most efficient way of

testing any current hypothesis[1], but that the learner should learn to distinguish negative from positive instances, regardless of:

a. whether or not instances of either sort have been deliberately created as part of a hypothesis testing process;

b. who creates them.

(b) turns out to be particularly important, I believe, as soon as we think about classroom learning, because it is clear, there, that any one learner is only one of a number of creators of positive or negative instances. The learner in a class can get information about what is or is not permissible in the target language, not only from feedback about personal attempts to use the language but also from:

1. everything the teacher says in the target language, on the assumption (not necessarily justified but at least understandable) that the teacher is always right;

2. everything the other learners say in the target language, in the light of the way the teacher reacts.

Neither must we forget:

3. everything the teacher says *about* the target language, again assuming the teacher is always right;

4. everything the other learners say *about* the target language, again in the light of the way the teacher reacts.

What this means in practice is that, if we want to study how any one learner learns in class, we must study everything that happens in class (note that we are assuming, for the sake of simplicity, but perhaps unwisely, that out-of-class activities are insignificant) to all the learners.

To focus in this paper on the teacher's treatment of learner error is, seen in this light, to adopt a rather narrow focus, because it means concentrating on what might be called the potential crisis points[2] in the process, ignoring all the other occasions on which any learner might get information about the target language. And

---

1. Thus we cannot expect that a learner will, say, deliberately form a passive in accordance with a hypothesis he assumes to be incorrect, although this procedure, from a strictly logical point of view, might enable him to very efficiently check the validity of the hypothesis he wishes to establish as a rule.

2. '*crisis* points' because an error is typically seen as evidence of failure of some sort (rather than as evidence of deliberate hypothesis-testing). Note it can be evidence of teacher failure, as well as, or rather than, learner failure. Thus the self-confidence of both teacher and learner are at risk. In addition, learner failure calls for remedial action and the teacher may add to his/her own failure if he/she is unable to provide treatment satisfactorily. The teacher has failed both to prevent the error and to provide a cure for it. Thus it seems reasonable to refer to the occasion of error as a potential (at least) crisis point in the classroom.

yet it is a much broader viewpoint than the one of conventional error analysis. First of all because it attempts to deal with the classroom context in which errors occur, as well as with the errors themselves. And secondly, because it attempts to take into account the social nature of this context, not in terms of an assumed 1:1 relationship between teacher and learner, but in terms of a complexity of relationships between teacher and learners.

The general hypothesis behind all this amounts to a hunch, at least, that, among Selinker's (1972) five processes of second language acquisition, transfer of training (loosely defined) may be even more important than is commonly assumed.

From another angle entirely, the sort of investigation under discussion could be seen as potentially contributing to research on teacher effectiveness. In the short term, at least, this is going to be the main focus of such investigations, given the relative ease with which teachers can be studied, compared to the methodological complexities of a longitudinal study of individual learners in full classroom context.

It certainly seems reasonable, assuming the argument so far has been coherent, to go from saying (a) that the making of an error by any learner constitutes a potential crisis point for that learner and any learner in the same classroom (and is, therefore, especially worthy of investigation if we wish to understand the process of classroom learning), to saying (b) that such crisis points are also crisis points for the teacher, in that the teacher's reaction to learner error will be the major factor in determining what the learners actually learn and (c) that therefore a teacher's way of handling these crisis points will be central to that teacher's effectiveness (see also note 2). Such a claim is undoubtedly optimistic, given how difficult it has been for educational researchers interested in classroom processes to isolate key variables in teacher effectiveness,[3] but at least, again assuming the foregoing arguments are valid, there are logical as well as intuitive reasons for a certain amount of optimism.

What we discover when we look at teachers in the classroom, is that, as Fanselow (1977 and personal communication) has argued, teachers are typically rather imprecise in their treatment of learner error, tending to repeat the correct model rather than provide any obviously adaptive treatment, and tending to fail to explicitly locate errors for the learners (i.e. indicate precisely at which point in the utterance the error occurred). It is intriguing that strong exceptions to this can be found among 'Silent Way' teachers, who may refuse to repeat the model of the correct utterance but who will locate the error to the nearest syllable. It appears, in this case, that a method,

3. For a full discussion of this problem, see Rosenshine 1971.

designed to force learners back on their own resources all the time, may actually give more precise help than is usual elsewhere.

The second point that emerges immediately from classroom studies is that teachers are not only imprecise, they are also inconsistent in their treatment of learner error. Mehan, at San Diego (1974) has shown how a teacher trying to apply a criterion such as 'only full sentences will be accepted' can appear very inconsistent on close analysis. Some of the inconsistency arises from an understandable lack of precision (as when a teacher accepts a partial utterance for what is in fact right about it, but fails to make explicit that it is some element of content that is being accepted, not the partial nature of the utterance itself). On other occasions the teacher may simply be relaxing the rule to help a particular learner, not because the learner has in fact produced a partial utterance with something in it worth encouraging, but because the teacher feels that that learner needs a more relaxed approach from the outset. At other times the inconsistency may be the product of a simple lack of self-discipline on the part of the teacher. The word 'inconsistent' has pejorative overtones that are not necessarily appropriate, of course. Teachers have a duty, perhaps, to be inconsistent in the sense that they must adjust their treatment of any error to the needs of the moment. At the very least teachers must reserve the right to adapt to the individual differences among their learners. To put it more directly: in order to be consistent in giving the appropriate treatment to all learners at all times, teachers must run the risk of appearing inconsistent in their application of criteria of acceptability.

There is no need, of course, to assume that teachers will be effective if they always provide the most precise treatment of learner errors, and, equally clearly, we cannot assume they will be effective if they always insist on exactly the same standard of acceptability. What we can perhaps assume is that teachers need to be aware of the potential they have for creating confusion in the minds of learners, given the typical lack of precision, on the one hand, and the inconsistency (if only apparent) that seem to characterize their treatment of learner error. This is no doubt familiar ground for any teacher trainer who gets involved in close analysis of student teachers' classroom performance. The type of investigation discussed here would not aim, perhaps, to do more than provide such teacher trainers with more refined tools for their analyses – analytical tools that might facilitate the identification of the different error and error-treatment types. More important, however, would be the potential contribution of such studies to our understanding of teaching/learning classroom processes, an understanding that might one day relate error treatments to learning outcomes in a way that would do justice to the complexities of the classroom situation.

There are, then, three distinct but closely related foci for any investigation. First of all (in logic if not in fact) there is the possibility of improving our understanding of learners' ways of learning in classrooms. Secondly, there is the possibility of improving our understanding of the teacher's contribution, for good or ill, to the learners' learning. And thirdly, there is the possibility of developing techniques that would play some part in helping teachers improve their classroom skills.

Of most importance, in retrospect, and thinking of later developments, is the fundamental point made at the beginning of the paper that a classroom error is a *social* event, and a social event not only in the life of the error-maker and the teacher, but also in the lives of all the other people in the classroom. This was an early indication of the importance of a properly social perspective on the language classroom.

It is no doubt obvious from the above extract that I was at that time trying to keep as many balls in the air as possible at the time – hoping that I would soon be able to contribute not only to our understanding of language learning processes but also to the world's stock of language teaching techniques. A good indication of the intermediate stage language classroom research was going through.

In the next part of my paper I began dealing with some of the many problems facing anyone contemplating research on classroom error treatment, starting with the fundamental and surprisingly complex problem of defining what is meant by an error in the language classroom context.

Whichever focus is adopted, methodological problems abound. Observational studies are clearly essential, and Fanselow has already given an example of how they might be conducted (1974 TESOL Convention), but Fanselow's seems almost the only example we have to date. Firstly, there is the question of the identification of error. Given a videotape recording and a detailed transcript of a lesson, can we locate all the 'error events' in it? Do we include 'failure to respond' as an error? If we do, then we have the problem of identifying 'failures to respond.' This may seem a trivial problem, until we reflect that one would presumably start by locating in the transcript those occasions where an elicitation was not followed by a student response of some kind. Perhaps, faced with such a failure, the teacher would have repeated the elicitation, or moved to another learner. Going back to the videotape recording we might then notice that failure to respond is perhaps necessarily teacher-defined (although we may be hoping to identify errors on external, teacher-independent, criteria). The teacher defines the failure by intervening at a certain point in time after the original elicitation. One moment later the learner might have begun a perfectly acceptable response.

T Eulyces (pause)
   I started
S2 I stotted
   (*Lines 190–2 of the transcript in the Appendix*).

In a sense, the teacher actually creates the failure, then. Again 'Silent Way' teachers present an intriguing exception, since they are trained to wait with infinite patience far beyond the point at which other teachers would intervene. In case it might appear that a trivial problem is being pointlessly exaggerated, reference should perhaps be made at this point to Brophy and Good's (1974) major survey of their own and others' work on expectancy effects:

> Teachers have been observed to provide more time for high achieving students to respond than for low achieving students. The determinants of this behaviour could include excessive sympathy for the student, teacher anxiety, and lack of probing skills, among others (1974, pp. 330–331).

Waiting time, therefore, is a variable on which teachers do vary and sometimes it would seem, inappropriately. It would be unwise, no doubt, to attempt to ignore it in our investigations of teachers' behavior, and equally unwise to attempt to ignore 'failure to respond' in our investigations of learners' behaviours. We include 'failure to respond' then, both on the grounds that it could represent learner error in an extreme form, and also on the converse grounds that it could represent an important aspect of teacher behaviour that one might want to characterize as 'error creating.'

Having accepted 'failure to respond' as worthy of investigation, but also having accepted that we may in so doing be investigating error as defined by the teacher's behaviour, we then return to the original problem of distinguishing between 'errors' and other classroom events. Is a teacher-behaviour-defined concept of error acceptable in general terms? Clearly we cannot define as errors only those events that get treated as errors, overtly, in the classroom, since that would beg all the important questions.

T I started at Essex on the fifth of October. When did you start?
   (Nominates by gesture)
S4 I start in Excess since the eleventh of January.
T When did you arrive? You arrived on the eleventh of January, did you? You must have started the next day, did you?
   (*Lines 176–9*)

We are forced, I believe, to adopt George's (1972) definition of an error as a form unwanted by the teacher or course designer. If we are focusing on the teacher we may wish to investigate his or her classroom behaviour by reference to his or her conception of the target language. We would then ask the teacher to study the videotape recording and the transcript and help us locate all the events that involved language not acceptable in his or her view. So we would be accepting a concept of error, defined by the teacher, but by the teacher's judgement on reflection, not by the teacher's classroom behaviour (the distinction is clearly important). In most circumstances that will probably be the most satisfactory procedure. It was followed for the purpose of establishing the pilot data on which this paper is based. But we will need to find teachers who are capable of viewing their own teaching objectively, and such teachers may not be representative of the majority. They may be expected, for example, to be more consistent in their acceptability judgements, if they are more 'objective' generally.

If we are focusing on the learner, then the above teacher-defined (but post-hoc) concept of error will appear even more problematic. Firstly, learners may have their own conception of the target language. Consider the case of English speakers in Montreal being taught French by teachers from France itself, when they, as Canadian learners, might be aiming at Canadian French norms. The transcript was made from a videotape recording of a class of Venezuelan undergraduates being taught, for the occasion, by a Canadian native English speaker, in an English university – a fairly complex pattern of target language was thus involved. In other circumstances, in an English grammar school, for example, it is going to be possible sometimes to find learners who are better informed about the target language (if only in minor and very particular ways) than the teachers or to find different learners in the same class having different target languages in view. The mere possibility of such cases makes it difficult to accept a purely teacher-defined concept of error.

A further possibility would be to take the views of an independent expert, if one is available, but here we run the risk of an analysis that misses the point because the target language, so defined, is the target neither of the teacher nor of the learners necessarily.

For simplicity's sake we are going to find ourselves trying to limit our investigations to situations where a high degree of conformity can be expected between the views of teachers and learners as to what constitutes the target language. If we can also have teachers who are native speakers of the target language, and make that language also the native language of ourselves the researchers (who can thus act as the relatively independent experts) the whole situation can thus be considerably simplified, but at some expense, of course, since most language teaching the world over is probably not in the hands of native speakers of the target language.

All of the above worries, however, may have suggested that errors need to be categorized only in purely linguistic terms. This is clearly not the case since even casual observations of teacher-behaviour make it apparent that the teacher is responding to more than the purely linguistic characteristics of errors, and we need to reflect this fact in our analyses. For example, the severity of a teacher's reaction may depend more on a judgement of the amount of effort the learner was using than on any judgement of the extent of the deviation from the target language norms. For this sort of reason a trivial deviation, in linguistic terms, may often be 'punished' more severely than a linguistically much more serious deviation, its very triviality being sufficient proof that only carelessness could have caused it.

The above discussion of the definition problem recalls Long *et al.*'s later struggles with their data, and represents well the very strong feeling at the time that everything we looked at was immensely complex and was not to be understood in the sorts of simple terms represented by the Flanders tradition. My paper continued with a suitably complex eighteen point analysis of possible error types, and then a sixteen point analysis of possible treatment types, all tentative, but generally relatable to some pilot classroom data.

Four major ways of categorizing errors seem relevant to any study of the treatment of error. These are summarized below:

Error type

A. Linguistic description:	1.	Content area.
	2.	Skill area.
B. Importance: **a** *Present*:	3.	Relevance to pedagogic focus.
	4.	Frequency.
	5.	Number of learners affected.
b *Future*:	6.	Accuracy.
	7.	Communicative effectiveness.
C. Source:	8.	Interlingual inference.
	9.	Intralingual inference.
	10.	L_2 learning strategy.
	11.	Communication strategy.
	12.	Teaching.
	13.	Carelessness (including obtuseness).
	14.	Stress (anxiety, fatigue, etc.).
	15.	Factual ignorance.

D. Ease of correction: 16. Teacher's competence.

17. Resources available.

18. Time available.

These are not mutually exclusive, of course. On the contrary, the teacher's behaviour may need to be based on a categorization in all four ways at once. Neither is the order in which they are presented above necessarily significant. It reflects logical simplicity, perhaps, but no more. The 18 sub-categories seem to be the minimal number that will do justice to the facts that observation has so far revealed. Most, if not all, of them can be illustrated by reference to the transcript. For example, it is clear, as far as one can tell, from the transcript that many errors have been completely ignored. Sub-category 3 (relevance to pedagogic focus) is probably highly relevant to the teacher's behaviour, since many of the ignored errors are in no obvious way related to the focus on dates and how to say them. Sub-category 15 (factual ignorance) is also frequently illustrated in the transcript, wherever the teacher attempts to insist, as in lines 178–9:

T When did you arrive? You arrived on the eleventh of January, did you? You must have started the next day, did you?

on adherence to the truth about learners' recent movements.

This analysis of types of errors will be refined as observational studies proceed. Already it suggests the complexity of the problem. It is the sort of analysis one might use in studying a transcript, but it is also an attempt to suggest the complexity of what lies behind the classroom behaviour of the teacher. The teacher's error analysis has to be 'instant'. He or she cannot, unlike the usual error analyst, just wait to see if an error is statistically frequent before he or she reacts to it. And any treatment given, typically, is public, a fact that has consequences of considerable complexity for the researcher as well as for the teacher.

The key task for the teacher, then, is firstly to sum up the whole situation on the spot, and then to react appropriately, in public, conscious of the need to treat the problems of the individual without misleading or confusing the other learners. In summing up the situation, the teacher may make simultaneous reference to any number of the 18 sub-categories of error type. He or she will also need very basic information of the following sort, and it may not be, in fact, readily available:

1. What was actually said or done.
2. Who said or did it.
3. What was meant by it.
4. What should have been said or done.

In addition, the teacher may need to know:

5. What the native-language equivalent would be.

Armed with as much of this information as is available (and the teacher may have to probe the learner to establish 3, for example), the teacher is now perhaps in a position to select from the various treatment options open to him or her. The basic seven treatment options so far established by observation are listed below, together with a further nine possible features of treatments. This analysis is particularly tentative, especially the distinction between 'basic options' and 'possible features,' hence the continuous numbering from 1 to 16.

Treatment type

A. Basic options:

1. To treat or to ignore completely.
2. To treat immediately or delay.
3. To transfer treatment or not.
4. To transfer to another individual, a sub-group, or to the whole class.
5. To return, or not, to original error-maker after treatment.
6. To call upon, or permit, another learner (or learners) to provide treatment.
7. To test for efficacy of treatment.

B. Possible features:

8. Fact of error indicated.
9. Blame indicated.
10. Location indicated.
11. Opportunity for new attempt given.
12. Model provided.
13. Error type indicated.
14. Remedy indicated.
15. Improvement indicated.
16. Praise indicated.

The transcript contains an intriguing example of options 3 and 4, when, in line 208:

T All together . . . (on the thirteenth of January)

the teacher apparently abandons a learner who almost wilfully, it seems, (see error type 13) repeats an error of fact. The teacher deals with the problem by asking the whole class to try to get it right. As soon as they do the sub-topic is changed.

There is an involuntary example of option 6, on lines 193–4:

T (started
    (
S1 (start

when one learner provides a model response at the same moment as the teacher. Unfortunately the learner's model is both incorrect and persuasive, as we see in line 196:

> I started on on Essess eh fourteen January

where the original error-maker copies his fellow-learner, rather than the teacher. The teacher takes up option 1 and ignores this particular misfortune.

Of the possible features of error treatments, this particular teacher tends to indicate errors by modelling what should have been said, but lines 185–9:

> S1 I start at Essex on the thirteenth of January.
> T   On the thirteenth of January.
> S1 Yes.
> T   Again.
> S1 I start at Essex on the thirteenth of January.

suggest, since there is no evidence of learner error in that bit of the utterance the teacher chooses to model, that this procedure is not entirely systematic. The learners cannot be sure that any repetition of what they have said necessarily indictates error, nor that absence of repetition indicates correctness – see lines 177–8:

> S4 I start in Excess since the eleventh of January.
> T   When did you arrive? You arrived on the eleventh of January, did you? You must have started the next day, did you?

The location of an error tends to be made by modelling of only a part of what the learner has said. This reduces the problem for the learner, perhaps, but does not necessarily locate the error with very much precision. Again the device is not used with absolute consistency, which could lead to considerable confusion. Lines 198–212:

> S2 Fourteenth January
> T   I started at Essex on the thirteenth of January. All right Eulyces: on the thirteenth of January ...
> S2 On the th
> T   Thirteenth
> S2 On the fourteenth of January
> T   of January
> S2 of January
> T   on the thirteenth of January.
> S2 On fourteenth of January.
> T   All together .... (on the thirteenth of January
>   (
> SSS   (on the thirteenth of January
>   on the thirteenth of January
> T   All right. I started at Essex (gesture for choral response)
> SSS I started at Essex on the thirteenth of January.

suggest a teacher focus on the factual incorrectness of the date quoted, but stress is not used to isolate the date (it would have produced an 'artificial' utterance, of course, which the teacher might well have wished to avoid). In addition line 204:

> T of January

could be interpreted as indicating a different location of the error under attack, although in fact it seems more reasonable, for us as observers, to interpret this line as indicating the teacher's desire to use what the learner had got correct to build up self-confidence and facilitate a fully correct utterance. It is not at all clear how the learner in question perceived the situation, but it is clear that the learner failed to change the date. Unfortunately what was said during the choral practice is not recoverable from the recording – lines 210–212:

> SSS on the thirteenth of January
> T   All right. I started at Essex (gesture for choral response)
> SSS I started at Essex on the thirteenth of January.

These few examples should serve to illustrate the suggested analysis of error treatments. None of the above comments on the transcript is intended of course, to be interpreted as constituting a statistically interesting description of typical teacher behaviour.[4] In fact, the original classroom recording was made simply for the purpose of providing pilot data that would be useful in establishing the above analytical frameworks.

Probably the most important and productive point in the above section was the point that all the complexity for the analyst meant a parallel amount of complexity for the classroom teacher, operating in real time in a social setting where all behaviour was public, and had therefore to make sense to a whole class of learners with all their different levels and ways of understanding, and not just to the original error-maker. Apart from indicating that classroom language teachers therefore deserved profound respect (a by no means trivial point in the otherwise inglorious history of relationships between teachers and researchers), this also indicated a new area for enquiry – the processes of teacher decision-making. The challenge was briefly taken up by Long (1977) and Chaudron (1977), but that was yet another area of apparently only passing interest (note, however, the later development in general education research of investigations into teachers' classroom decision-making – see, e.g. Calderhead 1984).

4. Nor, clearly, must the close analysis of one teacher's behaviour be interpreted as constituting a criticism of that behaviour. It *is* only (though not merely, I hope) an attempt at description and interpretation.

Also important was the adoption of the learner's perspective on the teacher's treatment of errors, and this provided the focus for the last section of my paper.

> To pursue the analysis a stage further, towards the problem of how learners may interpret any given treatment on any given occasion (and thus how a teacher will need to plan the treatment, however 'instantly', to ensure the appropriate interpretation) it will be helpful to move from the complexities of real data to the relative simplicity (if only for layout purposes) of constructed data. Consider the following simulated sample of classroom discourse:

> T   When's your birthday, Alvaro?
> Alvaro   Twelfth November
> T   Okay. Now, Santos, when's *your* birthday?
> Santos   Fourteenth of September
> T   No. Listen: *the* fourteenth. Again . . . . . .

> Assuming British English is the agreed target language, let us imagine that Alvaro is known to the teacher as a careless learner who does not repay individual attention, since he makes no attempt to learn from any feedback he gets. Let us further imagine that Santos is a keen student, the converse of Alvaro, as far as the teacher is concerned.

> So, looking back at the (artificial) data, we see that the teacher ignored the omissions in Alvaro's utterance, perhaps because he/she felt any time spent on them would be wasted; but the teacher refused to accept Santos' otherwise less deviant utterance, presumably because he/she felt Santos would respond well to correction.

> But, the following questions arise:
> 1. Does Santos know that Alvaro is careless?
> 2. Does Santos know that the teacher knows (or merely thinks) that Alvaro is careless?
> 3. Does Santos know that the teacher thinks that he (Santos) is serious and can be expected to react well to correction?
> 4. Does Santos know that the teacher has decided that Alvaro's carelessness is Alvaro's problem, not his, and therefore that the teacher's treatment of Alvaro is not to be considered reliable evidence of what is or is not acceptable?
> 5. Does Santos know, in fact, that the teacher's use of 'Okay' was not meant to indicate approval any more than his use of 'No' was meant to indicate complete rejection?

> If all the answers are affirmative, and if all the other learners, including Alvaro, are equally aware of the situation, no confusion will have been generated. But what right do we have to assume affirmative answers? For subjects other than languages it may seem

quite reasonable to assume that the learners in a class (especially after some years together) will know the rules of the game very well, given that they are familiar with each other and are operating in their native language. But language learners, especially learners away from home, are likely to find themselves among strangers, and trying to learn the rules of the game played in the very language they are learning. The fact that learners do cope, and do even learn something of the target language in class, is perhaps to be taken more as evidence of the highly complex patterns of behaviour humans take for granted (without a thought for the researcher!) than as evidence of any unnecessary complexity in the analysis.

If Santos, however, is unaware of the teacher's intentional differential treatment of himself and Alvaro, then all sorts of interpretations are open to him as to the facts of the language, and the meaning of the teacher's behaviour. For example:

1. Absence of *the* is wrong for *Fourteenth of September* but:
   a. optional for *Twelfth November*
   b. obligatory for *Twelfth November*,
   c. presence of *of* necessitates presence of *the* and
   d. absence of *of* necessitates absence or optionalizes presence of *the*, etc., etc.

2. Absence of *the* is always wrong but:
   a. T failed to notice with Alvaro, or
   b. T is victimizing Santos, or
   c. T is being easy on Alvaro,
   So: T is unreliable, unfair, inconsistent.

This additional type of analysis, in terms of the interpretations open to the learner (or learners) at any point, complicates the whole research problem considerably. It suggests a further set of problems for teachers, too, who must, we assume, attempt to avoid confusion in the classroom. Teachers need a way of predicting the interpretations their behaviour will give rise to. The effectiveness of their treatment of error will depend on how it is perceived rather than on what it 'is' or is intended to be. Teachers' behaviour, in turn, will depend on how they perceive the learner or learners they are dealing with. The following factors, at least, are going to be relevant:

1. Individual differences, **e.g. personality type**, first language, culture, cognitive style, intelligence, aptitude, etc.
2. Past history, **e.g.** academic record, errors previously observed, treatment types previously used, etc.
3. Current state, **e.g.** motivation, anxiety level, arousal level, level of aspiration, fatigue, etc.

Space does not permit the development of this type of analysis to the original logical problem of the learners' interpretation of negative and positive instances of the target language, and of the teacher's need to help the learners reach the correct interpretations of the target language.

This paper has attempted to indicate both the wealth of interest and the methodological complexity that confront the researcher investigating the language teacher's treatment of learner error. This preliminary work, based on pilot data only, has permitted the elaboration of analyses that need to be refined by further observational studies. Enough has been done already to lend support to the original judgement that the treatment of the error variable would prove extremely interesting to study (by the researcher) to establish the pedagogical importance of the variable. This remains a sadly distant aim, but one that must not be allowed to move out of sight.

Appendix

Extract from a lesson recorded at Essex University, England, February 1975

176	T	I started at Essex on the fifth of October. When did you start? (nominates by gesture)
	S4	I start in Excess since the eleventh of January.
	T	When did you arrive? You arrived on the eleventh of January, did you? You must have started the next day, did you?
180	S2	(the eleventh of January
	S5	(the twelfth
	S5	No, I we start at thirteenth
	T	on the thirteenth of January
		When did you start at Essex? (Nominates by gesture)
185	Sl	I start at Essex on the thirteenth of January.
	T	On the thirteenth of January.
	S1	Yes.
	T	Again.
	S1	I start at Essex on the thirteenth of January.
190	T	Eulyces (pause)
		I started
	S2	I stotted
	T	(started
	S1	(start
195	S2	I . . . ( ) Aside to S1 in Spanish
		I start on on Essess eh fourteen January.
	T	I
	S2	Fourteenth January.
	T	I started at Essex on the thirteenth of January.

200	All right, Eulyces: on the thirteenth of January ...
	S2 On the th
	T Thirteenth
	S2 On the fourteenth of January
	T of January
205	S2 of January
	T on the thirteenth of January.
	S2 On fourteenth of January.
	T All together ... (on the thirteenth
	SSS (on the thirteenth of January
210	on the thirteenth of January
	T All right. I started at Essex (gesture for choral response)
	SSS I started at Essex on the thirteenth of January.
	T Good. Good.
	Were you at University before?

Notes on transcript

Line

177	Many errors – relatively weak learner chosen
178	Above errors ignored, except for error against truth concerning date
180–2	Learners sorting out truth. Errors of pronunciation, person and tense form ignored subsequently
183	T models full correct date phrase
185	Tense form error
186	T confirms correct phrase, ignores tense form error
188	T requests repeat
189	Tense form error again
190	T ignores above error and renominates
191	S2 hesitates, T models start of utterance
192	Pronunciation error
192–3	T remodels but so does S1, repeating own tense form error
195–6	S2 seeks S1's help, in Spanish, then copies S1 rather than T
198	S2 spontaneously self-corrects 'fourteen' to 'fourteenth'
199	T remodels full correct utterance. No emphasis on factual error
200	T acknowledges S2's difficulties, and remodels final phrase
201	S2 pauses after 'th'
203	S2 repeats factual error
204	T ignores factual error, repeats what S2 got right
206	T remodels correct phrase
207	S2 repeats factual error, omits 'the'
208	T transfers treatment to whole class
213–4	T praises satisfactory choral responses and changes sub-topic

The final two points made in the paper, that there was as yet no established evidence for the *pedagogic* importance of the treatment of error, and that this was not to be forgotten, were symptomatic of the feeling, already described, that there was no lack of intriguing puzzles to look at, but a strong lack of sufficient reason for isolating any one of them for special consideration. And this was in spite of the connections explicitly made between error treatment and error analysis, between practical pedagogy and second language acquisition studies. Gaies was on firmer ground, perhaps, for his work on input, given the established and continuing role of this concept in both second and first language acquisition studies.

2 Teacher talk as input

Gaies may not have known he was on firmer ground, since he was one of the first to investigate teacher talk as input. Henzl had done some related work in 1973 and 1975, and Larsen-Freeman had entered the field in 1976, using the data I had used for my turn-taking study. In 1975, Wagner-Gough and Hatch had drawn attention to the importance of input studies, but in the context of natural (i.e. 'untutored') second language acquisition. In the circumstances it was appropriate for Gaies to start his paper, 'The Nature of Linguistic Input in Formal Second Language Learning: Linguistic and Communicative Strategies in ESL Teachers' Classroom Language', by emphasizing the topic's background in studies of first language acquisition.

> A recent and encouraging development in research in first and second language acquisition has been the renewal of interest in the role of the linguistic environment in language learning. For a number of years, many studies of language learning focused almost exclusively on the utterances which learners produced and paid little attention to the language directed at them. This neglect of language input data – this failure to pay attention to the language to which a learner is exposed – can be attributed in part to the methodological difficulties of such research, but even more so to the influence of the early nativist view of first and (as has been inferred by many) second language acquisition.
>
> While the nativist theory of language acquisition continues to enjoy general acceptance among psycholinguists and applied linguists, it has been argued (Landes 1975) that the early nativist view at least partially misrepresented the nature of language acquisition through its assumption that language learners are exposed to random, often ungrammatical, and essentially unstructured samples of language to be acquired. This notion led to the position

espoused most notably by McNeill (1966) that the kind of linguistic input to which a learner is exposed is basically irrelevant, because it is the learner's innate pre-disposition to learn language that guides and shapes the acquisition process. In studies of first and second language learning, the overwhelming emphasis has in many cases been on examining the processes and strategies employed by learners as they progress towards a closer approximation of full target language competence. The abundance of 'error analyses' of second language learners' utterances bears witness to the emphasis placed on learner strategies, to the primary focus on the language learner and the frequent accompanying neglect of the nature of the interaction of learner and linguistic environment.

Recently, however, the argument has been advanced (Campbell 1972; Clark 1974; Landes 1975) that while the behaviorist claim that external, environmental sources are the sole determinants of learning is inadequate as an explanation of how language is learned, it is equally simplistic to ignore almost altogether the linguistic context in which language learning takes place. This argument is based on an accumulating body of empirical data which suggests the following points about the linguistic input to which first language learners are exposed:

1 In terms of syntax, the language addressed to children by adults consists for the most part of consistently short, grammatical sentences. These sentences on the whole are transformationally simpler, involve far less subordination and self-embedding, and include a much greater number of interrogative and imperative sentences than those typical of adult-adult discourse.

2 There is a tendency on the part of adults to use a relatively restricted lexicon when addressing young children. The token-type ratio, which is a measure of vocabulary diversity, of adult-child interactions has been found to be far smaller than that of samples of adult-adult discourse (Drach 1969; Granowksy and Krossner 1970).

3 Characteristic phonological features of the language addressed to children by adults are a reduced rate of speech, clearer articulation, and an exaggeration of normal stress and intonation patterns.

These consistent adjustments in the language addressed to children by adults (and this includes parents, non-parents, and even older children) have been characterized by some researchers as constituting a special linguistic style called 'motherese.' It would thus be a situational register deemed appropriate for use when the interlocutor is a young child in the process of acquiring a language. It should be pointed out, however, that the degree of linguistic adjustment appears to be geared to either the changing age or the increasing skills of the child. That is, the older the child, the less radically the language addressed to him/her differs from that used between adults.

In addition to these linguistic modifications, adults employ a number of communicative and/or language training strategies in their verbal interactions with young children. One of the most salient of these strategies is *repetition*,[1] which is a recurrent technique thought to have potential accelerating effects on language acquisition. Snow (1972) has argued that repetition increases processing time, thus increases a child's chances of processing input. One study (Kobashigawa 1969) of first language acquisition revealed that in a corpus of utterances addressed by a mother to her twenty-six month old son, 15% of the statements, 35% of the questions, and 60% of the imperatives were repeated with no long intervening pauses or activity.

Prodding characterizes instances when a parent (or other adult) makes it verbally clear that he/she wants the child to say or repeat something. Such verbal directions typically take the form of 'Can you say . . .?' or 'Say . . . .'. A related device is *prompting*, in which, for example, a parent will show a child a picture of something which the child knows the word for and will ask, 'What's this?' or 'This is a *what?*' Prompting and prodding afford the child practice in using the language and are thought to have some effect on language acquisition, despite the fact that, as Slobin (1971) has pointed out, frequency of repetition sometimes weighs less heavily with children than the perception of an underlying pattern.

Another general strategy is *modeling*, which may involve something as simple as an adult's supplying the appropriate lexical item for a child who does not know the name of something in a picture. A more complex form of modeling takes place when an adult expands the child's utterances. These so-called 'imitations in reverse,' which are presumably performed by adults to check their understandings of children's utterances, have been thought to contribute to language development in that they recognize the truth value of a child's statements at the same time that they demonstrate to the child how those statements are encoded by his/her speech community at the very moment when the child is likely to be most attentive to such information. In contrast to responses to other forms of adult corrective feedback, children's imitations of adult expansions are frequently grammatically progressive. Empirical evidence for this was provided by Nelson *et al.* (1973), who found that syntactic development of an experimental group of forty-month-old children was significantly enhanced by their exposure to expan-

1. These categories are from Landes 1975.

sions which recast the subjects' sentences by providing a new syntactic structure.

Unfortunately, it is premature to make a precise statement of the way in which the linguistic and communicative adjustments characteristic of the speech addressed to children facilitates or otherwise influences the language acquisition process. The issue is clouded by the fact that though the relative amount of linguistic input versus input from child-child interactions and adult linguistic performance heard by, but not specifically addressed to the learner, varies considerably from child to child within a culture and from culture to culture, the acquisition process proceeds at a remarkably uniform rate. At the very least, we have evidence that children incorporate either literally or through recombination sentences or units of speech even larger than sentences into their own linguistic repertoire from the language they hear around them, often without first internally analyzing them and deducing the underlying structure. Beyond that, the provisional assumption that the relative simplicity and organization of adult linguistic input and the use by adults of the training strategies just listed have some facilitating effect on the acquisition process, in that the child may more easily discover, for example, the basic sentence patterns, major constituent categories, and salient phonological features of the language, does not seem unreasonable.

It is interesting, and indicative of how things were changing, that in his introductory survey of the issue Gaies made no appeal to a concern for practical pedagogy. That is not to deny that he had any such concern, of course (and in fact he did relate his study to pedagogy at the end – as we shall see), only to point out that at last here was someone with entirely sufficient motivation for his work from outside language pedagogy.

In the next part of his paper Gaies described his own study. The word 'observation' did not appear, but the word 'corpus' did – further evidence of the changes in progress.

> Does the input to which formal second language learners are exposed through the oral classroom language of their teachers involve linguistic and communicative adjustments analogous to those which are characteristic of much of the adult input in first language acquisition? This was one question which the present study examined. The study was primarily an investigation of the syntax of the oral classroom language of eight ESL teacher-trainees enrolled in a Practicum course offered by the Program in Applied Linguistics at Indiana University.
>
> Three of the subjects were highly proficient non-native speakers

of English who had had some experience teaching English in their home countries. The others were native speakers of English whose prior teaching experience was quite limited.

The subjects taught adult ESL classes as part of the Practicum course requirements. These classes, which are offered each semester, meet hourly four evenings a week for a period of ten weeks. In the Fall of 1975, when the data for the present study was collected, instruction was offered at four different levels. Each of these four levels was taught by two teachers, who shared the teaching responsibility equally. It should be mentioned that the subjects were given a great deal of freedom in making decisions about teaching materials and techniques (particularly the former, since no texts were used in these classes), curricular goals, and classroom management practices.

Each of the subjects agreed to let the researcher tape three of his/her classes: one each at the beginning, middle, and end of the ten-week period. In addition, the weekly meetings of the Practicum class, in which the subjects and their instructors discussed general and specific problems and approaches in teaching English to speakers of other languages, were taped so that samples of the language which the subjects used with each other – i.e., among linguistic peers – could be obtained.

From each of the twenty-four classroom tapes, a corpus was selected for analysis. In each case, the sample to be analyzed syntactically consisted of the first 500 words contained in utterances containing an independent clause spoken by the teacher during the actual class period. For the baseline language data collected in the Practicum class meetings, the first 500 words spoken in sentence-length utterances by a subject to the class as a whole and with the class's attention constituted the sample for that subject. For both the ESL classroom and baseline data, the nonsentential utterances – fragments, false starts, attention holders, etc. – which occurred in the corpus were tabulated separately.

Gaies was using the 'observational' technique of sound recording to construct a corpus of the speech of just one participant-type in multi-participant settings. Direct classroom observation was crucial to his research design, but as a means to a new sort of end: that of investigating an issue 'imported' into the language classroom from work firmly based outside it.

Gaies' data analysis, the subject of the next part of his paper, was equally novel from the perspective of the history of classroom observation as we have documented it in this volume.

> The samples were transcribed and analyzed by the researcher. Syntactic analysis proceeded by segmenting the 500-word samples

into T-units. A T-unit is defined as 'one main clause plus any subordinate clause or nonclausal structure that is attached to or embedded in it' (Hunt 1970, p. 4). This unit of syntactic analysis is objective and easy to compute, and in the last ten years it has gained increasing recognition as a far more valid index of syntactic complexity than other measures, including sentence length. A particularly attractive feature of the T-unit as an index of syntactic maturity (complexity) was revealed by O'Donnell, Norris, and Griffin (1967); in their study of syntax of the oral and written language of elementary schoolchildren, these researchers noted a close relationship between T-unit length and the number of sentence-combining transformations required to generate a T-unit. Differential mean length of T-unit, then, appears to reflect the relative degree to which users exploit the transformational resources of English.

Altogether, measures on six dependent variables were computed for each sample. These variables were: words per T-unit, ratio of clauses (main and subordinate) to T-units, words per clause, adjective (relative) clauses per 100 T-units, adverbial clauses per 100 T-units, and noun clauses per 100 T-units.

Table 1 presents a comparison of the means of the subjects' classroom language and their speech among linguistic peers. The data as measured by all six dependent variables indicates an overall process of syntactic simplification in the classroom language. The subjects spoke in shorter clauses and used fewer subordinate clauses per T-unit when addressing their students than they did

TABLE 1 Comparison of syntactic complexity of subjects' baseline (Practicum class meetings) language and their oral classroom language

| Variable | Source of language sample | |
	Baseline (N = 8)	ESL Classroom (N = 24)
w/T	10.97	6.19
c/T	1.60	1.20
w/c	6.84	5.10
AD/100	11.59	2.54
AV/100	20.27	5.33
N/100	28.54	11.16

w/T = words per T-unit
c/T = clauses per T-unit
w/c = words per clause
AD/100 = adjective clauses per 100 T-units
AV/100 = adverb clauses per 100 T-units
N/100 = noun clauses per 100 T-units

when speaking to highly proficient interlocutors. Multivariate analysis of variance performed on the data revealed that the overall difference in syntactic complexity was highly statistically significant (p = <.0001).

The next step in the analysis involved the comparison of the oral performance of the subjects according to the level at which they were teaching. What emerges from the data (see Table 2) is an unmistakable and statistically significant (p = <.0227) relationship between the syntactic complexity of the subjects' classroom language and the level of proficiency of their students. At any level, the syntax of the teachers' oral classroom language is more complex than at the level immediately below it and less complex than at the level immediately above it; and *this is true for every one of the six criterion variables.*

This syntactic adjustment evident in the subjects' oral classroom language is similar to that found both in previous studies (Henzl 1973, 1975) of the verbal performance of foreign language teachers and in samples of adult language addressed to children. Equally similar was the way in which the rate of speech and vocabulary diversity of the subjects' classroom language increased as a function of the level of proficiency of the students they were teaching.

TABLE 2   Comparison of syntactic complexity of subjects' oral classroom language by level

| Level | Variable | | | | | |
	w/T	c/T	w/c	AD/100	AV/100	N/100
L₁ (Beginner) (N =6)	4.30	1.02	4.20	0.00	0.76	1.60
L₂ (Upper Beginner) (N = 6)	5.75	1.14	5.04	1.46	3.64	6.92
L₃ (Intermediate) (N =6)	6.45	1.24	5.18	2.26	8.40	13.54
L₄ (Advanced) (N = 6)	8.26	1.38	5.98	6.47	8.51	20.91
X̄ₗ (N = 24)	6.19	1.20	5.10	2.54	5.33	11.16

These similarities between adult input to children and the speech addressed to adult second language learners by their teachers are not surprising. After research by Ferguson (1975) and others has led to the claim that modifications of the full adult system of this sort are consistently made by members of a speech community on behalf of all learners of the language, whether or not the verbal interaction has explicit instructional goals. What is particularly noteworthy, however, is the presence in the oral classroom language of the subjects of both linguistic adjustments and the very training strategies characteristic of adult input to children.

Consider first the strategy of repetition. As mentioned earlier, repetition is an alternative or complement to linguistic simplification as a means of facilitating comprehension. It was for this reason that sentence-length utterances which were exact and immediate – that is, which occurred with no intervening pauses, activity, or change of interlocutor – repetitions were marked and tabulated separately in the analysis of the data. Repetition was used most frequently at the two lower levels of instruction, and practically not at all at the advanced level. An indication of how prevalent this strategy was for communication and teaching at the beginner level is the fact that utterances containing a total of 660 words were exact repetitions. In other words, more than 20% of the subjects' sentences were repeated in exactly the same form. Thus, at the beginner level, students not only heard input which was far less syntactically complex than that directed at more proficient students, but also had in general more time to process that input.

Prompting and prodding are strategies which can also be observed at the lower levels of formal classroom language instruction. These strategies, however, seem, even more so than repetition, to be very transitional devices, and their use is predictably restricted to those classroom activities which involve naming concrete objects – i.e., to the initial stages of instruction.

A more important classroom strategy is modeling, which was accomplished through two complementary but very different procedures. The first involved the use of fragments. If a subject asked a student a question and the student made an appropriate and syntactically complete response, the subject would often supplement the reinforcement of that response by repeating the crucial lexical or other item in the response. For example, if a student answered the question, 'How did you come to class this evening?' by saying, 'I came to class by bus,' there was a tendency to respond, 'Yes, by bus.' Again, the strategy was most evident at the lower levels, which proceeded much more frequently than the more advanced levels through long series of short, teacher-initiated question–answer drills.

The alternative modeling technique – and the strategy which was most evident at all levels – was teachers' expansion of students' utterances. The strategy was often purely communicative – i.e, when it was used to check comprehension – but it served equally often, and again primarily at the lower levels, as a pedagogical strategy. The most obvious case of this was when a student responded to a question with a single word or phrase and the teacher expanded the response into a full independent clause.

Gaies' analytic categories came from the background work in first
and second language acquisition, and were not related in any way,
except by coincidence, to any of the category systems represented
elsewhere in this volume.

Finally Gaies considered the implications of his study, concluding
with comments from the perspective of language teaching.

> What implications can reasonably be drawn from the similarity in
> linguistic adjustments and communicative/training strategies of the
> input data to which first and second language learners are exposed?
> First of all, the observed 'training sessions' which result from the
> use of these strategies in a teacher's verbal interactions with his/her
> learners would be a major and identifiable criterion distinguishing
> formal from unstructured or 'natural' second language learning,
> since in the latter these strategies would presumably be considered
> less frequently employed by speakers of a language whose contact
> with a learner of the language has no explicit pedagogical goals.
>
> Again, there is additional support for Corder's (1967) position
> that the burden of proof remains with those who argue that first
> and second language learning proceed in a fundamentally different
> manner. This is not to suggest that there are no differences
> between first and subsequent language learning. One difference
> already alluded to is that many training strategies begin to be aban-
> doned relatively early – perhaps too early – in formal second
> language learning. And obviously, if we judge solely by the criterion
> of the relative percentage of instances on which first and second
> language learners attain full competence in the target language,
> there is a quantitative difference involved. However, just as a
> number of studies of second language learning have demonstrated
> that learners use processing strategies very similar to those
> employed by children acquiring their first language, we now have
> evidence, however preliminary, that the organization and presen-
> tation of the input with which they work is not unlike the primary
> linguistic input which children hear.
>
> Another implication arises from the relationship between the
> perceived proficiency of the learners and the nature of their
> teachers' oral classroom language. Elsewhere (Gaies 1976c), I have
> discussed the need for examining linguistic input as a factor in the
> development of transitional stages of competence or 'inter-
> languages.' Let me simply suggest here that as regards second
> language learning materials development, the principle that language
> drills should involve sentences which are increasingly longer and
> syntactically more complex (Stieglitz 1973) is indirectly validated
> by the findings of the present study. In view of the fact that
> teachers gear their own spoken language and communicative strat-

egies to the proficiency of their students, the claim that grading a series of oral manipulation drills from easy to difficult by itself leads to an 'artificial' exposure to the target language is not defensible.

A final and potentially the most immediately important implication of the relationship of the data from the present study to the linguistic input in first language learning is a revised notion of what is natural and what is artificial about formal (classroom) second language learning. Many of the kinds of foreign language classroom activities closely associated with the inductive or 'audio-lingual' approach to language teaching, as well as many of the concomitant teaching procedures, are not at all different from the kinds of language training sessions which adult linguistic input provides children with. At the early stages of formal second language learning – at the period when students are traditionally provided the training in skills acquisition which is thought to be essential to more creative, sophisticated uses of the target language – adult language learners are asked to repeat (this is equivalent to the strategies of prompting and prodding), have items repeated for them to facilitate processing, are given verbal signals to imitate – this is equivalent to modeling – and often have their responses expanded by their teachers (which constitutes a reinforcement of the truth value of their response as well as a model of how that response is fully elaborated in the target language). There is nothing inherently artificial about these activities, at least if we judge by their role in first language acquisition. What makes them 'unnatural' and perhaps more than anything else provokes dissatisfaction, is that these drills, these training strategies, are too often semantically divorced in every way from the classroom surrounding or the students' experience, past and present. Then they are unnatural and uninteresting. But this is no more necessarily the case in formal second language learning than it would be in first language acquisition.

It is significant that Gaies' conclusions in respect of language teaching did not concern themselves at all with possible 'new and improved' techniques for language pedagogy. That was not his world at all, for the purposes of this paper. If anything, we might notice that his concluding remarks would be more likely to give comfort to established teachers than to excite new ones with novelty.

Gaies' work on teacher talk as input did not lead to a whole series of replication studies on the topic. The interest it generated was of a different sort. The paper helped focus attention on the role of classroom input, and the field could move on and begin to deal more adequately with the social nature of that input, incorporating learners' contributions to it and redefining 'input' in the process. Chaudron did, however, stay closer to the teacher-centred focus of Gaies' work, with studies on, among other things, teacher talk as 'foreigner talk' (1983). Krashen, meanwhile, was developing his 'input hypothesis' (1985), and drawing attention more to the probable importance of input being comprehensible. Taken together with the topic of our third paper for Chapter 5, these were the origins of a major 'growth area' – the study of the relationships between input and interaction.

3 Learner interaction

Seliger's work on learner interaction was grounded in second language acquisition studies but also firmly related to a practical pedagogic issue, the perennial 'puzzle' of 'the common lack of transfer from the language lesson to natural language use contexts'. Seliger began his 1977 paper, 'Does Practice Make Perfect?: A Study of Interaction Patterns and L2 Competence', by setting out these two backgrounds, defining 'interaction' for his purposes, and then introducing his two learner types – high input generators (HIGs) and low input generators (LIGs).

> The cognitive effects of practice can be described as the counter-action of what Ausubel (1971) calls 'obliterative subsumption.' In other words, practice aids in the retention of those features which discriminate newly learned concepts from similar previously learned ones. The process of subsumption consists of subsuming or attaching new concepts to already existing networks. While subsumption aids retention, it has negative effects. In order to subsume new material within already existing cognitive networks, unique features or attributes of the new concept are often reduced or obliterated. While such a simplification strategy makes storage easier, it makes retrieval more difficult. Practice, in this context, serves the function of preserving the features unique to the new concept and thus preserving its entity.
>
> Within second language learning, overgeneralization errors resulting from L1 interference or the overextension of L2 rules can probably be traced to the obliterative effects which erase the contrastive features of one rule when it is subsumed under another already existing rule. Practice or further use of the language by the learner for his own purposes helps to distinguish the features of newly acquired rules whether they be rules of well-formedness or contextual appropriateness.
>
> Since formal instruction, because of time constraints, does not allow much practice of new language concepts in the manner described above, additional practice is necessary if the learner is to retain and completely acquire the feature system of a new language concept. Of course what this means is that much of what

must be learned, given even an optimal teaching system, must be acquired outside of formal instruction but perhaps built on what is acquired within a formal instructional framework.

This should not be taken to mean that formal instruction has little value for language practice. Rather, what will be shown is that some learners, because of certain cognitive or affective characteristics, are able to exploit formal learning environments for extensive practice while others derive only limited benefit from formal instruction. It also appears, based on the results of this study, that those who are capable of deriving the most benefit from formal learning environments may be the most likely to use this formally acquired base for further language development in informal or naturalistic learning environments.

In other words, an explanation for the common lack of transfer from the language lesson to natural language use contexts may reside not only in inadequacies of methods of instruction but in areas such as the motivation of the learner to seek and exploit opportunities for further practice and in limitations imposed on learners by different affective or cognitive styles. Such constraints prevent the learner from using potential practice situations for the further differentiation of subsumed concepts.

A simple conclusion from all of this is that the more one practices, the better his competence should become. Competence is defined in this study as well-formedness in the linguistic sense and as the general ability to understand and to make oneself understood by others. The criteria which were used in this study to reflect relative differences in language competence were language tests and the responses of subjects in an interview.

For the purposes of this study, the term practice has been defined as any verbal interaction between the learner and others in his environment. Usually such interaction consists of an output speech act by the learner and an input speech act from some other speaker. In some cases input will precede output and in other cases the reverse may be true. In the language classroom, those providing input to the learner may be the teacher or fellow class-mates. When the teacher directs a question to a specific learner, that input will usually elicit output from the learner. The learner himself may elicit input by asking questions or commenting aloud thus engendering language responses from other learners or from the teacher. Practice also consists of covert activity such as listening to the radio, watching television and reading. However, there is no way to tell when a learner is actively focused on language input in such situations.

In the sense used in this paper, practice has been measured quantitatively as the gross number of such interactions. The more interactions that take place, the more practice is said to take place. In addition, input/output speech acts which make up the interaction may vary in length from one word such as *yes* or *no* to several sentences in reply to an input question. In recording interactions for this study, no cognizance was taken of differences in length or complexity. Only the fact of an interaction having taken place was recorded. It is assumed that even in the case of a simple but meaningful *yes* or *no*, practice is taking place in the form of processing the input which generated *yes* or *no*.

This study tested the hypothesis that learners who practice by initiating interactions, and thereby cause a concomitant input from others, will benefit more from practice opportunities. These learners will be called *high input generators* (HIG). By initiating language interaction, the high input generator causes a reflexive response in the form of more language input to himself. Conversely, at the other extreme are language learners who play a relatively passive role in language interaction. Their behavior is reactive to input but they do little to initiate situations which cause more input to be directed to them. Such learners will be called *low input generators* (LIG). In language classes, low input generators prefer to be left alone. Often, the low input generator only interacts with the teacher during drill sessions. In a previous study (Seliger and Gingras 1976), low input generators had as much as 98% of their interactions with the teacher while high input generators, who produced more total output, had as little as 35% of their interactions with the teacher while 65% of their interactions were with other students and in the target language. In addition, because of the normal limitations of time and class size, those who wait to be spoken to before speaking will speak very little while those who take the initiative in such situations will practice much more.

It appears that small children at the language acquisition stage and adult second language learners exhibit similar kinds of interactive behavior and that such behavior may serve the same purpose for both kinds of language acquisition contexts. For example, a not yet two-year-old (the author's child) would often initiate language interaction even though it was obvious that little communication was taking place. She would often push her father's newspaper aside to get his attention and then direct a stream of gibberish at him mixed with a few hardly understood words. He, in turn, could discuss the weather, the stock market, her siblings or American foreign policy with her. It didn't seem to matter what was said as long as some interaction was taking place. As long as the child was answered, she would continue the game for quite some time. The question that must be asked is why a baby would participate in an activity in which very little was understood. One might explain such activity on the basis of Mowrer's (1960) autism theory of language acquisition and state that the baby was simply deriving pleasure from the vocal contact with a parent. However, it is possible that this very natural form of behavior might well be an important learning strategy in the language acquisition process. What the child was doing was getting language knowers to use language with her. Since she was dependent on the language knowers in her environment to provide her with appropriate models, she had a choice of sitting and waiting to be addressed or causing others to relate to her and feed her language. (For a similar view see Luria 1974/75.)

It is proposed here that a similar strategy is used by adult second language learners. In a program in which assumptions about minimal levels of education may be made and in which students are grouped homogeneously by placement tests, one still finds different rates of acquisition for different learners. What becomes obvious if one teaches or observes such classes is that there are differing degrees of learner involvement in the language lesson. Some students, the high input generators, are actively involved and, like the child, cause input to be directed at them by calling out, answering out of turn, and working out answers to questions or drill cues directed to others. Such students can often be observed talking to themselves during language drills. Still other students, the low input generators, sit quietly but rarely and in some extreme cases never participate unless specifically asked to do so.

As for Gaies, it is worth noting that Seliger made no appeal to the 'traditional' literature on classroom interaction, neither to the tradition of Flanders nor to any of the 'alternatives to Flanders' introduced in Chapter 4. Like Gaies, he had a quite different, and independently justified, source for his approach and for his terminology.

Seliger continued by stating his 'primary hypothesis' – an extremely rare case for the time of classroom research into language teaching and learning having a hypothesis to test – and describing the design and methodology of his study.

Design and methodology

The Primary Hypothesis

The purpose of this experiment was to test the primary hypothesis that high input generators (HIG) would tend to be higher achievers than low input generators (LIG) when rankings of the HIG and LIG were compared for intensity of interaction and achievement.

H_1: HIG > LIG when compared for interaction and achievement.

Achievement was defined as the learner's performance on examinations given at the end of a fifteen week semester when compared with his performance on placement examinations given at the beginning of the same semester. The same examinations were given as pretest and post-test: a discrete point test of English structure (Lado-Fries) and the Queens College English Language Institute Test of Aural Comprehension which is an integrative measure. In addition, all subjects were tested with a cloze test at the end of the semester.

Subjects and Classroom Environment

The adult subjects for this study were selected from an upper intermediate level class in the English Language Institute which is an intensive ESL program for foreign students at Queens College, C.U.N.Y. The six subjects who contributed the data for this study were selected from a class of twelve students after four hours of class observation. They were selected on the basis of being classified as either high interactors or low interactors. (See below for description of interaction measurement.) The subjects were: two Iranians, one Japanese, one Greek, one Israeli, and one Spanish speaker.

The observations for interaction took place in regular classes of the Institute. The only condition placed on which classes were to be observed was that the lesson allow for as much verbal interaction as possible. For this reason, only classes concerned with teaching oral skills were observed. All observed classes were what might be called 'frontal' in the sense that the students sat in rows facing the teacher.

The Measurement of Verbal Interaction

Language interaction was observed by two observers during four hours of classes. Two observers were used to control for observer reliability. A previous study, Seliger and Gingras (1976), found inter-observer agreement on the relative ranking of student interaction to correlate at .984. In this study, inter-observer correlation was .917. Even though the exact numbers of interactions tabulated for each student differed for the observers, the overall ranking of students showed the above levels of agreement. The discrepancy in interaction scores between observers can be explained on the basis of size of the group that was being observed and the positions of the observers. Observers usually sat on opposite sides of the classroom so that, while there was some overlapping of fields of vision, interactions which happened close to one observer might be missed by another. Group size is also a determining factor. Bales (1970) suggests that no group be greater than seven for such observations.

Any speech act by a student in the class was counted as an

interaction. Speech acts considered as one interaction might be a single word or several sentences in a discourse. Using a code, the following information about each interaction was recorded on a tabulation sheet devised for the experiment.

a. Which student spoke? Did he/she address another student? the teacher? the whole group?

b. Did the student initiate the interaction (shown by +) or was he responding (shown by /)?

c. Was the student using English or his L1 in the interaction? (Shown by (+) for initiated but in L1 and (/) for respondent but in L1.)

The number of these interactions was tabulated for each student in the observed class at the end of each observation session. At the conclusion of the four hours of observation, the students were ranked according to the total number of interactions and the type of interactions in L2. Three of the highest interactors (HIG) and three of the lowest interactors (LIG) were then selected from the class of twelve for further study. These six were then interviewed and administered a language contact and motivation questionnaire and an embedded figure test.

The Language Contact Profile

The Language Contact Profile (LCP) is a revised version of a previous questionnaire devised by Seliger and Gingras (1976) for the study of language contact and motivation. It is a self-report questionnaire administered by the experimenter. The LCP quantifies the learner's motivation and the extent of contact with the second language (potential practice opportunities) outside of regular language classes. While numerical values are obtained in response to the variously weighted questions, the LCP admittedly provides only approximate measures and they should be interpreted as such. (See Appendix for LCP.)

The results obtained from the LCP were compared with other measures to examine the relationship between out-of-class language activity and classroom interaction patterns. Hypothesis 2 was that HIG differed from LIG in the amount of such out-of-class language activity.

H_2: HIG > LIG for LCP scores.

Cloze

A cloze test consisting of 50 items in which every fifth word in the test was left out was administered to all E.L.I. students as part of the final examination battery. This test was not used as part of the placement battery. The test was marked using the exact word method. The scores that appear in Table 1 are percentages.

TABLE 1   Raw scores on criterion measures and percent change for pre-test and post-test*

		Student					
		M	A	N	D	Z	G
1	A	39	40	62	12	8	0
	B	77	71.5	92.5	31.5	24.4	11
	C	51%	56%	67%	38%	32%	0%
2		45	46	52	30	20	20
3	A	84	63	64	71	75	80
	B	92	89	91	89	83	74
	C	8%	41%	42%	25%	11%	−8%
4	A	30	62	64	36	44	46
	B	74	90	86	56	52	56
	C	147%	31%	34%	56%	18%	21%
5		43	44	41	39	29	32
6		60	48	48	36	44	28

*1   Interactions, 1A. Initiated interactions, 1B. Total interactions, 1C (percentage of total which were initiated).
2   Language Contact Profile Score (LCP)
3   Structure test, 3A. Placement, 3B. Final, 3C (percentage of change between Placement and Final).
4   Aural comprehension, 4A. Placement, 4B. Final, 4C (percentage of change between Placement and Final).
5   Cloze
6   Group Embedded Figures Test (% of 25).

Rankings for interaction and cloze were correlated (Table 2) for the six subjects. It was hypothesized that HIGs would score higher than LIGs. This is based partially on DeFazio's (1973) findings that field independents (see below) perform better on the cloze test and the generally accepted notion that cloze is a reliable measure of integrative or functional abilities in L2.

H$_3$: HIG > LIG for cloze.

Field Sensitivity

Subjects were administered the Group Embedded Figures Test. Adjustments were made in time allotments per section of the test. The Group Embedded Figures Test is a corresponding form for the individual Embedded Figures Test. In this test, the subject is asked to find a designated figure which is embedded in another figure. The task is similar to those found in children's books and magazines in which the child is asked to find the shape of an object such as an animal when it is part of a larger figure. In the case of the Embedded Figures Test, the subject is asked to find a geometric shape which is embedded within another geometric shape.

The Embedded Figures Test is a further development of the concept of field sensitivity originally proposed by Witkin and his associates (1954). In the last few years, many studies have examined the personality and cognitive style parameters of this concept (see for example, Witkin, Cox and Friedman 1976). Two general psychological types which relate to other affective and cognitive variables have been identified from these studies. Individuals are thought to be on a continuum of what is termed field independence to field dependence. The relative ability to perceive figures within a context is called field independence. The relative inability to perform this task is termed field dependence. In other words, a confounding context has different effects on the perceptual abilities of individual subjects.

A recent study by Lefever and Ehri (1976) found a positive correlation between field independence and sentence disambiguation ability. DeFazio (1973) found that field independents tended to perform better than field dependents on cloze tests. Because of these and similar findings, it was suspected that the HIGs might be able to induce more from any language context and therefore felt less of a need to depend on structured drill than did the LIGs. In addition, the fact the HIGs might be more intensely interacting with L2 outside the language classroom might be taken as an indication of their success in dealing with perceptually embedded language data. This success would in turn encourage further interaction. LIGs, on the other hand, if they are also field dependent, would be likely to experience difficulty in functioning in natural language environments and tend to avoid interaction.

Ramirez and Castaneda (1974) write that field dependent types are much more sensitive to the approval and disapproval of authority figures. Suzman (1973) states that field independent types use inner guides for action rather than relying on such external cues as authority. Suzman also found that field independents were more willing to take risks than field dependents. All of this would tend to predict that HIGs would be field independent, less fearful of experimenting with language, less afraid to make mistakes and less afraid to speak out. Field dependent subjects, on the other hand, would be more likely to speak only when asked to in the language class and more fearful of disapproval because of mistakes.

In summary, because of the affective and cognitive variables associated with the field sensitivity construct, it was hypothesized that HIGs would also tend to be field independent while LIGs would tend toward field dependence.

H₄: HIG > LIG for measures of field independence.

It is striking that even in his detailed description of his data collection procedures Seliger did not need to relate his study to the classroom observation 'tradition'. It is perhaps significant that his only reference to outside sources here was to Bales, whose work on interaction processes was already extremely well established (see Bales 1950), but in the field of business management studies rather than in education.

It is also striking, as an example of a further change in the role of classroom observation, that for Seliger the observations served only to isolate six learners for further study *by other means*. In the remainder of Seliger's paper there was no need for further reference to the original classroom data – a strong contrast to the other two papers in this chapter, as well as to those in previous chapters.

Analysis of results

H₁: HIG > LIG for Interaction and Final Examination Results
This hypothesis was supported. It will be noted from Table 2 that negative or low correlations respectively were found for rankings based on the total number of interactions (Total Interactions) and rankings based on the percentage of interactions which were initiated (% initiated) when these were correlated with structure placement and aural comprehension placement. Based on these initial comparisons, it would not have been possible to predict the performance of subjects on the basis of placement tests. That is, placement test results would not have predicted final test results (p = −.014).

The negative or low correlations obtained for interaction and placement tests is problematic in light of the fact that strong positive correlations were found for interaction and final tests. In fact, the structure test which correlated negatively with interaction was very high in correlating as a final test. The following interpretations might be considered:

1   The discrete point test of specific rules does not measure communicative or functional abilities while aural comprehension does and the HIG may initially lack control of specific grammar rules while performing better on measures of functional ability. Therefore

TABLE 2 Correlations of interaction measures with measures of achievement, language contact, and field sensitivity*

	Total Interaction	% of Initiated Interaction
Total Interaction		0.942
Structure Placement	−0.314	−0.600
Structure Final	0.929	0.728
% Change	0.943	1.000
Aural Comprehension Placement	0.200	0.429
Aural Comprehension Final	0.829	0.886
% Change	0.657	0.486
Cloze	0.714	0.771
Language Contact Profile	0.936	0.971
Embedded Figures	0.843	0.757

* For all of the above, p is significant at .829 for a one-tailed test (see G. A. Ferguson 1959, *Statistical Analysis in Psychology and Education*. New York: McGraw-Hill Book Company, Inc.)

it would be expected that aural comprehension scores (placement and final) would show the same trend.

2   These subjects had had little exposure to intensive English as a second language. Their previous experience with English had been limited to the study of English as a foreign language taught by non-native speakers. It might be surmised that the HIGs were able to capitalize on practice opportunities in and out of class to improve not only functional ability as measured by the comprehension test but also to improve upon previously acquired passive knowledge in grammar as measured by the discrete point structure test.

H_2: HIG > LIG for Language Contact Profile (LCP)

This hypothesis was also supported. An item analysis of the results of the LCP reveals that HIGs tended to score higher than LIGs on items 15, 16 and 17. Item #15 asked subjects to name three of their closest friends in New York City and the language which they spoke with each friend. It was assumed that social contact with English would enable speakers to practice more of those skills related to the communicative use of language. It may also be taken as a measure of the personality type that the HIG represents. That is, he is a learner who seeks out opportunities for the use of 1.2.[1]

No relationship was found between the amount of time in the United States and the number of close English speaking friends. As an example, M and Z had been in the United States for approximately five months and both lived within communities which allowed easy access to speakers of their own L1. M, a Japanese woman, named two non-Japanese as her closest friends while Z, an Iranian woman, had no non-Persian speaking friends with whom she spoke English.

Item #16 asked the subjects to list three English speaking Americans with whom they have the most contact. This item distinguished contact with Americans (#16) from contact with anyone with whom English would be the language of communication (#15). In addition, subjects were asked to describe the kind of relationship they had with the person named. Suggested types of relationships were: teacher, storekeeper, friend, relative, landlord, etc. HIGs tended to list friends as their American contacts while LIGs tended to list teachers or doctors.

H_3: HIG > LIG for Cloze

This hypothesis was not supported by the data. The ranking correlations between total interactions or initiated interactions and the cloze test results did not reach significance. However, the results (Table 2) do indicate a healthy trend in the direction of a relationships between a cloze integrative measure and interaction.

H_4: HIGs Tend toward Field Independence; LIGs Tend toward Field Dependence

The results as seen from Table 2 only partially support this hypothesis. Total interactions correlate significantly with field independence while rankings for initiated interaction do not. It should be noted that levels of significance are for a one-tailed test. A two-tailed measure would be significant. However, given the small number of subjects, the general direction of the results is encouraging.

1. One might be led to a conclusion from this statement that the HIG is an integratively motivated learner. However, Seliger and Gingras (1976) found no differential effects for integrative/instrumental motivation. This may simply mean that since all learners in these studies are foreign students in the L2 environment for a very short time, the measurement of integrative/instrumental motivation is inappropriate for this population. That is, interaction type and motivation type are not interacting variables for this kind of population. Further study of this problem with bilingual children is warranted.

Conclusions

This study examined the relationship between external language behavior in the form of intensity of verbal interaction between the learner and his language environment and the effects of this inter-action on language abilities as measured by language tests. While it may seem obvious at first glance that practice has an effect on language competence, it should also be obvious that different kinds of practice have different effects on developing competence. Teachers have long been frustrated with the phenomenon of near perfect performance in formal drill in class and the lack of transfer of this performance to real communicative ability.

This study has shown that learners may be classified into two main types:

1 Active learners who utilize all language environments, both formal and natural, for practice by interacting and getting others to use language with them are termed *high input generators*. The end result of their behavior is a competence which develops at a faster and perhaps qualitatively better rate. By getting more focused input, the *high input generator* is able to test more hypotheses about the shape and use of L2.

2 Passive learners who do not exploit practice opportunities and retreat from interaction are termed *low input generators*. This type of learner will avoid intensive contact with the second language. For this reason, the *low input generator is heavily dependent on language learning environments such as the classroom* which are artificially contrived to force him into contact with L2. Because of the limitations of formal learning environments, the *low input generator* will receive a limited amount of focused input and will not seek out additional practice opportunities when left to his own devices. This 'avoidance' behavior affects the rate of L2 achievement.

The results of this research apply only to the group studied. It focused on subjects who were at two extremes on the interaction continuum. It must be assumed, as with other learner variables, that the Input Generator concept is a continuum. It is also not incon-ceivable that learners who are typed as *low input generators* in the classroom could compensate for the disadvantages of this behavior by other forms of language contact outside the classroom. No such exceptions were found in the group studied here.

The results of this study do raise important questions about previous research concerned with the role of formal instruction versus exposure to language in natural situations. At one extreme are those like Newmark and Reibel (1968) who have claimed that structuring in the normal sense is unnecessary. Others like

Macnamara (1975) have claimed that adults can learn like children from exposure and that there are no real differences between child and adult abilities. Other studies (Krashen and Seliger 1975, 1976 and Seliger 1975) have argued that exposure is not the determining variable in adult success but instruction is.

It appears that the primary problem with all of these studies has been a simplistic view of both the learner's role and the term 'exposure' or its synonyms – 'practice opportunities' or 'natural language settings.' The term *exposure* is neutral. Being exposed to language is not like being exposed to a virus. One doesn't catch it automatically. Children seem to catch a first language automatically but one can hardly imagine a normal child retreating from language interaction. The adult apparently has the option. The learner must do something active that involves him cognitively in the process. The distinction that has been made between 'input' and 'intake' captures this.

This study has examined two extreme types of learners – those who intensively interact with their language environment and those who do not. Based on the results of this study, it may be concluded that *high input generators* will benefit from instruction because they are maturationally able to do so. However, they will also exploit other practice opportunities beyond what is presented formally. *Low input generators* on the other hand, do not interact intensively in language classes or outside of language classes. While they too are maturationally capable of benefitting from formal instruction, it appears that they are also dependent on it.

Appendix

Language Contact Profile

E. _____

Date _____

Program _____ Level _____

Score 1. Student's name _____ Sex M/F

2. Country of origin _____ How long in U.S.?
   _____

3. Educational level (grade school, h.s., college, etc.) ____

4. Native language _____

5. Age _____

_____ 6. About how much time do you spend speaking English outside of class every day? (circle one)

   a. none = 0
   b. very little (directions, shopping etc.) = 1
   c. occasionally (with friends) = 2
   d. most of the time = 3

7. How well do you think you speak English now?

a. poorly b. fair c. good d. very good e. excellent
(E. do you agree or disagree with S's evaluation _____

8. How many years have you studied English? _____
Where? _____

_____ 9. Do you live with anyone who speaks *only* English? ____
How much time do you spend with them on a daily basis?
a. less than one hour (2 points)
b. one or two hours (4 points)
c. more than two hours (6 points)

_____10. Are newspapers and magazines available in your first
language? Y/N
How often do you read them?
a. seldom = 4
b. once in a while = 3
c. weekly = 2
d. daily = 1

_____11. When you have homework in English do you
a. do it as soon as you can = 4
b. do it if you find time = 3
c. do it at the last possible moment = 2
d. do it but turn it in late = 1
e. (none of these) _____

_____12. During English classes do you
a. have a tendency to daydream about your country = 0
b. have to force yourself to listen to the lesson = 0
c. listen at all times, even when it's not your turn = 4
d. listen when it's your turn but do other things when
it's not = 2

_____13. Do you watch television programs in English?
a. as often as you can = 3
b. once in a while = 3
c. not very often = 1
d. never = 0
e. prefer watching programs in your native language.
Otherwise you do not watch television at all = 0

_____14. If you have a choice between listening to a radio program
in your native language or in English do you
a. prefer English = 3
b. sometimes listen to the English programs and sometimes to those in your language = 2
c. would not listen to the English programs = 0

_____15. List your three closest friends in New York City.
name of friend   language usually
                           spoken with friend
a. _____   _____
b. _____   _____
c. _____   _____

(score: 3 points for each friend with whom English is
used, 0 points for language other than English)

_____16. List the three *English speaking Americans* that you speak English with the most. In what capacity do you know them? (e.g. teacher, busdriver, friend, neighbor, landlord, storeclerk, boss, relative, etc.).

　　　　name of American　　　　relationship

　　a. _____　　_____
　　b. _____　　_____
　　c. _____　　_____

(score: friend = 2 points, relative = 2 points, teacher = 1 point, other formal relationships such as busdriver, landlord, clerk, etc. = 1)

_____17. Do you spend time trying to improve your English outside of class? _____ How? (list all activities, e.g. watching t.v., reading, writing, speaking with friends, going to movies, etc.)

_____

_____

About how much time each day *for each activity*?
a. one hour = 1 b. two hours = 2 c. three hours = 3 etc.
(score: 4 points for each active or productive activity, 2 points for each passive or receptive activity. Multiply each of these by the amount of time spent in this activity per day; add up.)

As noted in the concluding comments to the previous section, Seliger's paper was one of those that gave the initial impetus to studies of the relationships between input and interaction. As for teacher talk there was no rash of follow-up studies, although Seliger did publish an updated version of his 1977 paper in 1983, and in 1984 Day published a study that incidentally failed to reproduce Seliger's original results. It does no credit at all to researchers on classroom language learning and teaching to be so uninterested in undertaking replication studies. Elsewhere (Allwright 1983) I have suggested a 'prima donna' mentality as characteristic of our field, but there is also the major factor that in a new and rapidly developing area any initial study, however much in need of careful replication, is likely to be so suggestive that its tentative results will be largely accepted and the field will move on. In such a context it was important that Day's attempt to replicate Seliger's study did in fact challenge Seliger's findings. Because of the unavoidable differences between the two studies we cannot say that Day's results necessarily 'overturn' Seliger's, of course. Both may be true results. But we are now much less likely to make unwarranted generalizations about the role of learner interaction. (My own turn-taking study had already specu-latively challenged the generalizability of Seliger's findings, of course, with Igor participating most but not making noteworthy progress, and another learner participating very little but making most progress.)

One final point to note in connection with Seliger's paper is that it paralleled the others in this chapter in its avoidance of conclusions tailored to the immediate and practical expectations of language teachers or of language teacher trainers. The intended audience for these papers was primarily fellow researchers, quite clearly, and fellow researchers in second language acquisition studies as well as those in the more restricted area of classroom language learning and teaching.

Summary

This chapter opened with the image of systematic classroom observation as 'a procedure looking for a purpose', and it is now time to review that rather unkind suggestion. We looked at how three different researchers had used classroom observation to investigate three topics drawn primarily from work in second (and first) language acquisition. There seems little doubt that acquisition studies were successful in supplying adequate purposes for the three studies. What remains in doubt is whether or not systematic classroom observation survived the process in a recognizable form. The application of exisiting category systems, for example, or the development of new ones for the field, disappeared almost completely from these studies, to be replaced by references to categories of analysis that would for the most part be applied to the immediate data only, and certainly not offered as a ready-made system for other researchers to adopt (hence, in part, some of the difficulties of replication already referred to). The reason is probably the obvious one – that, at least in the cases of Gaies and Seliger, existing work in acquisition studies provided not only the topics for research but also the categories of analysis and the basic research procedures. In my own case, which came nearest to proposing a category system anyhow, the inter-disciplinary nature of the background was perhaps more substantial, since there did exist several pedagogically motivated observational studies of error treatment, and many second language acquisition studies in the area of error analysis.

The common ground remains firm, however. What unites all the studies in the volume is faith in the observable, and the conviction that the route to the answers to our questions, whether we ask them as teachers, teacher trainers, or as researchers, lies primarily in the systematic study of the events of the language classroom. It is the status of these two beliefs that we will have to question in our final chapter.

Follow-up activities and points for discussion

1. What is a category system? Does Allwright's eighteen point analysis of error types constitute a category system? Try analysing the pilot data sample at the end of his paper in terms of the eighteen categories he suggests. What problems arise? How might they be solved, and to what purpose, if any?

2. Does Allwright's sixteen point analysis of error treatment possibilities constitute a category system? Try analysing the data sample at the end of his paper in terms of his suggested sixteen categories. What problems arise? How might they be solved, and to what purpose, if any?

3. Does it make any difference how teachers treat errors? How might the pedagogic importance, or otherwise, of the treatment of errors be established empirically? Make specific proposals for how you would undertake such an investigation (or for how you would argue against it, if you think it would be a pointless enterprise). Note: it may help to divide into small teams and to plan to pit the teams against each other eventually.

4. What are 'communicative strategies'? Take any language classroom data sample and assess the practical issues that arise in the use of Gaies' categories for the analysis of teacher talk. Do you find his categories for 'communicative strategies' generally to be high-inference or low-inference ones? Could they be turned into a workable category system? If so, how, and to what purpose?

5. What is 'interaction'? Discuss the advantages and disadvantages of Seliger's definition of the term. Did he choose the best definition for his purposes? If not, what definition would you have preferred?

NB: It would be useful to have Day's 1984 paper available for comparison purposes. Day develops Seliger's analytical apparatus. In addition, consider the use of the term 'interaction' in the work of Long (1981), Allwright (1984), and Ellis (1984 and 1985).

6. What is 'classroom observation'? Do you accept that all three papers in this chapter are essentially 'observational' in nature? If not, how would you classify them?

7. Do you have 'faith in the observable'?

8. Rate the three papers in this chapter in terms of their standing on the 'prescriptive/descriptive' dimension. If you prefer, consider them instead in terms of their 'exploratory' and/or 'explanatory' status.

9. Whatever happened to the 'non-judgementality' issue? Is it entirely irrelevant to research studies? Are the three papers in the preceding chapter 'non-judgemental', anyway?

10. Is 'objectivity' still an issue? If not, why not? If so, how would you apply it to the three papers in this chapter?

Classroom observation and second language learning 241

6 Classroom observation – retrospective, introspective and prospective

What we have seen throughout this volume is the story of how a 'faith in the observable' became translated into new ways of conducting both teacher training and research in the field of classroom language learning and teaching. This 'faith in the observable' was twinned with an equal but more precise faith in the events of the language classroom to hold the answers to the major questions in the field. Naturally enough, as experience accrued so views on what these questions were could themselves change considerably. And so the story of the faith is also the story of the field's view of itself – both in terms of its subject matter and of its methods. In this chapter we shall first review this story and then bring it somewhat more up to date, before finally speculating on the direction or directions it might take in the future.

First of all, however, it may be as well to look in more detail at the general background to this 'faith in the observable'. A 'faith in the observable' implies, conversely, a lack of 'faith in the *un*observable' – anything which cannot be directly experienced through the physical senses. Related distinctions in more or less familiar (and 'popular') terms would be 'scientific' versus 'unscientific', and 'objective' versus 'subjective'. Such an exclusive faith in the observable goes well beyond what Russell had in mind in the introduction to his Sceptical Essays (1935) when he proposed the 'subversive' doctrine 'that it is undesirable to believe a proposition when there is no ground whatever for supposing it true' (1960 edition, page 9), but the reference to Russell does suggest a third pair of contrasting terms: 'rational' versus 'irrational'. Taken in the abstract, then, a 'faith in the observable' is 'rational', 'objective', and 'scientific', all of which are naturally seen as undeniably positive descriptors by its adherents. Whether or not they are necessarily to be seen as such positive attributes is of course a matter for legitimate debate.

Such a debate could take place at the purely conceptual level, but what we are dealing with here is not just a philosophical issue, in fact it is more a matter of social history – the story of more than a decade in the lives of people trying to make sense of classroom language teaching and language teacher training. For this reason we need a historical perspective on the interpretation we give to 'a faith in the observable'. We need to try to understand why such a faith appealed at the time it became current, and how, to preempt my conclusions somewhat, subsequent developments eventually took away some of that original appeal.

The status of observational data in research in the 1960s

If we start, as we did in Chapter 1, with language teaching research, then immediately we need to distinguish a faith in the 'observable' from a faith in the 'measurable'. This is to relate the notion of 'observability' more closely to the other 'faith' mentioned at the start of this chapter – the faith in the study of classroom events to hold the answers to major questions. There is no doubt that the researchers who conducted the experiments comparing different methods believed in measurement. Indeed they expected measurements of learner behaviour, in the form of test results, to constitute what we might call the 'core' data for their research projects. Observations of classroom events had a quite different, and lower status. In the case of Scherer and Wertheimer's study in Colorado (1964) no observational data were reported, although the 'group leaders' did visit classes, and we are told that 'these visits convinced the leaders that a reasonably uniform mode of instruction was being pursued within each of the two groups'. The status afforded classroom observations in the Pennsylvania Project was clearly much higher, since special observation schedules were devised and used, and results were reported, but as we saw in Clark's criticisms, not enough was done to ensure that this essential 'corroborative' data could be used for the crucial purpose of interpreting the core test data.

When we turned to the work of Jarvis, Politzer, and Rothfarb, in the second part of Chapter 1, we found a quite different status for observational data, which now became the 'core' of the studies. And yet there was no evidence that these three researchers were reacting to deficiencies identified in the methodological comparisons work. Rather they seemed to ignore such work, and base themselves more upon the research tradition in education in general, where direct observation had for some time been an accepted way of gathering core research data (see, for example, the coverage given the topic in the important Handbook of Research on Teaching, edited by Gage in 1963). From this perspective it now looks as if the methodological comparison studies were something of a temporary aberration, induced by the need for audiolingualism (and later 'cognitivism') to justify itself, and representing a retrograde step in terms of their research methods, perhaps because the research question they were addressing was itself a retrograde one. 'Progressive' educational research had already moved on, having established, to its satisfaction at least, that methodological comparisons were doomed to be unproductive. Jarvis, we may recall, referred in his first paragraph to systematic observation as 'the most obvious approach to research on teaching', and presumably thought he could take his readers' agreement for granted, since he offered no justification for the assertion.

Before we leave Jarvis, Politzer, and Rothfarb, we should note where all three stood in terms of their faith in measurement. Politzer stood out because for him test results and observations together comprised his core data, to be related to each other as equals. Jarvis gave much less weight to the measurement of achievement, and offered 'congruence to an ideal' of teacher behaviour as a preferred focus for future work. Rothfarb worked on the basis of assumptions about what sorts of teacher behaviour would lead to enhanced learner achievement, and so for her the observational data was everything. All three, we should also note, clearly believed in the necessity of being able to 'measure' their observations against external criteria of some sort.

Jarvis and Rothfarb were also different from Politzer in that they related their conclusions to the issue of encouraging behaviour change in teachers. This indicates a further aspect of the 'faith in the observable', as it is represented in this volume – the faith that teachers would, upon observing their own lessons in a systematic way, be better able to bring about desirable changes in their classroom behaviour. The key term here was the word 'systematic', which is where 'rational', 'scientific', and above all 'objective' come in, bringing us on to deal with teacher training.

The status of observational data in teacher training

Systematic classroom observation came into teacher training originally (before our period) as an answer to the problems faced by supervisors who had to evaluate their trainees' classroom performance, but, as we have seen, it became much more closely associated with research on learner achievement and on teacher behaviour change – both represented in this volume largely in the person of Flanders, whose work was particularly well-established and particularly influential on people concerned with language teaching and learning, although he did not work in that area himself.

The status of observational data on the research on learner achievement need not concern us for long here, since its results seem to have been largely taken for granted, and adopted somewhat uncritically as the basis for assumptions about desirable teacher behaviour (as noted in the reference to Rothfarb, above). Suffice it to say that such research paralleled Politzer's in its design, gathering both observational data and achievement data and then looking for correlations between them, but differed from Politzer's in drawing the categories of its analysis from thoughts about 'authoritarian' versus 'democratic' teaching styles, rather than from thoughts about the types of practice drills involved in the implementation of a particular teaching method.

The status of observational data in teacher training itself was considerably more complex. An early compendium of category systems summed the situation up well in its title 'Mirrors for Behavior' (Simon and Boyer 1967). The fundamental contribution of systematic observation was to act as a mirror, in which a teacher would see his or her behaviour with a clarity never before achieved, and, thus prompted to change, would be able to keep on looking in this objectively perfect mirror to make sure that the desired changes had indeed been brought about. Such a 'systematic mirror' would act not merely as a motivator for change (a property of all mirrors?), but crucially also as a source of information feedback, a measure of change. Originally, given its origins in Flanders' work on learner achievement, it was natural that the information feedback role should be related directly, as in Rothfarb's work, to assumptions about teacher effectiveness, but increasingly, as confidence in Flanders' findings receded, and, indeed, confidence in the whole field of work on teacher effectiveness, it was more reasonable to emphasize the non-judgemental possibilities of information feedback, and its motivational role. In such circumstances Bailey's critical comments about the use of systematic observation techniques in the Flanders tradition were perhaps best countered by de-emphasizing the importance of the categories themselves, and by placing more reliance on the motivating effects of the process of systematic self-observation. Certainly there seems to have been no direct response to Bailey's paper, although we should not ignore Moskowitz's assertion of her interest in teacher effectiveness, in the form of an extremely interesting 1976 study of 'the classroom interaction of outstanding foreign language teachers' (recommended for detailed consideration at the end of Chapter 3).

It is worth noting here that for this work Moskowitz chose to measure teacher effectiveness in terms of learners' reports, rather than in terms of Flanders' direct and indirect influence concepts.

Systematic observation in teacher training came in, then, as a way of getting over the problems of the impressionistic subjectivity of earlier ways of evaluating teaching practice (for convincing evidence that there really were such problems see Morrison and McIntyre's 1969 account of the situation). But the role of systematic observation changed rapidly, as, in conjunction with the development of micro-teaching, the nature of teacher training itself changed to focus much more on the fundamental nature of the process of behaviour change in teachers.

The status of observational data in research in the 1970s

In Chapter 4 we looked at three alternatives to the Flanders tradition. The first of these, Fanselow's FOCUS system, was presented in isolation from any instance of its use, but Fanselow made it clear that he was expecting his system to be useful for research that would seek relationships between interaction and outcomes, or in his terms, 'help us examine the effects different communications have on learning'. For him, then, much as for Moskowitz, the interest in teacher effectiveness was still very much a live one, although Fanselow did make it clear that what he expected in the first instance was research on the relationships between communications (between one move and the next), rather than on the relationships between communications and learning. In his own 1977 study on error treatment, for example, (recommended as valuable additional material at the end of Chapter 4) Fanselow took some observational data as his core data, provided a description of the treatment of error in his data samples, and used that description as the basis for speculations about possibly more effective ways of treating errors than those found in his data.

The other two 'alternatives to Flanders' presented in Chapter 4 both took observational data as their core data and then allowed themselves only the most general of speculations about language pedagogy. For Long *et al.* the problems of devising an adequate category system predominated, suggesting that they foresaw future research for which a fully developed system would be necessary and valuable, whereas in my own work the whole question of the value of category systems was raised, and some intensive text analysis was offered as an alternative possibility for the last and most delicate stage of the investigation. For Fanselow and for Long *et al.* the observational data was the only data, while in my study I was able to base some final speculations on the additional 'data' of the teacher's largely impressionistic rankings of the learners on a variety of relevant parameters.

If self-observation was coming to be seen as 'its own reward' for teachers in teacher training, there was at that time no parallel expectation that the sorts of research advocated in Chapter 4 would be 'their own reward' for the learners under investigation. Such ideas were to develop later, however.

The role of the observational data in the studies of Chapter 5, when 'classroom observation met second language acquisition', was already briefly discussed in that chapter but now needs additional comments. Clearly systematic observational data had core status for Gaies and myself, and was not backed up by any other sorts of data. Any thought of relating the research to learner achievement (or to any other 'measures' for that matter, prompting the rather uncharitable thought that the earlier 'faith in the measurable' had been reduced to a 'faith in the merely countable' – see Allwright 1986) remained very distant, and was replaced by a concern for throwing light on issues that were certainly of general pedagogic interest but probably of more specific relevance to the field of second language acquisition research. In my own work, and in that of Long *et al.*, what was most impressive to the researchers themselves was the enormous complexity of the observational data. This suggested that Fanselow's hope of finding consistent relationships between 'communications' and 'learning' was decidedly optimistic, and that we would do better to look forward to a perhaps indefinitely extended period of research that would concentrate on trying to understand the data itself. Following this line of reasoning, the status of the observational data was now that it was to be the unique object of study.

Seliger, however, had a quite different role for his observational data. He needed it only to isolate subjects for further study, in a research design that permitted relationships to be sought directly between interaction and achievement, and which therefore depended on the gathering of other sorts of data, including language test results. To that extent his design could appear 'old-fashioned', putting an unreasonable amount of trust in 'discredited' procedures like achievement testing (it seemed at the time that the available tests could be of only very limited interest since they could handle only a very little of what was held to be involved in knowing a language).

Apart from Seliger there was a move, then, that could be characterized as a move to divorce the faith in the observable from the faith in the measurable. There was only the observable to study, and whether or not the observable was also measurable, even if it was demonstrably countable, was a matter for some doubt.

The status of observational data since the mid-seventies

Although this is not the place to go into it in any detail, the rise of challenges to the primacy of observational data (already mentioned in connection with my own work in Chapter 4) is an important part of the story. One of the first moves came in 1976, when the Schumanns undertook a 'diary study' of their experiences as language learners in Iran and Tunisia (Schumann and Schumann 1977). Diaries substituted retrospective accounts for class-time observations. These retrospective accounts were systematic in their own way (i.e. produced in accordance with specific procedural recommendations), but their thematic content, instead of being specified in advance, as with any systematic observation schedule, was left to 'emerge'. In this way diary studies could be used to reveal variables that might otherwise have been neglected. K. M. Bailey, for example, in reviewing a number of such diary studies, found 'competitiveness' and 'anxiety' to be prominent in learners' retrospective accounts of their experiences (Bailey 1983), but these were certainly variables that had not received more than passing research attention, if any, in observational studies. It could easily be objected that diary studies might be an appropriate way of uncovering variables, but might not be an appropriate way of continuing the investigation of any variables so uncovered. Proponents of diary studies, however, could equally easily answer back that it was not at all clear how any sort of observational study could hope to pursue the investigation of such 'unobservables' as 'competitiveness' and 'anxiety'. What has happened is that diary studies have continued to throw light on the situations they have been used in, have not uncovered very many 'new' variables, but have been developed as a form of relatively 'informal' research that can be of direct value to all those who take part in them (for an imaginative extension of the idea see the newsletter on dialogue journal writing, published by the Center for Applied Linguistics, Washington, under the title: 'Dialogue'). Diary studies constitute a first move towards research that is indeed its own reward.

Another challenge to the primacy of observational data came from Hosenfeld's introduction into the second language field of the so-called 'think-aloud' technique for classroom research (Hosenfeld 1975). Here the data was now the learner's talk, while a learning task was in progress; an introspective rather than a retrospective account. Eventually, as noted briefly in Chapter 4, as more techniques were developed for obtaining learners' accounts of their experiences, all such techniques were grouped together as sources of 'mentalistic' data (Cohen and Hosenfeld 1981). Seliger (1983a) took up the challenge on behalf of observational data, questioning the possible status, as valid and reliable evidence, of learners' attempts to report their own mental activity, but, whatever their epistemological status, learners' reports have proved interesting material to contemplate. Also, as mentioned under diary studies, such procedures for data collection can be argued to be productive for the learners who take part (as in the case of Hosenfeld's subject 'Cindy', for example, Hosenfeld 1979). The same cannot be said of the typical procedures for systematic classroom observation, which are more easily and probably more usually seen as intrusive and parasitic.

Ochsner raised the whole issue of what might constitute appropriate ways of investigating language learning in his 1979 paper, intriguingly and significantly entitled 'A Poetics of Second Language Acquisition', in which he drew attention to a 'hermeneutic' alternative to the 'nomothetic' tradition that appeared to him to be dominant in the field at that time. He called for a realization that the 'truth' is not to be found exclusively, if at all, in numbers, although in so doing he was probably reacting more to the prevalence of 'morpheme counting' in general second language acquisition research than to 'event counting' in language classroom research as it is represented in this volume. In the following year Long, under the slightly more prosaic title of 'Inside the "Black Box": methodological issues in classroom research on classroom language learning', also stressed the existence of potentially valuable alternatives to straightforward classroom observation. Much more recently, in 1985, Breen has argued persuasively that an understanding of classroom language learning (and teaching) will only come if we go far beyond the merely observable in our research and at least make a serious attempt to account adequately for the social as well as the cognitive aspects of classroom language learning, treating the class as a culture in and of itself, whose investigation will require an anthropologist's rather than a statistician's expertise.

It is intriguing to draw parallels between this 'history' of classroom observation and that of the somewhat related field of psychology. Both started in a way that was 'subjective', relying on subjects' own reports of their mental states in psychology, or on supervisors' impressionistic observations and subsequent subjective reports of their trainees' classroom skills in teacher training. Both came in for severe criticism on account of their 'unscientific' subjectivity, and both experienced an objectivist revolution that established observable, countable, and measurable data as the only sort of data worth collecting. Both, in time, experienced a counter-revolution as the limitations of objectively observable data became increasingly apparent. In both cases it is arguable that the return to 'subjectivity' was facilitated by the development of new research procedures making use of new technical capabilities. In both cases, again, it is also arguable that this counter-revolution was at least partly motivated by the desire to bring a more 'human' approach to the subject matter. The final parallel to be drawn is the fact that in neither case did the counter revolution totally eliminate the old regime. The objectivists in psychology (the behaviourists, obviously) carried on working, though from a much less dominant position, and so have the systematic classroom observers.

But what have they been working at? In teacher training the place of systematic classroom observation seems assured, as a practical and helpful way of providing detailed feedback to trainees about their classroom behaviour. The proliferation of category systems for such a purpose has stopped, however, with no major new system to report since the publication of Fanselow's FOCUS in 1977. What is new in the field is the availability of publications devoted to helping language teacher trainees with precisely the language they need for the purposes of the language classroom (see, for example, Edmondson and House 1981, Hughes 1981, Sinclair and Brazil 1982 and Willis 1981). In two cases (Sinclair and Brazil, and Willis) the material is based on research into classroom language use employing Sinclair and Coulthard's discourse analytic categories and procedures. In another (Edmondson and House) the research was conducted using a model of analysis for spoken discourse developed by the first author (see Edmondson 1981).

Also in teacher training, but with a quite different perspective on the field, is the major Danish work on language learner language that has been built into a language pedagogy text by Faerch, Haastrup, and Phillipson (1984). Faerch *et al*. base their text on a corpus of learner language that, curiously, did not include ordinary classroom interaction, and so their work falls to some extent outside the definition of systematic classroom observation adopted for this volume. It is relevant here, however, and interesting, for its coverage (in Chapters 18 and 19) of data collection and data analysis procedures for classroom language teachers to use with respect to their own language teaching, in their own classes. It is a very positive move to encourage teachers to see themselves as researchers, and to bring teaching and research close together. Faerch *et al.*'s volume is also interesting as a text representative of the move away from studying teacher behaviour towards taking learner behaviour as the central object of study (a move clearly implicit in the mentalistic data collection procedures outlined earlier).

Observational research, then, but not necessarily research conducted in the classroom, has provided language teacher training with some new inputs. It has also pursued fundamental issues in the field, still stimulated mostly, if not exclusively, by work in second language acquisition (now frequently referred to as 'interlanguage' studies, see Davies, Criper and Howatt 1984). The background question that dominates the field is this: if, as seems indicated by research so far, a classroom learner's linguistic progress is in crucial ways, if not totally, independent of the context in which it occurs, such that sequenced language syllabuses are rendered basically irrelevant, how is it that classroom learners learn whatever it is that they do learn while under instruction? One hypothesis, derived directly from Krashen's claim (1985) that input comprehensibility is the key, suggests that learners may make linguistic progress in proportion to the extent to which their interlocutors make conversational adjustments in their speech to them (i.e. make it comprehensible to them). This hypothesis has been investigated principally by Long, returning to his earlier interest in group work. In Long and Porter (1985) the authors first review the traditional pedagogic arguments in favour of group work in the language classroom, and then turn to interlanguage studies for a psycholinguistic rationale based on the finding that certain types of task, performed in small groups, give rise to enhanced figures for conversational adjustments. No causal connection has yet been demonstrated between the quantity of conversational adjustments and linguistic progress, but, as the authors point out (1985, p. 214), there is a 'substantial amount of evidence consistent with' such a claim. (See Aston 1986, for a strong note of caution, however). The authors further state: 'What many researchers do agree upon is that learners must be put in a position of being able to *negotiate* the new input, thereby ensuring that the language in which it is heard is modified to exactly the level of comprehensibility they can manage' (1985, p. 214, authors' original emphasis). However, this claim that the negotiation process is itself the key element makes it impossible to account for the tentative findings of my 1980 study (already discussed in detail in Chapter 4) in which a learner who was one of the least frequent contributors to classroom interaction was also the learner judged by the teacher to have made the most linguistic progress. To account for such cases we need an approach which permits the possibility that, for at least some of the learners some of the time, classroom language learning can be a 'spectator sport'.

At Lancaster we have been working on such an approach for some time, taking as our starting point the possibility that language lessons are best seen not as opportunities to negotiate so much as opportunities to attend to (and perhaps even learn) whatever it is that classroom interaction makes available as input. This is not the place to describe the work in any detail, but it is at least relevant to this story of systematic classroom observation to note that our core data is twofold – on the one hand we have learners' specific claims about what they have learned from a particular lesson, and on the other hand we have transcribed recordings of the lessons themselves. The research task is to try to account for the learners' claims in terms of the specific events of the classroom, which necessarily involves us in trying to find relevant and systematic ways of characterizing those events. From this brief description it should be clear by now that we are mixing direct classroom observation with more 'mentalistic' procedures (see Allwright 1984a, for a fuller description of the research design involved), but that we are still relying on our observational data to hold the answers to key questions. We must imagine, however, that we might well be mistaken in this. We are therefore taking our optimism rather as a 'working hypothesis', and taking the research itself as an opportunity to test the limits of direct classroom observation in such investigations.

A further hypothesis to account for the characteristics of classroom language learning has been put forward by Ellis, also working in Britain. Ellis is looking to variability as the key, with interaction as the mechanism. For him, as for Long, interaction offers the opportunity to negotiate which is itself crucial to linguistic progress (Ellis 1984), whereas in work at Lancaster we are obtaining some evidence that the process of negotiation may inhibit some learners, to the extent that they will learn more when not actively involved in the negotiation process (Slimani 1987). The main theoretical difference between Ellis and Long is Ellis's suggestion that the relevant characteristic of input is not so much the quantity of conversational adjustments it displays, as its variability in terms of the different levels of discourse planning involved (Ellis 1985). A further difference between Ellis and Long, and one of particular interest here, is that Ellis's work, like that in progress in Lancaster, depends crucially on observational data obtained in the language classroom, while Long has demonstrated that much can be done starting with data obtained in artificial, more laboratory-like, settings. In the Long and Porter review cited above, for example, only Long *et al.* (1976), and one or two very much more recent studies, are based on classroom data. It is an important part of Long's approach to research that phenomena are best studied first in controlled settings, and so even his classroom data is obtained under relatively controlled conditions (with a set task for learners to perform, for example). Ellis, too, has worked with controlled classroom data, as in his 1984 study of the effects of formal instruction on the acquisition of WH-questions by children, but the bulk of his work is with naturally occurring classroom discourse. The Lancaster work is exclusively with naturally occurring classroom data.

The above three approaches can all be characterized as dealing with the role of formal instruction in second language acquisition. In this connection it is worth recalling that Long's authoritative research survey on the topic (published in 1983 under the title: 'Does Second Language Instruction Make a Difference?') reviewed more than a dozen research studies, none of which was based on observational data, for the very good reason that there were no observational studies that addressed the issues as directly as Long needed for his survey. The result, of course, was a repetition of the sort of descriptive problem that arose in the late sixties over the interpretability of the methodological comparisons studies. Long was able to conclude that there was enough research evidence to support a not so tentative 'yes' in response to the question in the survey's title, but there was no way for a reader to interpret this as support for any particular form of instruction, since no information was available about the type or types of instruction that 'made a difference'. That, as Long himself made clear, was a different question.

Others had been investigating the role of instruction more qualitatively, by collecting naturally occurring classroom data. Felix, for example, in Germany, studying the linguistic output in the language classroom of school learners was able to conclude that much of their output could only be understood as essentially random behaviour, but that otherwise their classroom use of language suggested that they were using 'natural' processes of language acquisition rather than those the teaching was designed to promote (Felix 1981). It is arguable that classroom conditions prevented the learners from displaying their true command of the target language, which amounts to suggesting that Felix had the wrong data for his purposes. Certainly other studies have tended to take data elicited outside the classroom setting as evidence for linguistic command, and then to look inside the classroom for explanations for the characteristics of the elicited data. Lightbown, for example, in her extensive work in Canada, has elicited target language data from schoolchildren over several years and made a large number of classroom recordings in order to be able to study the classroom input available to these learners (Lightbown 1983). Her conclusions are somewhat more negative than Long's, and perhaps even more impressive given their grounding in classroom observation:

> One important observation of this study is that there was relatively little improvement over time in the accuracy of learners' use of the six grammatical morphemes in obligatory contexts even though grammatical accuracy was always the focus of their ESL classes. (1983, p. 240).

This review of research studies investigating questions directly relating second language acquisition 'theory' to classroom instruction has tried to give at least the flavour of their substance, while emphasizing their position with regard to the use of observational data. It is time to attempt a summary of the uses of observational data that the survey has revealed. The most important point to make at the outset is that the collection of observational data is obviously central to work in the field. Where studies do not have an observational component they suffer from the same interpretation problem that we saw in experimental research in the late sixties. But it is also apparent that observational data are not always expected to suffice on their own. Increasingly frequently performance data are also required by the research design and it is now usual for such data to be obtained by elicitation procedures rather than by the use of 'traditional' tests. Other studies combine classroom observations with more 'mentalistic' data. Typically observational data represent the core data for a project, then, either alone or in combination with other forms of data. But we must distinguish at least three types of observational data in use currently. At one extreme there is the 'Long' approach based on the systematic observation of learners in controlled non-classroom settings, and in which there is no longer a distinction to be made between 'observational' and 'elicited' data. At the other extreme there is the 'Lancaster' approach, based on the systematic observation of naturally occurring language classroom events, with virtually no attempt at control. In the middle there is the systematic observation of controlled classroom data, as exemplified in some of Ellis's work, and in Long and Porter's. Finally, we should also note that the term 'systematic observation' is now being used somewhat more broadly than it was when it was originally coined decades ago. Modern recording techniques make real-time coding quite unnecessary, and permit the use of vastly more complex systems of analysis. But analyses can also be more focused, as foreseen by Fanselow, there being no need in most research projects for an analysis that claims to be exhaustive (note that Flanders' ten categories were quite clearly intended to provide such an exhaustive analysis of any classroom lesson). The term 'systematic' can now be used to refer to any observation which is subjected to a detailed analysis for the purpose of classifying in some explicit way the events and/or utterances recorded.

The above definition of 'systematic observation' did not deal with the issue of the possible purposes that might lay behind the wish to classify. So far we have given examples of classification for the purpose of pursuing the investigation of fundamental research questions. We have therefore neglected another purpose that was first mentioned in connection with Rothfarb's work in Chapter 1 – the provision of a description of the state of language teaching in a particular setting. In Britain there is a particularly interesting example in the work of the team at the University of Stirling. Mitchell *et al.* (1981) developed a 'lesson analysis system' which they applied to 147 French lessons involving seventeen different teachers. The result is a detailed and very informative 'picture' of the state of French language teaching in that area at that time. Mitchell *et al.* relate that picture to the 'communicative' ideas current in discussions of language pedagogy and find little evidence that these ideas have made much of an impact on what happens in the language classroom. Such research may appear less 'exciting' because of its distance from the sorts of psycholinguistic questions addressed by others, but it is extremely important research from the point of view of educational decision making, if such decision making is to be informed not only by the latest 'theories' but also by reliable information about what is currently going on in the classroom.

There remains one further research project to discuss as an example of the recent development and use of systematic classroom observation. In Canada, Fröhlich, Spada and Allen (1985, see also Allen, Fröhlich and Spada 1984) have developed an observation system for the specific purpose of capturing 'differences in the communicative orientation of L2 classrooms in a variety of settings' (1985, p. 27). Like Mitchell *et al.*, they base their observations exclusively in naturally occurring language lessons. Their work could clearly also be used in the same way as that of the team in Scotland – to provide pictures of the state of language teaching in particular educational settings – but the team in Canada is considerably more ambitious, and its ambitions make a fitting conclusion for this survey. The ultimate goal of their research project is to find relationships between the communicative orientation of classrooms and learner achievement, and for the team the successful development of a descriptive system 'is an important step towards identifying what makes one set of instructional procedures more effective than another' (1985, p. 50).

This work in Canada brings us neatly back to almost the place we started at in Chapter 1. Then the problem was to discover which method was 'best'. Twenty years later the precise form of the question has changed, since we are now asking about 'what makes one set of instructional procedures more effective than another', but the underlying problem remains the same: 'What advice can we give teachers about how to teach?'. It seems very likely that the new form of the question, and the new procedures developed to investigate it, will prove much more productive than the methodological experiments were in the mid-sixties, and that perhaps the team in Canada have achieved what I seemed to be looking for in my 1972 paper when I was calling rather vaguely for a descriptive approach to a prescriptive question.

It would be wrong, however, to end on this particular note, since it does a considerable injustice to the overall picture of the current state of observational work on language teaching and learning.

Final comments

What can be said, finally? The clue is probably in the last word of the last section. The work in Canada is focusing on 'instructional procedures'. Almost all of the other work reported in the previous section of this last chapter focused on the language learner, and on the language learning process rather than on the instructional process. That represents a fundamental change of emphasis over the years, and one that relates directly to the powerful argument that we cannot hope to usefully understand the *instructional* process until we have established for ourselves a much greater understanding of the *learning* process. It is however a linear argument, one that relies on a sequential view of the acquisition of knowledge. My own position is that we can usefully work on both at the same time, and preferably not in separate teams but collectively. This is what observations of naturally occurring classroom lessons make possible. We can use them to investigate learner behaviour, but in so doing we are necessarily involved in trying to make sense of instruction itself, since, following the view that classroom lessons, like any other form of interaction, are co-produced, learner behaviour is a vital part of what constitutes instruction, of what determines the learning opportunities that learners get (see Allwright 1984).

Where does that leave the 'faith in the observable' with which this chapter started, and the faith in the events of the classroom to hold the answers to the key questions? The answer must surely be that the faith in the observable has survived the challenges to it implied by the development of 'mentalistic' alternatives, but lost some of its exclusivity in the process. It no longer appeals so strongly as the only possible approach. It now has to share the territory, and this is working well to the ultimate benefit of the whole field, but it is holding on to the centre of the territory, and showing few signs of giving any more ground in the very near future. As to the faith in the events of the classroom to hold the answers to the key questions, this faith seems only to be strengthened by recent developments. It would be appropriate to end on a note of caution, however. The answers to our questions may lie somewhere in classroom events, but that does not mean that we shall be able to *understand* these classroom events simply by studying their objectively observable characteristics. We shall perhaps have to find a way, following Breen's suggestions (as reported above), of treating the language classroom as a whole culture. And it must remain possible that the answers to our questions will in any case be found to lie too deep within the minds of the participants in the events for any investigator to be able to get at them.

Meanwhile, language classroom research needs to run to catch up with educational research in general. It is arguable (see Breen 1985 again) that the SLA connection may have actually hindered our progress in terms of research method, since it has fostered what is in some respects a fundamentally asocial view of the language acquisition process, at a time when educational research in other fields has been busy accommodating itself to a thoroughly social view of classroom learning.

What can we do? Certainly we cannot just abandon the connection with second language acquisition research, since the commonality of interests must in the long run be potentially beneficial to both parties, but we should clearly be very wary of our tendency to let the procedures and concepts of second language acquisition research determine our own. Meanwhile, we could at least follow Faerch, Haastrup and Phillipson (and Breen, incidentally), and do everything possible to encourage teachers to join in the research enterprise. We could also follow the lead set by some of the 'mentalist' researchers and do everything possible to encourage forms of investigation that would not only be productive for the learners, but that would also bring the learners in as partners in the research enterprise. Good research can be good pedagogy, and good pedagogy can itself be good research.

Follow-up activities and points for discussion

1. Of all the papers in this volume, which one exhibits the strongest 'faith in the observable', and which the weakest? Use the discussion to sharpen your own standpoint, and your own definition of what is involved.

2. Can you see people being competitive? Formulate proposals for an observational reseach project to investigate competitiveness in the language classroom.

Alternatively, prepare arguments against any such proposals. If both viewpoints are represented in the group, take the opportunity to pit them against each other, but only after the proposals and counter-arguments have been properly formulated.

3. How do you think the issue of teacher effectiveness is best investigated? Is there a paper in this volume that illustrates your position?

Alternatively, does the term 'teacher effectiveness' suggest the wrong question? If so, what would the right question look like?

4. How would you distinguish between a 'faith in the observable', a 'faith in the measurable', and a 'faith in the countable'? Are there any papers in this volume that represent the distinctions particularly well?

5. Can you *report* your own learning processes? Can anyone else *observe* your learning processes? What would constitute the data in either case?

6. What is the difference between a 'method' and a 'set of instructional procedures'? If you have access to copies of the Allen *et al.* papers referred to in this final chapter, try to take the issue out of the context of their particular work at first, and bring their views in only when your own have been formulated.

7. Why do researchers ask the questions they ask, and use the research methods they use? Now that you have read their papers, do you feel that you know what the researchers represented in this

volume are like as people? *Should* it be possible to discern their personalities in their reports?

8. In your personal experience has language learning been a 'participator sport' or a 'spectator sport'? What difference, if any, might such views make to your own perspective on research, either as a consumer or as a producer of it?

9. What objections could be raised to the suggestion that teachers should see themselves as researchers in the classroom? How could you counter such objections? If both viewpoints are represented in the group, take the opportunity to pit them against each other, but only after the objections and the counter-arguments have been properly formulated.

10. Can research be good pedagogy? Can pedagogy be good research? Do you know of any examples of either? Are there any such examples amongst the papers in this volume?

11. Acting as a Research Council, with funds to distribute, which of the research projects in this volume would you have been happy to have funded, if any? If this becomes too depressing, think instead of future research projects you would wish to promote!

Further reading

The six chapters of this volume have included sixteen papers published between 1968 and 1980. The focus has been on the years during which classroom observation became established in the field of language teaching, rather than on the most recent years and the most recent developments in the field. Even here, in this final section, it seems more appropriate to attempt to fill in the gaps left in the coverage of early papers, rather than to try to bring the reader up-to-date with the newest ones. What follows, then, is a brief annotated bibliography to remind the reader of some of the references already given in each chapter, and to add to those wherever this seems appropriate and helpful. Generally speaking, these additional references will be restricted to items directly concerned in some way with language classroom observation.

1 Observation 'arrives' in language teaching research.

1. Anyone wishing to obtain a more complete background to the earliest alternatives to the methodological comparisons research paradigm of the sixties should read:

Hayes, A S, Lambert, W E and Tucker, G A 1967 Evaluation of Foreign Language Teaching. *Foreign Language Annals* 1(1): 22–44

The authors' abstract is worth citing in full here to give the full flavour of the enterprise being undertaken:

> The standard technique for evaluating a language teaching program is to obtain objective measures of pre- to post-training changes in students. A potentially faster and more useful technique would be the evaluation, based on direct observation, of actual training in progress to ascertain whether the course design, program administration, and individual teaching performance conform to certain principles, policies, and procedures that have been demonstrated to play a role in successful language learning. A research plan has been devised for developing such an evaluation technique. The preliminary phase of the first step in this plan has been accomplished through an analysis of the ratings which 364 faculty members at NDEA institutes gave to 324 features believed to be important in developing second-language proficiency. The

consensus strongly favored an audio-lingual approach. The next step will be to validate those features which are apparently important. (An appendix lists the 324 features and gives the mean rating, standard deviation, and % of negative responses to each.)

This project (a collaborative venture between the Center for Applied Linguistics, Washington DC, and McGill University, Montreal) seems not to have been pursued through all the planned stages, but it is well worth reading about and relating to the work of the Stanford Center for Research and Development in Teaching, out of which came Politzer and Weiss's 1969 volume 'Improving Achievement in Foreign Language', their 1969 report entitled 'Characteristics and Behaviors of the Successful Foreign Language Teacher', a series of language teacher training manuals, and of course the Politzer paper on 'good' and 'bad' teaching behaviours included in the second part of Chapter 1.

2. For the earliest European use of systematic classroom observation to do research on language classroom interaction the reader should go to:
    Wragg, E C 1970 Interaction Analysis in the Foreign Language Classroom. *Modern Language Journal* 54(2): 116–120
    Quite apart from its interest as the first evidence of Flanders' influence outside north America, Wragg's work is noteworthy for his particularly ingenious modification to Flanders' original system. He needed to be able to distinguish between uses of the target language and of the learners' mother tongue and so he simply used the numbers 1 to 10 for Flanders' original categories when the native language was being used, and the numbers 11 to 20 for the same categories when the target language was involved. Wragg did not have either achievement or attitudinal data to relate his observations to (unlike Sister Mary William, below), but was proposing his modification to Flanders' system as a research tool and as a form of feedback for 'the language teacher wishing to modify his own behavior'.

3. For a research study that appears to 'turn the clock back' by using Flanders' Interaction Analysis categories unmodified, but that confounds both critics and cynics by finding significant differences in support of Flanders' claims about the relative value of 'direct' and 'indirect' influence, see:
    Sister Mary William 1973 Interaction Analysis and Achievement: An Experiment. In Green, J R (ed.) *Foreign Language Education Research: A Book of Readings*. Chicago, Center for Curriculum Development, Rand McNally: 153–165

Twelve classes were involved, taught by twelve different teachers. Both achievement measures and attitude measures were applied and related to the classroom observations made by two trained observers (with reliability coefficients calculated according to Scott's formula).

4. An important area of related research not represented in this volume is that concerned with interaction in bilingual classrooms, an area developed very strongly in the more recent work of Politzer (see his 1982 study: 'Linguistic and communicative competence, language dominance, selected pupil characteristics and their relation to achievement of bilingual pupils'. Final Report of NIE Grant G-79-0130. Stanford, California: Stanford University.) As an introduction to work in this area see:

Townsend, D R and Zamora, G L 1975 Differing Interaction Patterns in Bilingual Classrooms. *Contemporary Education* **46** (3)

Townsend and Zamora's work is especially interesting for its use of a category system devised to capture 'non-verbal affective' behaviour (in addition to a Flanders type 'instructional' behaviour category system).

2 Observation 'arrives' as a feedback tool in teacher training

1. Anyone who wishes to have details of how Moskowitz intended her FLint system to be used in language teacher training should consult:

Moskowitz, G 1971 Interaction Analysis – A New Modern Language for Supervisors. *Foreign Language Annals* **5** (2): 211–221

This paper has already been referred to in the main text as the best source of information about FLint and how it was to be used. In it Moskowitz sets out both the system and the very important post-observation analytical procedures associated with it.

2. In a further contribution to teacher training Moskowitz presented an intriguing example of her FLint system in use:

Moskowitz, G 1976 The Classroom Interaction of Outstanding Foreign Language Teachers. *Foreign Language Annals* **9** (2): 135–157

This paper has also been referred to already in the main text, but it deserves additional mention here as a highly positive but also highly provocative statement about teacher quality. In it Moskowitz lists those behaviours (identified in terms of FLint categories) that distinguished 'outstanding' from 'typical' language teachers in her Philadelphia area study.

3 Second thoughts

Three years before Bailey published her doubts about Flanders' Interaction Analysis a team at the University of Birmingham, England, included a thorough and critical review of classroom interaction systems in a research report that introduced what later became known as the Sinclair/Coulthard model of discourse analysis (see Sinclair and Coulthard 1975):

Sinclair, J McH, Forsyth, I J, Coulthard, R M and Ashby, M 1972 *The English Used by Teachers and Pupils.* Final report to SSRC for the period September 1970 to August 1972. Department of English Language and Literature, University of Birmingham. See especially Section Two: Educational Studies of Language Interaction in the Classroom: 11–34

Flanders' Interaction Analysis system is only one of many reviewed by the Birmingham team. Their criticisms reflect problems of principle rather than the problems of practicality and interpretation emphasized by Bailey in 1975. In particular, they challenge the appropriateness of an arbitrary time unit and propose instead that the units of analysis should be inherently discoursal in nature.

4 First alternatives to Flanders

1. The Birmingham team's work, introduced above, could also be considered as proposing an alternative to Flanders, and is certainly worth reading from this point of view. In the event, however, their analytical system was taken up more as a contribution to the development of the whole field of discourse analysis, than as a direct contribution to observation in the language classroom.

Well before 1972, in Canada, Mackey had been developing his ideas on language classroom analysis (having published his major work: Language Teaching Analysis, in 1965). The picture of early alternatives to Flanders would not be complete without reference to Mackey's radically different approach to the problems of classroom observation:

Mackey, W F 1978 Cost-Benefit Quantification of Language Teaching Behaviour. *Die Neueren Sprachen* 1: 2–32

Mackey's concern to respect the enormous complexities of language classroom behaviour led him to develop both a technology to permit simultaneous multidimensional tallying (in Mackey's terms 'polychronometry') and a complex system of data interpretation to permit the 'measurement of cost-benefit'. He began work on it in the sixties, at about the same time as Moskowitz started to develop FLint.

2. Fanselow's FOCUS system, already represented in Chapter 4, was also highly complex, too complex to be used in its entirety in real-time (but Fanselow always intended it to be used very selectively). His interest in the Competency-Based Teacher Education movement did not lead him in the direction of 'cost-benefit' analyses, however. Instead, Fanselow emphasized the potential value of his system to the individual language teacher. For an example of his work to encourage language teachers to engage in classroom observation see:

Fanselow, J F 1978 Breaking the Rules of the Classroom Game Through Self-Analysis. In Light, R L and Osman, A H (eds.) *Teaching English as a Second Language and Bilingual Education: Themes, Practices, Viewpoints*. New York, New York State ESOL/BEA: 145–166

The paper constitutes in part a training manual for the use of FOCUS, and as such will be of especial interest to anyone wishing to learn more about using the system.

5 Classroom observation and second language acquisition

Chapter 5 included three papers – one on the treatment of error, one on input, and one on practice. Each of these three areas will be taken separately here.

A. *The treatment of error*

1. The pioneer study in this field is still well worth consulting:

Holley, F M and King, J K 1971 Imitation and Correction in Foreign Language Learning. *Modern Language Journal* 55 (8): 494–8

The authors report their relatively informal observational findings from experimentation with a variety of correction procedures. They make explicit appeal to work in first and second language acquisition.

2. The first detailed quantitative study in this area is also still of considerable interest:

Fanselow, J F 1977 The Treatment of Error in Oral Work. *Foreign Language Annals* 10 (4): 583–593

As noted in the main text of this volume Fanselow is here reporting work done much earlier in the decade (and presented orally at the 1974 TESOL Convention). In this 1977 paper he reports the results of using a sixteen category analysis of treatment types on lessons taught by eleven teachers all using the same lesson plan with different classes. He also makes a number of suggestions about potentially more useful ways of treating errors than those most commonly found in his data. Unlike Holley and King he does not make explicit appeal to language acquisition research, but he does include such sources in his references.

3. Following Fanselow's descriptive work, and my own consideration of some of the problematic issues involved in any work on the treatment of error, there came two papers that developed the conceptual background further. The first of these was by Chaudron:

Chaudron, C 1977 A Descriptive Model of Discourse in the Corrective Treatment of Learners' Errors. *Language Learning* 17: 29–46

Chaudron was concerned with the proper definition of 'correction', and with the appropriate description of classroom interaction. He devised a model of discourse that came from a 'synthesis of the descriptive system for classroom discourse developed by Sinclair and Coulthard (1975), and of Allwright's (1975) suggestions for the basic options open to the teacher in corrective reactions' (page 33).

4. Published in the same year was Long's contribution:

Long, M H 1977 Teacher Feedback on Learner Error: Mapping Cognitions. In Brown, H D, Yorio, C A and Crymes, R H (eds.) *On TESOL '77*. TESOL, Washington, DC: 278–293

Long built on the earlier work but took it in a different direction – towards a systematization, for descriptive purposes, of the decision-making involved in the treatment of oral errors. He proposed a 'model of the decision-making process prior to the teacher feedback move' (page 289).

5. Another direction entirely was chosen by the authors of our last selection on the topic of the treatment of learner error:

Cathcart, R L and Olsen, J W B 1976 Teachers' and Students' Preferences for Correction of Classroom Conversation Errors. In Fanselow, J F and Crymes, R H (eds.) *On TESOL '76*. TESOL, Washington, DC: 41–53

Cathcart and Olsen seem to have been the first to take learners into consideration as people with a right to an opinion. Their descriptive study would be of particular value for this reason alone, but it can also be seen as offering teachers a way of finding out about their learners' preferences. In this respect it approaches Fanselow's position with regard to the use of FOCUS – that teachers could perhaps use research techniques to obtain locally relevant findings of their own, instead of depending on 'professional' researchers to hand down generalizable findings to them.

B. Input in the language classroom

1. The pioneer in this area seems to have been Henzl:

Henzl, V 1973 Linguistic Register of Foreign Language Instruction. *Language Learning* 23: 207–22

As her title suggests, however, Henzl was at the time more interested in teacher talk as a 'register' than as a vital source of input to the language learner.

2. The first person to do classroom observational research on the basis of a language acquisition perspective on the characteristics of teacher talk as input seems to have been Larsen-Freeman (following perhaps the lead given by Wagner-Gough and Hatch in their 1975 paper: The Importance of Input Data in Second Language Acquisition Studies):

Larsen-Freeman, D 1976 ESL Teacher Speech as Input to the ESL Learner. *UCLA Workpapers in Teaching English as a Second Language* 10: 45–49

Larsen-Freeman, using the same data-base as the one I had collected for my 'Turns, Topics and Tasks' study, provided a morpheme analysis of teacher speech and related it to what was known at that time about input in informal language acquisition settings and about accuracy orders in learners' oral production. She found positive correlations suggesting frequency of occurrence in input as a potentially explanatory factor. Since this early work the notion of input has become increasingly important in classroom second language learning research, with Krashen devoting a whole book to his 'input hypothesis' (1985), and a major conference taking input as its entire theme (see Gass and Madden (eds.) 1985).

C. Practice

It is very striking that there is very little to report of further work under this heading. Both of the following items have already been referred to in the main text, but they do deserve extra mention here, and it is to be hoped that more people will be encouraged to work in this area. It is odd that classroom teachers seem to see practice as a major concern, and to be less concerned about input, whereas researchers typically have their priorities quite the other way round.

1. Seliger, H W 1983 Learner Interaction in the Classroom and its Effects on Language Acquisition. In Seliger and Long (eds.) 1983 *Classroom Oriented Research in Second Language Acquisition.* (Newbury House, Rowley, Massachusetts: 246–267

In this 1983 revision of his earlier paper Seliger refines his categories of analysis but confirms his previous results and their interpretation.

2. Day, R R 1984 Student Participation in the ESL Classroom, or Some Imperfections in Practice. *Language Learning* 34 (3): 63–98

Day's paper reports a follow-up study to Seliger's 1977 work, but casts doubt on the generalizability of Seliger's findings, since Day failed to obtain the expected positive correlation between learner participation and achievement.

6 Classroom observation – retrospective, introspective, and prospective

Suggestions for further reading were implicit in Chapter 6, making it unnecessary to add yet more here. Suffice it to say at this point . . .

Now read on

Bibliography

Allen, D W and Ryan, K A 1969 *Microteaching*. Addison-Wesley, Palo Alto
Allen, J P B Fröhlich, M and Spada, N 1984 The Communicative Orientation of Language Teaching. In Handscombe, Orem and Taylor (eds.): 231–252
Allwright, R L 1972 Prescription and Description in the Training of Language Teachers. In Qvistgaard *et al.* (eds.) 3: 150–166
Allwright, R L 1975a Problems in the Study of the Teacher's Treatment of Learner Error. In Burt and Dulay (eds.): 96–109
Allwright, R L 1975b An Attempt to Model the Role of Cognitions in Language Learning. Volume on Pragmalinguistics, *Fourth AILA Congress Papers*. Hochschulverlag Stuttgart
Allwright, R L 1976 *Language Learning Through Communication Practice*. ELT Documents 3, British Council: 2–14
Allwright, R L 1980 Turns, Topics and Tasks: Patterns of Participation in Language Learning and Teaching. In Larsen-Freeman (ed.): 165–187
Allwright, R L 1983 Classroom-Centred Research on Language Teaching and Learning: a Brief Historical Review. *TESOL Quarterly*, 17(2): 191–204
Allwright, R L 1984a The Importance of Interaction in Classroom Language Learning. *Applied Linguistics* 5(2): 156–171
Allwright, R L 1984b Why Don't Learners Learn What Teachers Teach? – The Interaction Hypothesis. In Singleton and Little (eds.): 3–18
Allwright, R L 1986 *Classroom Observation: Problems and Possibilities*. Paper presented at RELC Seminar, Singapore
Amidon, E J 1966 *Using Interaction Analysis at Temple University*. Paper presented at the Conference on the Implications of Recent Research on Teaching for Teacher Education, Rochester, New York
Amidon, E J *et al.* 1967 *Project on Student Teaching: The Effects of Teaching Interaction Analysis to Student Teachers*. US Office of Education, Cooperative Research Project No 2873, Temple University, Philadelphia
Amidon, E J and Flanders, N A 1962 *The Role of the Teacher in the Classroom*. Temple University, Philadelphia
Amidon, E J and Flanders, N A 1967 Interaction Analysis as a Feedback System. In Amidon and Hough (eds.) 1967: 5–11
Amidon, E J and Giammateo, M 1965 The Verbal Behaviour of Superior Teachers. *Elementary School Journal* 65: 283–285
Amidon, E J and Hough, J B 1964 *Behavioral Change in Pre-Service Teacher Training: An Experimental Study*. Temple University, Philadelphia
Amidon, E J and Hough, J B (eds.) 1967 *Interaction Analysis: Research, Theory and Application*. Addison-Wesley
Aston, G 1986 Trouble-Shooting in Interaction with Learners: the More the Merrier? *Applied Linguistics* 7(2): 128–143

Ausubel, D P 1971 Some Psychological Aspects of the Structure of Knowledge. In Johnson (ed.)

Bailey, D C 1965 Foreign Language Teaching: The Human Gap. *French Review* 39: 116, 118

Bailey, K M 1983 Competitiveness and Anxiety in Adult Second Language Learning: Looking AT and THROUGH the Diary Studies. In Long and Seliger (eds.): 67–104

✓Bailey, L G 1975 An Observational Method in the Foreign Language Classroom: A Closer Look at Interaction Analysis. *Foreign Language Annals* 3(4): 335–344

Bales, R F 1950 *Interaction Process Analysis: a Method for the Study of Small Groups*. Addison-Wesley

Bales, R F 1970 *Personality and Interpersonal Behavior*. Holt, Rinehart and Winston, New York

Banathy, B H 1968 The Design of Foreign Language Teacher Education. *Modern Language Journal* 52(8): 490–500

Barnes, D 1969 Language in the Secondary Classroom. In Barnes (ed.): 9–77

Barnes, D (ed.) 1969 *Language, the Learner and the School*. Penguin

Barnes, D 1973 *Language in the Classroom*. Open University Press

Barnes, D and Todd, F 1975 *Communication and Learning in Small Groups*. A Report to the Social Science Research Council. University of Leeds. Republished in 1977 by Routledge and Kegan Paul

Bartley, D E and Politzer, R L (no date) Practice-Centered Teacher Training: Spanish. Center for Curriculum Development, Philadelphia

Beattie, N M and Teather, D C B 1971 Microteaching in the Training of Teachers of Modern Languages. *Audio-Visual Language Journal* 9(3): 117–121

Bellack, A A, Kliebard, H M, Hyman, R J and Smith, F L 1966 *The Language of the Classroom*. Teachers College Press, New York

Borg, W R, Kelley, M L, Langer, P and Gall, M 1970 *The Minicourse: A Microteaching Approach to Teacher Education*. Macmillan Educational Services, Beverley Hills, California

Borne, W (ed.) 1979 *The Foreign Language Learner in Today's Classroom Environment*. Northeast Conference, Montpellier, Vermont

Braine, M D S 1971 On Two Types of Models of the Internalization of Grammars. In Slobin (ed.): 153–186

Breen, M P 1985 The Social Context for Language Learning – A Neglected Situation? *Studies in Second Language Acquisition*. 7(2): 136–158

Brophy, J E and Good, T L 1974 *Teacher-Student Relationships*. Holt, Rinehart and Winston, New York

Brown, H D, Yorio, C A and Crymes, R H (eds.) 1977 *Teaching and Learning English as a Second Language: Trends in Research and Practice*. Selected papers from the 1977 TESOL Convention. TESOL, Washington DC

Burkhart, R C (ed.) 1969 *The Assessment Revolution: New Viewpoints for Teacher Evaluation*. Teacher Learning Centre, Buffalo State University College

Burt, M K and Dulay, H C (eds.) 1975 *On TESOL '75: New Directions in Second Language Learning, Teaching and Bilingual Education*. TESOL, Washington DC

Calderhead, J 1984 *Teachers' Classroom Decision-Making*. Holt, Rinehart and Winston, New York

Campbell, R and Wales, R 1972 The Study of Language Acquisition. In Lyons (ed.): 242–260

Carpenter, E 1974 *Oh, What a Blow That Phantom Gave Me!* Bantam, New York

Carroll, J B and Sapon, S 1959 *Modern Language Aptitude Test (MLAT)*. Psychological Corporation, New York

Castaños, F 1976 The Discourse of Science and Teaching English for Special Purposes at the Elementary Level. *Language for Special Purposes*. Universidad Autónoma Metropolitana, Xochimilco

Cathcart, R L and Olsen, J W B 1976 Teachers' and Students' Preferences for Correction of Classroom Conversation Errors. In Fanselow and Crymes (eds.): 41–53

Chastain, K 1969 Prediction of Success in Audiolingual and Cognitive Classes. *Language Learning* 19: 1, 2, 27–39

Chaudron, C 1977 A Descriptive Model of Discourse in the Corrective Treatment of Learners' Errors. *Language Learning* 17: 29–46

Chaudron, C 1983 Foreigner Talk in the Classroom – An Aid to Learning? In Seliger and Long (eds.): 127–145

Chomsky, N 1959 Review of Skinner's 'Verbal Behaviour'. *Language* 35: 26–58

Cicourel *et al.* 1974 *Language Use and School Performance*. Academic Press, New York

Clark, J L D 1969 The Pennsylvania Project and the 'Audio-Lingual vs Traditional' Question. *Modern Language Journal* 53: 388–396

Clark, R 1974 Performing Without Competence. *Journal of Child Language* 1: 1–10

Clements, R D 1964 *Question Types, Patterns and Sequences Used by Art Teachers in the Classroom*. Co-operative Research Project No S-161, July–December, The Pennsylvania State University

Cohen, A D and Hosenfeld, C 1981 Some Uses of Mentalistic Data in Second Language Research. *Language Learning* 31: 285–313

Corder, S P 1967 The Significance of Learners' Errors. *IRAL* 5(4): 161–170. Reprinted in Richards, J C: 19–27

Creore, A E and Hanzeli, V E 1960 *A Comparative Evaluation of Two Modern Methods for Teaching a Spoken Language*. University of Washington, Seattle

Davies, A, Criper, C and Howatt, A P R (eds.) 1984 *Interlanguage*. Edinburgh University Press

Day, R R 1984 Student Participation in the ESL Classroom, or Some Imperfections in Practice. *Language Learning* 34(3): 63–98

DeFazio, V J 1973 Field Articulation Differences in Language Abilities. *Journal of Personality and Social Psychology* 25: 351–356

Dodl, N R 1965 *Pupil Questioning Behavior in the Context of Classroom Interaction*. Unpublished doctoral dissertation, Stanford University

Drach, K 1969 The Language of the Parent: A Pilot Study. In *The Structure of Linguistic Input to Children*. Working Paper No 14, Language Behavior Research Laboratory, University of California, Berkeley

Dubin, R and Taveggia, T C 1968 *The Teaching-Learning Paradox.* Center for the Advanced Study of Educational Administration, University of Oregon, Eugene

Dulay, H C and Burt, M K 1974 You Can't Learn Without Goofing. In Richards (ed.): 95–123

Edmondson, W 1981 *Spoken Discourse: A Model for Analysis.* Longman

Edmondson, W and House, J 1981 *Let's Talk and Talk About It.* Urban und Schwarzenberg, Munich

Educational Testing Service 1939–41 *MLA French and German Tests.* Princeton, New Jersey

Educational Testing Service 1963 *Cooperative Foreign Language Tests.* Princeton, New Jersey

Elam, S 1971 *Performance-Based Teacher Education; What is the State of the Art?* American Association of Colleges for Teacher Education, Washington DC

Ellis, R 1984a Can Syntax Be Taught? *Applied Linguistics* 5(2): 138–155

Ellis, R 1984b *Classroom Second Language Learning Development.* Pergamon Press

Ellis, R 1985 *Understanding Second Language Acquisition.* Oxford University Press

Faber, H von 1971 Modellfilme zur Lehrerausbildung mit den Mitteln der Unterrichtmitschau. *AV-Praxis* 21(10): 5–10

Faerch, C, Haastrup, K and Phillipson, R 1984 *Learner Language and Language Learning.* Multilingual Matters Ltd., Clevedon

Fanselow, J F 1974 *The Treatment of Learner Error.* Paper presented to TESOL Denver

Fanselow, J F 1977a Beyond *Rashomon* – Conceptualizing and Describing the Teaching Act. *TESOL Quarterly* 11(1): 17–39

Fanselow, J F 1977b The Treatment of Error in Oral Work. *Foreign Language Annals* 10(4): 583–593

Fanselow, J F 1978 Breaking the Rules of the Classroom Game Through Self-Analysis. In Light and Osman (eds.): 145–166

Fanselow, J F and Crymes, R (eds.) 1976 *On TESOL '76.* TESOL, Washington DC

Felix, S W 1981 The Effect of Formal Instruction on Second Language Acquisition. *Language Learning* 31(1): 87–112

Ferguson, C A 1975 Toward a Characterization of English Foreigner Talk. *Anthropological Linguistics* 17: 1–14

Fink, S R 1972 *Dialog Memorization in Introductory Language Instruction; A Comparison of Three Different Strategies.* In Qvistgaard *et al.* (eds.): 273–289

Flanders, N A 1960a *Interaction Analysis in the Classroom: A Manual for Observers.* University of Michigan Press, Ann Arbor

Flanders, N A 1960b *Teacher Influence, Pupil Attitudes and Achievement.* US Office of Education Cooperative Research Project No 397, University of Minnesota, Minneapolis

Flanders, N A 1961 Analyzing Teacher Behavior. *Educational Leadership* 19(3):173

Flanders, N A 1967a The Problems of Observer Training and Reliability. In Amidon and Hough (eds.) 1967

Flanders, N A 1967b Lecture on Interaction given at Stanford University California

Flanders, N A 1970 *Analyzing Teaching Behavior*. Addison-Wesley

Flanders, N A 1971 Künftige Entwicklungen bei der Analyse der verbalen Kommunikation in der Klasse. *PL* 8: 133–148

Fröhlich, M, Spada, N and Allen, J P B 1985 Differences in the Communicative Orientation of L2 Classrooms. *TESOL Quarterly* 19(1): 27–57

Furst, N and Amidon, E J 1963 *Teacher-Pupil Interaction Patterns in the Elementary School*. Unpublished article, Temple University, Philadelphia

Furst, N 1965 *The Effects of Training in Interaction Analysis on the Behavior of Student Teachers in Secondary Schools*. Paper read at the annual meeting of the American Educational Research Association, Chicago. Reprinted in Amidon and Hough (eds.) 1967: 315–328

Gage, N L 1963 Paradigms for Research on Teaching. In Gage (ed.)

Gage, N L (ed.) 1963 *Handbook of Research on Teaching*. Rand McNally, Chicago

Gaies, S J 1976a *The Syntax of ESL Teachers' Classroom Language: A Preliminary Report*. Paper presented at the Summer Conference of Second Language Learning and Teaching, SUNY, Oswego

Gaies, S J 1976b *ESL Teachers' Classroom Speech: Support for the L1 = L2 Hypothesis*. Paper presented at the Sixth Annual Conference of the New York State English to Speakers of Other Languages and Bilingual Education Association, Albany

Gaies, S J 1976c Gradation in Formal Second Language Instruction as a Factor in the Development of Interlanguage. *Lektos: Interdisciplinary Working Papers in Language Sciences*. Special Issue. St Clair and Hartford (eds.): 29–41

Gaies, S J 1977a *Linguistic Input in First and Second Language Learning*. Paper presented at the Sixth Annual University of Wisconsin-Milwaukee Linguistic Symposium

Gaies, S J 1977b The Nature of Linguistic Input in Formal Second Language Learning: Linguistic and Communicative Strategies in ESL Teachers' Classroom Language. In Brown, Yorio and Crymes (eds.): 204–212

Galloway, C 1967 *Nonverbal Communication*. Paper presented at the American Association of College Teachers of Education Education Media Project, University of Maryland

Gallwey, T W 1974 *The Inner Game of Tennis*. Random House, New York

Gamta, T 1976 *Selected Behaviors in Four ESL Classrooms*. EdD dissertation. Teachers College, Columbia University, New York

Gass, S M and Madden, C (eds.) 1983 *Input in Second Language Acquisition*. Newbury House, Rowley, Massachusetts

George, H V 1972 *Common Errors in Language Learning*. Newbury House, Rowley, Massachusetts

Gibb, G 1970 CCTV: Some Guide Lines for the Future Use of Videotapes in Professional Training. *Education for Teaching* 81: 51–56

Gingras R C (ed.) 1978 *Second-Language Acquisition and Foreign Language Teaching*. Center for Applied Linguistics, Arlington

Goodman, L A 1954 Kolmogorov-Smirnov Tests for Psychological Research. *Psychological Bulletin* 51: 160–168

Granowsky, S and Krossner, W 1970 Kindergarten Teachers as Models for Children's Speech. *The Journal of Experimental Education* 38: 23–28

Green, J R (ed.) 1973 *Foreign Language Education Research: A Book of Readings*. Rand McNally, Center for Curriculum Development, Chicago

Grittner, F M 1968 Letter to the Editor. *Newsletter of the National Association of Language Laboratory Directors (NALLD)* 3(2): 7

Grittner, F M 1969 *Teaching Foreign Languages*. Harper and Row, New York

Guberina, P 1965 La Méthode Audio-visuelle Structuro-globale. In *Revue de Phonétique Appliquée* 1: 35–64

Guilford, J P 1954 *Psychometric Methods*. McGraw-Hill, New York

Hall, E T *The Silent Language*. Fawcett, New York

Halliday, M A K 1973 *Explorations in the Functions of Language*. Edward Arnold

Handscombe, J, Orem, R A and Taylor, B P (eds.) 1984 *On TESOL '83. The Question of Control*. TESOL, Washington DC

Hayes, A S, Lambert, W E and Tucker, G A 1967 Evaluation of Foreign Language Teaching. *Foreign Language Annals* 1(1)

Henzl, V 1973 Linguistic Register of Foreign Language Instruction. *Language Learning* 23: 207–22

Henzl, V 1975 *Speech of Foreign Language Teachers: a Sociolinguistic Analysis*. Paper presented at the Fourth International Congress of Applied Linguistics, Stuttgart

Hoetker, J P and Ahlbrand, W 1969 The Persistence of the Recitation. *American Educational Research Journal* 6: 145–169

Holley, F M and King, J K 1971 Imitation and Correction in Foreign Language Learning. *Modern Language Journal* 55(8): 494–8

Hosenfeld, C 1975 The New Student Role: Individual Differences and Implications for Instruction. In Jarvis (ed.) 1975

Hosenfeld, C 1979 Cindy: A Learner in Today's Foreign Language Classroom. In Borne (ed.): 53–75

Hough, J B and Amidon, E J 1967 Behavioral Change in Student Teachers. In Amidon and Hough (eds.) 1967: 307–314

Hough, J B and Duncan, J K 1965 *Exploratory Studies of a Teaching Situation Reaction Test*. Paper read at the Annual Meeting of the American Educational Research Association, Chicago, February

Hough, J B and Ober, R 1967 The Effects of Training in Interaction Analysis on the Verbal Teaching Behavior of Pre-Service Teachers. In Amidon and Hough (eds.) 1967

Hughes, G S 1981 *A Handbook of Classroom English*. Oxford University Press

Hunt, K W 1970 Syntactic Maturity in Schoolchildren and Adults. *Monographs for the Society for Research in Child Development* 35(134)

IFS 1971 *Dokumentation Fremdsprachen- und Sprachlehrinstitute.* Arbeitstagung, Marburg

Jakobovits, L and Gordon, B 1974 *The Context of Foreign Language Teaching.* Newbury House, Rowley, Massachusetts
Janacek J 1969 Réflexions sur la pédagogie de la formation. *Voix et Images du CREDIF* 2: 1–4
Jarvis, G A 1968 A Behavioral Observation System for Classroom Foreign Language Skill Acquisition Activities. *Modern Language Journal* 52: 335–341
Jarvis, G A 1975 Perspective: A New Freedom. *ACTFL Review of Foreign Language Education.* National Textbook Company, Skokie, Illinois
Johnson, P E (ed.) 1971 *Learning: Theory and Practice.* Thomas Y Crowell, New York

Keating, R F 1963 *A Study of the Effectiveness of Language Laboratories.* Institute of Administrative Research, Columbia University Teacher's College, New York
Kirk, J 1964 *The Effects of Teaching the Minnesota System of Interaction Analysis on the Behavior of Student Teachers.* Unpublished dissertation, Temple University, Philadelphia
Kobashigawa, B 1969 Repetitions in a Mother's Speech to her Child. In *The Structure of Linguistic Input to Children.* Working Paper No 14, Language Behavior Research Laboratory, University of California, Berkeley
Koehring, K H 1970 Zur Beobachtung und Beurteilung von Englischunterricht. *Englisch* 4: 97–103
Krashen, S D 1978 The Monitor Model for Second-Language Acquisition. In Gingras (ed.): 1–26
Krashen, S D 1985 *The Input Hypothesis: Issues and Implications.* Longman
Krashen, S D and Seliger, H W 1975 The Essential Contributions of Formal Instruction in Adult Second Language Learning. *TESOL Quarterly* 9: 173–183
Krashen, S D and Seliger, H W 1976 The Role of Formal and Informal Learning Environments in Second Language Learning. *International Journal of Psycholinguistics* 6: 15–21
Krumm, H J 1973a Interaction Analysis and Microteaching for the Training of Modern Language Teachers. *IRAL* 11(2): 163–170
Krumm, H J 1973b *Analyse und Training fremdsprachlichen Lehrverhaltens.* Weinheim

Landes, J 1975 Speech Addressed to Children: Issues and Characteristics of Parental Input. *Language Learning* 25: 355–79
Larsen-Freeman, D E 1976 ESL Teacher Speech as Input to the ESL Learner. *UCLA Workpapers on TESOL* 10: 45–49
Larsen-Freeman, D E (ed.) 1980 *Discourse Analysis in Second Language Research.* Newbury House, Rowley, Massachusetts
Lefever, M M and Ehri, L C 1976 The Relationship Between Field Independence and Sentence Disambiguation Ability. *Journal of Psycholinguistic Research* 5: 99–106
Light, R L and Osman, A H (eds.) 1978 *Teaching English as a Second Language*

and Bilingual Education: Themes, Practices, Viewpoints. ESOL/BEA, New York

Lightbown, P M 1983 Exploring Relationships Between Developmental and Instructional Sequences in L2 Acquisition. In Seliger and Long (eds.): 217–245

Lindblad, T 1969 *Implicit and Explicit – An Experiment in Applied Psycholinguistics.* GUME Project 1 Report 11, Gothenburg

Lohman *et al.* 1967 A Study of the Effect of Pre-Service Training in Interaction Analysis on the Verbal Behavior of Student Teachers. In Amidon and Hough (eds.) 1967

Long, M H 1975 Group Work and Communicative Competence in the ESOL Classroom. In Burt and Dulay (eds.): 211–223

Long, M H 1976 Group Work in the Teaching and Learning of English as a Foreign Language: Problems and Potential. *English Language Teaching Journal* 31(4): 285–292

Long, M H 1977 Teacher Feedback on Learner Error: Mapping Cognitions. In Brown *et al.* (eds.): 278–293

Long, M H 1980 Inside the 'Black Box': Methodological Issues in Classroom Research on Language Learning. *Language Learning* 30(1): 1–42

Long, M H 1981 Input, Interaction and Second Language Acquisition. In Winitz (ed.): 259–278

Long, M H 1983 Does Second Language Instruction Make a Difference? *TESOL Quarterly* 17(3): 359–382

Long, M H *et al.* 1976 Lockstep and Small Group Work. In Fanselow and Crymes (eds.)

Long, M H and Castaños, F 1976 Towards Non-Interference: Making Second Language Learning More Like The First. *MEXTESOL Journal* 1(1): 36–48

Long, M H, Adams, L, McLean, M and Castaños, F 1976 Doing Things with Words – Verbal Interaction in Lockstep and Small Group Classroom Situations. In Brown, Yorio and Crymes (eds.) 1977: 137–153

Long, M H and Seliger, H W (eds.) 1983 *Classroom Oriented Research in Second Language Acquisition.* Newbury House, Rowley, Massachusetts

Long, M H and Porter, P A 1985 Group Work, Interlanguage Talk and Second Language Acquisition. *TESOL Quarterly* 19(2): 207–228

Luria, A R 1974/75 Scientific Perspectives and Philosophical Dead Ends in Modern Linguistics. *Cognition* 3(4): 377–385

Lyons, J (ed.) 1972 *New Horizons in Linguistics*, Penguin, Baltimore

Mackey, W F 1965 *Language Teaching Analysis.* Longman

Mackey, W F 1978 Cost-Benefit Quantification of Language Teaching Behaviour. *Die Neueren Sprachen* 1: 2–32

Macnamara, J 1975 Comparison Between First and Second Language Learning. *Working Papers on Bilingualism* 7: 71–94

Marxheimer, E 1969 Comments on the Pennsylvania Project: Challenge for the Secondary School Laboratory. *Newsletter of the National Association of Language Laboratory Directors (NALLD)* 3(3): 20–22

Mary William, Sister 1973 Interaction Analysis and Achievement: An Experiment. In Green (ed.): 153–165

McLean, M and Castaños, F 1976 Discourse of Language Learning. *MEXTESOL Journal* 1(3)

McNeill, D 1966 Developmental Psycholinguistics. In Smith and Miller (eds.): 15–84

Medley, D M and Mitzel, H E 1963 Measuring Classroom Behavior by Systematic Observation. In Gage (ed.): 247–328

Mehan, H 1974 Accomplishing Classroom Lessons. In Cicourel *et al.* (eds.): 76–142

Mitchell, R, Parkinson, B and Johnstone, R 1981 *The Foreign Language Classroom: an Observational Study.* Stirling Monographs No 9, Stirling University

Morrison, A and McIntyre, D 1969 *Teachers and Teaching.* Penguin

Moskowitz, G 1966a *College Students React to Foreign Language.* Unpublished article, Temple University, Philadelphia

Moskowitz, G 1966b Toward Human Relations in Supervision. *Bulletin of the National Association of Secondary School Principals* 50: 98–114

Moskowitz, G 1967a The FLint System: An Observational Tool for the Foreign Language Classroom. In Simon and Boyer (eds.)

Moskowitz, G 1967b The Attitudes and Teaching Patterns of Cooperating Teachers and Student Teachers Trained in Interaction Analysis. In Amidon and Hough (eds.) 1967

Moskowitz, G 1967c *The Foreign Language Teacher Interacts.* Association for Productive Teaching, Minneapolis

Moskowitz, G 1968a The Effects of Training Foreign Language Teachers in Interaction Analysis. *Foreign Language Annals* 1(3): 218–235 (First presented as a paper at the Annual Meeting of the American Educational Research Association, New York 1967)

Moskowitz, G 1968b *The Attitudes and Teaching Patterns of Foreign Language Student Teachers Trained and Not Trained in Interaction Analysis.* Temple University, Philadelphia

√ Moskowitz, G 1971 Interaction Analysis – A New Modern Language for Supervisors. *Foreign Language Annals* 5(2): 211–221

Moskowitz, G 1972 Paper presented at the International Microteaching Symposium, Tübingen

√ Moskowitz, G 1976 The Classroom Interaction of Outstanding Foreign Language Teachers. *Foreign Language Annals* 9(2): 135–157

Moskowitz, G 1978 *Caring and Sharing in the Foreign Language Class.* Newbury House, Rowley, Massachusetts

Mowrer, O H 1960 *Learning Theory and the Symbolic Processes.* John Wiley, New York

Naiman, N, Fröhlich, M, Stern, H H and Todesco, A 1977 *The Good Language Learner.* Ontario Institute for Studies in Education, Toronto

Nearhoof, O 1969 *Teacher-Pupil Interaction in the Foreign Language Classroom: A Technique for Self-Evaluation.* Unpublished research paper cited in Grittner 1969: 328–330

Nelson, K E, Carscaddon, G and Bonvillian, J 1973 Syntax Acquisition: The Impact of Experimental Variation in Adult Verbal Interaction with Children. *Child Development* 44: 497–504

Neujahr, J K 1972 Classroom Observational Research. *The Educational Forum*: 221–228

Newmark, L and Reibel, D A 1968 Necessity and Sufficiency in Language Learning. *International Review of Applied Linguistics* 6(2)

Ochsner, R 1979 A Poetics of Second Language Acquisition. *Language Learning* 29(1): 53–80

O'Donnell, R C, Norris, R C and Griffin, W J 1967 *Syntax of Kindergarten and Elementary Schoolchildren: a Transformational Approach*. Research Report No 8, National Council of Teachers of English, Champaign-Urbana, Illinois

Otto, F 1969 The Teacher in the Pennsylvania Project. *Modern Language Journal* 53: 411–420

Paulston, C B 1975 Linguistic and Communicative Competence. *TESOL Quarterly* 8(4): 347–362

Paulston, C B 1975 *Teaching English to Speakers of Other Languages in the United States, 1975: A Dipstick Paper*. Paper presented at the UNESCO Meeting of Experts on the Diversification of Methods and Techniques for Teaching a Second Language, Paris

Phillips, M and Shettlesworth, C 1976 Questions in the Design and Use of Courses in English for Specialised Purposes. In Nickel (ed.) *Proceedings of the Fourth International Congress of Applied Linguistics, Volume 1*: 249–264. Hochschulverlag, Stuttgart

Pirsig, R M 1975 *Zen and the Art of Motorcycle Maintenance*. Bantam, New York

PMLA 1955 70(4/2): 46

Politzer, R L (no date) *Practice-Centered Teacher Training: French*. Center for Curriculum Development, Philadelphia

Politzer, R L 1966 Toward a Practice-Centered Program for the Training and Evaluation of Foreign Language Teachers. *Modern Language Journal* 50

Politzer, R L 1967 *Performance Criteria for the Foreign Language Teacher*. Technical Report No 1A, Stanford University

Politzer, R L 1970a On the Use of Aptitude Variables in Research on Foreign Language Teaching. *IRAL* 8(4): 330–340

Politzer, R L 1970b Some Reflections on 'Good' and 'Bad' Language Teaching Behaviors. *Language Learning* 20(1): 31–43

Politzer, R L 1982 *Linguistic and Communicative Competence, Language Dominance, Selected Pupil Characteristics and Their Relationship to Achievement of Bilingual Pupils*. Final Report of NIE Grant G-79 – 01 30, Stanford University

Politzer, R L and Weiss, L 1969a *Characteristics and Behaviors of the Successful Foreign Language Teacher*. Stanford Center for Research and Development in Teaching, Technical Report No 5, Stanford University

Politzer, R L and Weiss, L 1969b *Improving Achievement in Foreign Language*. Center for Curriculum Development, Philadelphia

Qvistgaard *et al.* (eds.) 1972 *Applied Linguistics: Problems and Solutions*. AILA Proceedings Copenhagen, Julius Groos Verlag, Heidelberg, III

Ramirez, M III and Castaneda, A 1974 *Cultural democracy, bicognitive development, and education.* Academic Press, New York

Richards, J C (ed.) 1974 *Error Analysis.* Longman

Rivers, W M 1964 *The Psychologist and the Foreign-Language Teacher.* Chicago University Press, Chicago

Rosenshine, B 1970 Interaction Analysis: A Tardy Comment. *Phi Delta Kappa* 51: 445–446. Reprinted in Sperry 1972: 246–250

Rosenshine, B 1971 Teaching Behaviors Related to Pupil Achievement: A Review of Research. In Westbury and Bellack (eds.): 51–98

Rothfarb, S H 1970 Teacher-Pupil Interaction in the FLES Class. *Hispania* 53: 256–260

Rubin, C B 1976 *Self Instructional Materials for Learning Bellack's Moves.* Unpublished. Teachers College, Columbia University, New York

Rubin, J 1975 What the 'Good Language Learner' Can Teach Us. *TESOL Quarterly* 9(1): 41–51

Russell, B 1960 (First published 1935) *Sceptical Essays.* Unwin Books

Rwakyaka, P 1976 *Teacher Student Interaction in ESL Classes in Uganda.* EdD dissertation, Teachers College, Columbia University, New York

Sacks, H, Schlegoff, E and Jefferson, G 1974 A Simplest Systematics for the Organisation of Turn-Taking in Conversation. *Language* 50(4): 696–735

Scherer, G A C and Wertheimer, M 1964 *A Psycholinguistic Experiment in Foreign Language Teaching.* McGraw-Hill, New York

Schumann, F M and Schumann, J H 1977 Diary of a Language Learner: An Introspective Study of Second Language Learning. In Brown, Yorio and Crymes (eds.): 241–249

Schumann, J H 1978 *The Pidginization Process: A Model for Second Language Acquisition.* Newbury House, Rowley, Mass.

Scott, W A 1955 Reliability of Content Analysis. *Public Opinion Quarterly* 19: 321–25

Seliger, H W 1975 Inductive Method and Deductive Method in Language Teaching: A Re-examination. *International Review of Applied Linguistics* 13(1)

Seliger, H W 1977 Does Practice Make Perfect?: A Study of Interaction Patterns and L2 Competence. *Language Learning* 27(2): 263–278

Seliger, H W 1983a Learner Interaction in the Classroom and Its Effects on Language Acquisition. In Seliger and Long (eds.): 246–267

Seliger, H W 1983b The Language Learner as Linguist: A Metaphor and Its Realities. *Applied Linguistics* 4(3): 179–191

Seliger, H W and Gingras, R 1976 *Who Speaks How Much and To Whom?: A Study of Interaction Patterns in Second Language Classrooms.* Unpublished paper presented at Colloquium on Verbal and Non-Verbal Behavior in Second Language Learning, National TESOL Convention, New York

Seliger, H W and Long, M H (eds.) 1983 *Classroom-Oriented Research in Second Language Acquisition*: 246–267. Newbury House, Rowley, Massachusetts

Selinker, L 1972 Interlanguage. *IRAL* 10(3): 209–231

Simon, A and Boyer, E G 1967 *Mirrors for Behavior: an Anthology of Classroom Observation Instruments.* Research for Better Schools and Center for the Study of Teaching, Temple University, Philadelphia

Sinclair, J McH, Forsyth, I J, Coulthard, R M and Ashby, M 1972 *The*

English Used by Teachers and Pupils. First report to the SSRC for the period September 1970 to August 1972. Department of English Language and Literature, University of Birmingham

Sinclair, J McH and Coulthard, R M 1975 *Towards an Analysis of Discourse.* Oxford University Press

Sinclair, J McH and Brazil, D 1982 *Teacher Talk.* Oxford University Press

Singleton, D M and Little, D G (eds.) 1984 *Language Learning in Formal and Informal Contexts.* IRAAL, Dublin

Skinner, B F 1957 *Verbal Behavior.* Appleton-Century-Crofts, New York

Slimani, A 1987 Doctoral research in progress.

Slobin, D I 1971 *Psycholinguistics.* Scott Foresman and Company, Glenview, Illinois

Slobin, D I (ed.) 1971 *The Ontogenesis of Grammar: A Theoretical Symposium.* Academic Press, New York

Smith, F 1975 *Comprehension and Learning.* Holt, Rinehart and Winston, New York

Smith, F and Miller, G (eds.) 1966 *The Genesis of Language.* MIT Press, Cambridge, Massachusetts

Smith, P D 1968 How Effective the Language Laboratory. *Newsletter of the National Association of Language Laboratory Directors (NALLD)* 3(1): 5–8

Smith, P D 1970 *A Comparison of the Cognitive and Audiolingual Approaches to Foreign Language Instruction; the Pennsylvania Project.* Center for Curriculum Development, Philadelphia

Snow, C 1972 Mothers' Speech to Children Learning Language. *Child Development* 43: 549–65

Sperry, L 1972 *Learning Performance and Individual Differences.* Scott Forsman and Company, Glenview, Illinois

Staton, J, Kreft, J and Gutstein, S (eds.) *Dialogue.* Newsletter, Center for Applied Linguistics, Washington

St Clair, R and Hartford, B (eds.) 1976 *Error Analysis and Language Testing.*

Stephens, J M 1967 *The Process of Schooling.* Holt, Rinehart and Winston, New York

Stevick, E W 1976 *Memory, Meaning, and Method.* Newbury House, Rowley, Mass.

Stieglitz, F 1973 *Teaching a Second Language: Sentence Length and Syntax.* Research Report No 14, National Council of Teachers of English, Champaign-Urbana, Illinois

Suzman, R M 1973 Psychological Modernity. *International Journal of Comparative Sociology* 14: 273–287

Thompson, M P *et al.* 1961 *Audio-Lingual Materials.* (First Edition) Harcourt, Brace and World Inc., New York

Townsend, D R and Zamora, G L 1975 Differing Interaction Patterns in Bilingual Classrooms. *Contemporary Education* 46(3)

Valette, R M 1969 Some Conclusions to be Drawn from the Pennsylvania Study. *Newsletter of the National Association of Language Laboratory Directors (NALLD)*, March 3(3): 17–19

Vleck, Ch (no date) *Classroom Simulation and Teacher Training.* Research paper

Wagner, A C 1972 *Is Practice Really Necessary? An Experimental Study on the Role of Practicing Vs. 'Cognitive Discrimination Learning in Behavioral Change.* Paper presented at the International Microteaching Symposium, Tübingen

Wagner-Gough, J and Hatch, E 1975 The Importance of Input Data in Second Language Acquisition Studies. *Language Learning* 25: 297–308

Wason, P C 1971 Problem Solving and Reasoning. *Cognitive Psychology, British Medical Bulletin* 27(3): 206–210

Westbury, I and Bellack, A (eds.) 1971 *Research into Classroom Processes.* Teachers College Press, New York

Widdowson, H G 1972 The Teaching of English as Communication. *English Language Teaching* 27(1): 15–19

William, Sister Mary 1973 See Mary William, Sister 1973

Willis, J 1981 *Teaching English Through English.* Longman

Winer, B J 1962 *Statistical Principles In Experimental Design:* 136–138. McGraw-Hill, New York

Winitz H. (ed.) 1981 *Native Language and Foreign Language Acquisition.* New York Academy of Sciences, New York

Witkin, H A, Lewis, H B, Hetzman, M, Machover, K, Meissner, P B and Wagner, S 1954 *Personality Through Perception.* Harper and Brothers, New York

Witkin, H A, Cox, P W and Friedman, F 1976 Field-dependence-independence and Psychological Differentiation: a Bibliography with Index. Supplement Number 2. *Educational Testing Service, Research Bulletin 76–28.* Princeton, New Jersey

Wragg, E C 1970 Interaction Analysis in the Foreign Language Classroom. *Modern Language Journal* 54(2): 116–120

Wragg, E C 1971 The Influence of Feedback on Teachers' Performance. *Educational Research* 13(3): 218–221

Wright, E M J 1967 *Interaction Analysis in the Minnesota National Laboratory Mathematics Field Study.* Paper read at the Annual Meeting of the American Educational Research Association, New York

Zifreund, W 1966 *Konzept für ein Training des Lehverhaltens mit Fernse-haufzeichnungen in Kleingruppen-Seminaren.* Berlin, 1:18

Index

Mission and Money goes beyond the common focus on elite universities and examines the entire higher education industry, including the rapidly growing for-profit schools. The sector includes research universities, four-year colleges, two-year schools, and non–degree-granting career academies. Many institutions pursue mission-related activities that are often unprofitable and engage in profitable revenue-raising activities to finance them. This book contains a good deal of original research on schools' revenue sources from tuition, donations, research, patents, endowments, and other activities. It considers lobbying, distance education, and the world market, as well as advertising, branding, and reputation. The pursuit of revenue, although essential to achieve the mission of higher learning, is sometimes in conflict with that mission itself. The tension between mission and money is also highlighted in the chapter on the profitability of intercollegiate athletics. The concluding chapter investigates implications of the analysis for public policy.

Burton A. Weisbrod is John Evans Professor of Economics and Faculty Fellow of the Institute of Policy Research at Northwestern University, Evanston, Illinois. His publications include 15 authored, coauthored, or edited books, including the landmark study *The Nonprofit Economy* (1988) and *To Profit or Not to Profit: The Commercial Transformation of the Nonprofit Sector* (Cambridge University Press, 1998), as well as nearly 200 articles in journals such as the *American Economic Review, Quarterly Journal of Economics, Journal of Political Economy*, and the *Journal of Policy Analysis and Management*.

Professor Weisbrod is an elected member of the Institute of Medicine of the National Academy of Sciences as well as Fellow of the American Association for the Advancement of Science, and he is a former elected member of the Executive Committee of the American Economic Association. A former Guggenheim Foundation and Ford Foundation Fellow and senior staff member of the U.S. Council of Economic Advisers, he recently completed terms as a member of the National Advisory Research Resources Council of the National Institutes of Health and as Chair of the Social Science Research Council Committee on Philanthropy and the Nonprofit Sector. Professor Weisbrod has received the Lifetime Research Achievement Award of the Association for Research on Nonprofit Organizations and Voluntary Associations and the American Public Health Association's Carl Taube Award for Outstanding Contributions to the Field of Mental Health Services Research. He is included in biographical listings such as *Who's Who in Economics, Who's Who in Science*, and *Who's Who in the World*.

Jeffrey P. Ballou is an economist at Mathematica Policy Research, Inc., in Cambridge, Massachusetts. Prior to joining Mathematica, he held faculty positions at Northeastern and Northwestern Universities. Dr. Ballou's professional research spans multiple industries, including higher education and health care, areas in which he consults regularly for policymakers and institutional stakeholders. He received his Ph.D. from Northwestern University.

Evelyn D. Asch is Research Coordinator at the Institute for Policy Research at Northwestern University. She has also taught research and writing in the humanities and social sciences at Loyola University Chicago, DePaul University, and Shimer College. Dr. Asch is the author (with Sharon K. Walsh) of three college texts in the Wadsworth Casebook in Argument series: *Just War* (2004), *Civil Disobedience* (2005), and *Immigration* (2005). She received her Ph.D. from the Committee on the History of Culture of the University of Chicago.